NEW PERSPECTIVES
ON ANCIENT JUDAISM

Studies in Judaism

NEW PERSPECTIVES ON ANCIENT JUDAISM

VOLUME FIVE

SOCIETY AND LITERATURE IN ANALYSIS

Senior Editors
Jacob Neusner   Ernest S. Frerichs
William Scott Green   Gary Porton

Editors
Alan J. Avery-Peck   Roger Brooks
Paul V. M. Flesher   Amy-Jill Levine

Volume Editor
Paul V. M. Flesher

UNIVERSITY
PRESS OF
AMERICA

Lanham • New York • London

BM
177
.S6
1990

Copyright © 1990 by

University Press of America,® Inc.

4720 Boston Way
Lanham, MD 20706

3 Henrietta Street
London WC2E 8LU England

Printed in the United States of America

British Cataloging in Publication Information Available

Library of Congress Cataloging-in-Publication Data

(Revised for volume 5)

New perspectives on ancient Judaism.
(Studies in Judaism)
Includes bibliographical references and index.
Contents: v. 1-2. Religion, literature, and society in ancient Israel,
formative Christianity and Judaism—v. 3. Judaic and Christian interpretation
of texts / edited by Jacob Neusner and Ernest S. Frerichs—
v. 5. Society and literature in analysis /
volume editor, Paul Virgil McCracken Flesher.
1. Judaism—History—Talmudic period, 10–425.
I. Neusner, Jacob, 1932–   . II. Series.
BM177.N485   1987   296'.09'01   87–16073

ISBN 0–8191–7614–1 (v. 5 : alk. paper)

The paper used in this publication meets the minimum requirements of American
National Standard for Information Sciences—Permanence of Paper for Printed Library
Materials, ANSI Z39.48–1984.   ∞

For

William Scott Green

Table of Contents

Preface

It is a methodological commonplace in the study of antiquity that a document must always be studied in its context. But that commonplace does not offer the final word on this relationship, for a dialectical interplay exists between text and context. Certainly, the context helps interpret a text, but the interpreted text describes elements of its context—whether those elements be aspects of the text's historical, cultural, social or religious context, or the characteristics of its authorship. The studies in this volume address the issue of what a text reveals about its context.

The essays in Part One, Social and Literary Analysis, focus on a particular problematic with regard to the text in its context. This problem can be simply stated: frequently, a document's known context can be delineated only in such general terms that it is practically useless in interpretation. It is helpful to know, for example, whether a document comes from first-century or sixth-century Palestine, but not very. It would be more helpful to know whether it was composed by Qumran sectarians, Pharisees, or Christians. The more scholars know about a text's context, therefore, the more accurately they can interpret it. When scholars know little about its context, the usefulness of that knowledge is limited. But how can this knowledge be increased?

The opening articles of this volume investigate this hermeneutical problem. Using different methods, different texts, different perspectives and different questions, they surprisingly all come to the same conclusion. The answer, in their view, is this: the authorship constitutes the primary operative context for any document. (Authorship is a term that encompasses whoever creates texts, whether it be single authors, multiple authors, editors or redactors.) Why? Because the authorship has determined the shape of the text. It comprises the creative and formative force behind the text. That is, since the text could not have come into existence without the work of the authorship, the authorship constitutes the most important—and most telling—aspect of the context.

The best source of knowledge about the authorship, of course, is the text itself. By knowledge, I do not mean what the author explicitly recorded in the text about himself and his concerns (which may in fact be pure propaganda, as Joseph Healey argues with regard to the Books of the Maccabees). Rather, I refer to the implicit hints and clues that derive from the very nature of the text. By going beyond *what* is said to include the study of *how* it is said, scholars can discover information about the people who formulated the document. The goal is not, therefore, to describe and name the authors, but to understand their character as revealed in the text, whether this character is of a social, economic, religious or intellectual nature. Once we understand an authorship's nature, we can bring that specific knowledge of the text's context to bear when interpreting the text itself.

Of course, as this volume's papers suggest, even assuming this single process, there are many ways to pursue the problem of authorship. The study by Harold Van Broekhoven (Chapter One) focuses on two wisdom texts, Ben Sira and the Wisdom of Solomon, with the goal of discovering a fuller and more accurate portrayal of the writers behind them. Using methods initially set forth by Mary Douglas, Van Broekhoven characterizes the social order to which the authors belong, explores the extent to which the writers believe in that order and ascertains how satisfied they are with the roles that order grants them. Van Broekhoven's positioning also reveals important insights into the cosmology articulated in the two documents, and enables the correlation between the social description and their understanding of the cosmos. Vernon K. Robbins (Chapter Two) takes a different tack. Using the method of socio-rhetorical criticism which he has developed, Robbins analyzes the gospel of Mark to discover the extent to which its forms derive from both Jewish and Greek forms of rhetoric. In so doing, he enables interpretation to go beyond the usual claims that Mark's author moves in either a Jewish or hellenistic context. He shows, in a specific and detailed manner, how Mark's author is familiar with and makes use of both rhetorical and literary tropes native to both Judaism and Hellenism.

Jacob Neusner's contribution (Chapter Three) represents an important departure for the study of the Mishnah, one which again reveals the character of a document's authorship by clarifying its nature. Specifically, Neusner argues that the Mishnah's concept of intention can be found not only where the words for intention are invoked, but more extensively where relationships between a person's actions and the result of those actions are discussed. By listing the places where the issue is debated, despite the lack of explicit mention, Neusner shows that the framers, who provide the only context into which the Mishnah can be placed, imbedded their thought in the analysis of cases rather than in explicit statements of definition. Roy Kreitner (Chapter Four) also addresses the question of the relationship between a text's nature and its context, but he takes a radically different perspective. Kreitner brings reader-response criticism to bear on the question of the nature of the Babylonian Talmud. This enables him to show that the Bavli is a text that requires reader participation and thus requires the reader to formulate his or her own responses to its issues. The implications of this result are significant, for it means that the Bavli was not designed by its authorship to be a magnum opus of traditional material, but instead questioned that material and initiated a new program.

The four articles in Part Two, Society and Literature, address a different issue of the dialectic between text and context. They focus on the question of how to use the data found in a text to describe historical events and entities. They do not attempt to delineate a more specific or particular context within which to interpret a text. Instead, they use interpreted texts to reconstruct the specific character of the explicit context.

Stephen D. Ricks' study of the magician (Chapter Five) looks at different portrayals of magic in the Hebrew Bible and attempts to discern the criteria that distinguish magic from divine acts. He argues that the definition of magic is not related to the type of act performed, but instead stems from the social identity of the person who performs it; "they" do magic, "we" perform miracles. In contrast, the study of the Chronicler's law book by Judson R. Shaver (Chapter Six) investigates the identity of a book rather than a class of persons. The Chronicler frequently quotes from an authoritative text—which he indicates through phrases such as "according to the Torah of Moses," "as it is written in the book of Moses," and others. Shaver asks whether the text to which these refer can be identified. Specifically, he investigates whether it is equivalent to one of the legal collections now in our possession and he discovers that it is not. Joseph P. Healey's article (Chapter Seven) begins by arguing that the books of the Maccabees are partisan political documents and if their description of the events of the period following 175 B.C.E. are taken seriously, the scholar will be buying into a propaganda ploy. Borrowing models from Norman Gottwald and others, Healy argues that the proper reconstruction of the conflict is primarily one of feuding between economic classes within the Jewish people themselves, rather than one of religious and political conflict between the Jews and the empire. Finally, Michael D. Swartz' study of *Ma'aseh Merkavah* analyzes its prayers (Chapter Eight). Using form critical analysis, Swartz delineates the changing function of prayers from their formulation to their incorporation in the *hekhalot* texts. These changes, he shows, ultimately transform the divine appeals from communal recitations to prescriptions for individual ascent into the heavens.

As a collection, then, these eight articles reveal the changing nature of the study of ancient Judaism. In proper scholarly fashion, "received wisdom" is being questioned by dedicated and imaginative thinkers—not to tear down but to build up. In this way, our understanding of Judaism in antiquity continues to grow and increase.

This volume could not have been prepared without the assistance of a number of people. I am grateful for the wisdom and advice supplied by William Scott Green, Alan J. Avery-Peck, and Caroline McCracken-Flesher. Also invaluable were the proofreading talents of Beverly Patton Mortensen and Ronald Michael Campbell, and the word-processing skills of Joshua Bell and the staff at Verbatim Word Processing of Providence, R.I.

I am also thankful for the counsel and support of Jacob Neusner, my teacher, and for the opportunity to publish this volume in the series, Studies in Judaism, of which he is the Editor in Chief.

I dedicate this volume to William Scott Green who, when I was an undergraduate, introduced me to the scholarly study of religion, to the exciting world of ancient Judaism, and to the skills and enjoyment of scholarly publishing.

Northwestern University   Paul Virgil McCracken Flesher
June 8, 1989

Abbreviations

b.	Babylonian Talmud
BJRL	Bulletin of the John Rylands Library
BZAW	Beihefte zur Zeitschrift für die alttestamentliche Wissenschaft
C.P.Jud.	*Corpus Papyrorum Judaicarum*
CBQ	*Catholic Biblical Quarterly*
Chr.	Chronicles
Congr.	Philo, *De Congressu Eruditionis Gratia*
Cont.	Philo, *De Vita Contemplativa*
D	Deuteronomic Source of the Pentateuch
Dan.	Daniel
Decal.	Philo, *De Decalogo*
Deut.	Deuteronomy
E	Elohist Source of the Pentateuch
Ex.	Exodus
Ezek.	Ezekial
HCJ	V. Tcherikover, *Hellenistic Civilization and the Jews* (Philadelphia: Jewish Publication Society, 1959)
Heb.	Hebrew
HUCA	*Hebrew Union College Annual*
J	Yahwist Source of the Pentateuch
JBL	*Journal of Biblical Literature*
JJS	*Journal of Jewish Studies*
Josh.	Joshua
JQR	*Jewish Quarterly Review*
JSJ	*Journal for the Study of Judaism*
Kgs.	Kings
Lev.	Leviticus
LXX	Septuagint
M.	Mishnah
Mem.	Xenophon, *Memorabilia*

MGWJ	*Monatsschrift für Geschichte und Wissenschaft des Judentums*
Mk	Mark
MT	Masoretic Text
NEH	National Endowment for the Humanities
Neh.	Nehemiah
Num.	Numbers
P	Priestly Source of the Pentateuch
Rhet. ad Her.	*Rhetorica ad Herennium*
RSV	*Revised Standard Version*
SBL	Society for Biblical Literature
Sir.	Sirach
Spec.	Philo, *De Specialibus Legibus*
TDNT	*Theological Dictionary of the New Testament*
VT	*Vetus Testamentum*

Part One

SOCIAL AND LITERARY ANALYSIS

Chapter One

A New Social Model for Discerning Wisdom: The Case of Sirach and Pseudo-Solomon

Harold Van Broekhoven, Jr.
Denison University

The social context for *literary* wisdom appears to be the courtier elite, perhaps even a professional class of sages.[1] The biblical setting

---

[1] I hold to this conclusion despite serious doubts that Israelite wisdom originated in the Hebrew court. G. von Rad, *Wisdom in Israel* (Nashville: Abingdon, 1972): 24-50, considers the sages a professional class, as does G. Fohrer, *T.D.N.T.* VII:477-483, although he acknowledges a nationalization and popularization of wisdom in the life of Israel. Similarly, J. L. Crenshaw concludes that "a group of professional sages existed in ancient Israel...(although in time) the narrow concerns of the royal court have given way to more universal interests" in *Old Testament Wisdom: An Introduction* (Atlanta: John Knox, 1981): 12. See also W.A. Brueggemann, "The Epistemological Crisis of Israel's Two Histories (Jer. 9:22-23)," in *Israelite Wisdom: Theological and Literary Essays in Honor of S. Terrien*, ed. by J.G. Gammie (N.Y.: Union Theological Seminary, 1978): 85-105; H. J. Hermisson, *Studien zur israelitischen Spruchweisheit* (WMANT 28; Neukirchen-Vluyn: Neukirchener Verlag, 1968); R.B.Y. Scott, who denies Solomonic origin but accepts a courtly setting for literary wisdom, in "Solomon and the Beginnings of Wisdom in Israel," reprinted in *Studies in Ancient Israelite Wisdom*, ed. by J.L. Crenshaw (N.Y.: KTAV, 1976): 84ff. R.N. Whybray argues against a professional class of sages but acknowledges a small literate class of "intellectuals" in *The Intellectual Tradition in the Old Testament*, BZAW 135 (Berlin: Walter de Gruyter, 1974): esp. 69-70. J.-P. Audet was one of the first to argue against the origination of wisdom in the court and for an original folk setting of wisdom in "Origines comparees de la double tradition de la loi et de la sagesse dan la proche-orient anciens," *International Congress of Orientalists* (25th), (Moscow: 1960): 352-357. Compare W. Richter's thesis that

of the Solomonic *Aufklarung* or enlightenment and the opportunity for a flourishing of wisdom thought provided by the cosmopolitan life of the monarchy suggests a court setting is likely.[2] Parallels between biblical wisdom and instruction literature for the training of courtiers in Egypt also point to a Hebrew court setting.[3] The aesthetic merit of the wisdom literature,[4] the concerns addressed and the ethical as well as social guidelines expressed indicate a concern for the proper socialization of young courtiers of the "upper class."[5]

R. Gordis' classic analysis of the upper class social background for wisdom exemplifies scholarly views up to now.[6] The sages are upper class, according to Gordis, and their schools, like those of the sophists, were intended for sexually mature, young men of wealth (the warnings are of kept mistresses and not street walkers) and their preparation for government service. Gordis noted the sages' utilitarian ethics focuses on success, their emphasis on wealth as a sign of God's blessing and their concern for issues of commerce and property (warning against boundary markers that are moved and scales that are rigged). He argued that their theology affirms free will (the assumption of self-made men), omits or denies any dependance upon the afterlife (which is the comfort of the poor), and is generally indifferent to the temple cultus. Social

---

wisdom took shape in the school in *Recht und Ethos* (StANT 15; Munich: Kogel Verlag, 1966) or E. Gerstenberger's thesis that it emerged from the family/tribal education in *Wesen und Herkunft des Apodiktischen Rechts* (WMANT 20; Neukirchen-Vluyn: Neukirchener Verlag, 1961, 1966).

[2] R.B.Y. Scott argues against the Solomonic origins of wisdom but acknowledges the later court setting for the literature in "Solomon and the Beginning of Wisdom in Israel," *VTSup* 23 (1972): 262-79.

[3] C. Bauer-Kayatz, *Studien zu Proverbien 1-9* (Neukirchen-Vluyn: Neukirchener, 1966) presents the most convincing parallels. See R.J. Williams, "Scribal Training in Ancient Egypt," *JAOS* 92 (1972): 214-21.

[4] Von Rad, *Wisdom in Israel*: 24-50.

[5] For example, see W. L. Humphries, "The Motif of the Wise Courtier in the Book of Proverbs," in *Israelite Wisdom: Theological and Literary Essays in Honor of S. Terrien*, ed. by J. Gammie, et. al. (Missoula: Scholars Press, 1978): 177-90; W.A. Brueggemann, "The Epistemological Crisis of Israel's Two Histories," *Israelite Wisdom*: 85-105; B. Malchow, "A Manual for Future Monarchs," *C.B.Q.* 47(1985): 238-45; B.W. Kovacs, "Sociological-Structural Constraints Upon Wisdom: The Spatial and Temporal Matrix of Proverbs 15:28-22:16," Ph.D. Dissertation, Vanderbilt University, 1978; Kovacs, "Is There a Class Ethic in Proverbs?" in *Essays in Old Testament Ethics*, ed. by J.L. Crenshaw and J.T. Willis (New York: KTAV, 1974): 171-89.

[6] R. Gordis, "The Social Background of Wisdom Literature," *H.U.C.A.* 18 (1943/44): 77-118.

injustice, when noticed, elicits only upper class skepticism and not the active concern of the victim.

This class analysis and many of its conclusions have become nearly axiomatic in wisdom scholarship. But it is drawn with too wide a brush stroke. It fails to address such questions as whether wisdom was a school phenomenon (before Ben Sira), whether it represented the same *sitz in leben* throughout the period of its writing, whether all the writings reflect the same world view or even whether the application of class analysis is not anachronistic. In other words it treats all wisdom as a monolithic entity and limits the options for social description to class experience.

While Gordis' class analysis has the merit of noting that texts communicate not merely ideas but social worlds,[7] we still need to make finer distinctions. Gordis' definition of the wisdom tradition as upper class, individualistic and eudaemonistic, for example, leads him to gloss over the social conscience of Sirach. His conclusion that the wisdom tradition has an upper class disinterest in the afterlife excludes the Wisdom of Solomon from that tradition. What we need is a model that explains both the data that Gordis summarizes *and* the data which his class analysis cannot explain. I find such an analytic model in the grid-group paradigm of Mary Douglas.[8] Applying this paradigm of Douglas to the later wisdom literature of Sirach and the Wisdom of Solomon allows further refining of established notions concerning the social background of the sages.

I

Douglas argues that all social experience (regardless of the presence or absence of class distinctions) may be analyzed according to

---

[7] "If we ask of any form of communication the simple question, What is being communicated? the answer is: information from the social system. The exchanges which are being communicated constitute the social system." Mary Douglas, "Do Dogs Laugh? A Cross-Cultural Approach to Body Symbolism," in *Implicit Meanings* (London: Routledge and Kegan Paul, 1975): 87. See also Peter Berger and Thomas Luckmann, *The Social Construction of Reality: A Treatise in the Sociology of Knowledge* (Garden City: Doubleday & Company/ Anchor Books, 1966): 34ff., hereafter, Berger and Luckmann.

[8] The important work for this study is *Natural Symbols: Explorations in Cosmology* (New York: Pantheon, 1982). B.J. Malina, *Christian Origins and Cultural Anthropology: Practical Models for Biblical Interpretation* (Atlanta: John Knox, 1986), provides convenient summaries of Douglas's thought. Douglas's paradigm is being used with greater frequency in biblical studies, although usually with emphasis on "Purity and Danger" and community boundaries.

the categories of group identity and ego-centered identity. By group identity she means the degree to which one's sense of self is found in relations with other people or is subject to the pressure to conform to others' notions of proper behavior. We may think of teenagers flocking together in a shopping mall, wearing the same clothes and jewelry and speaking the same language, as having strong group affiliation. On the other hand, we might picture a young computer whiz, more comfortable with computers than with people and who sits alone at a computer screen for hours writing complicated programs, as having weak group affiliation. Or again, we might contrast the happily married man, devoted to wife and family, with the bachelor who is unable or unwilling to sustain an enduring relationship. The former is dyadic (part of the dyad composed of wife and husband) while the latter is individualistic. In a religious context, the member of a sectarian commune has a strong group identity, while the hermit in a cave possesses a weak group identity. The former happily finds religious meaning in community defined behavior and values, while the latter finds meaning in solitary meditation. In each example, Douglas would term the first case "high group" (meaning that the individual has a *high* tendency for *group* affiliation) and would term the second case "low group" (indicating that the individual has a *low* tendency towards *group* affiliation).

In addition to measuring group affiliation, Douglas uses a grid to measure the degree to which one's identity is found in terms of community-affirmed roles. She is speaking here of the extent to which one's experience fits socially determined norms. We may take for examples sex or age roles. In a patriarchal society, if a woman accepts a norm that woman's labor is in the home and that she submit to the husband and find fulfillment through her children, then she identifies with her socially defined role and therefore falls into Douglas' classification of high grid; her relationship with her husband may be defined in terms of socially approved roles irrespective of deep love and attachment to her spouse. Similarly, the well behaved youth is high grid when his relationship to parents is determined by socially approved rules of silence ("seen but not heard"), deference and obedience to elders. High grid does not necessarily involve high status; indeed, the socially approved role of submissive wife may not give the wife high status. The term "high grid" indicates only that a person has a *high* predilection towards fulfilling his or her socially defined role within a *grid* of such roles. By contrast, where the sex role provides not domestic bliss but horror and alienation, the woman may reject the role of submissive wife, moving from high grid to low grid. Similarly, the runaway teenager who flees from parental authority or abuse is low grid. In both of these latter cases, the individuals reject the family role designed for them by social convention. The term "low grid" signals a person who has a *low* predilection for fulfilling the role assigned to them within the *grid* of such roles.

In Douglas' classification, role-centered identity is not the opposite of group-centered identity but rather a different yet related dimension of human experience; the two forms of identity must be measured concurrently. The young computer whiz who relates better to his machine than to other people (that is, weak group) may at the same time be a model of adolescent submission to his parents or represent a socially approved type of achiever (high grid); he is likely to succeed in the vocation of computer programmer. The husband who finds his fulfillment in his marriage relationship and in his wife may nonetheless have few skills or inclinations to support his wife or relate to her at home in socially approved ways; their relationship may be intimate but unstructured, at least in terms of social conventions (strong group but low grid). Of course, a person may fulfill socially approved roles in the home *and* be intensely committed to his or her spouse (both strong group and high grid). Conversely, the lonely computer whiz may not be able to translate his solitary skills into an acceptable vocation and may end up as a misfit (both weak group and low grid). Douglas' method provides a means for analyzing both dimensions of social experience rather than just one.

These two dimensions may be plotted on a diagram (see below). The horizontal axis indicates the degree of group identity—from weak identity on the left (individualism) to strong identity on the right. The vertical axis indicates the degree of one's acceptance of socially approved roles—from low role identification on the bottom to a high degree of such identification with the current social roles and values at the top of the diagram, that is, from low to high grid. Again, high-grid does not in itself indicate high-status, but only the individual's complete acceptance of the socially approved roles and his or her self-definition in terms of those roles. Douglas' diagram, then, shows four quadrants.

High Grid	A	C
Low Grid	B	D

Low   High
Group   Group

A = High role definition but little group identity.
B = Low role identity and low group identity.
C = Both high role and high group identity.
D = High group identity, but low role definition.

Figure 1

Two categories are inherently unstable. First, since most people need social connections, "A" type individualism is not stable. Second, since most groups need structure, "D" type groups are not stable. Obviously, "B" is anti-social, for these individuals are neither connected nor structured. Douglas argues that "C" is the typically most stable social identity—one of both social cohesion and social order. Although she does not typically use this paradigm to describe movement from one category to another, she would suggest that societies tend to move toward both high group and high role definition.

This paradigm measuring the importance of role and group centeredness works best in face-to-face relationships and other more or less homogenous social groups. In modern pluralistic societies the paradigm must be used with care. For one thing, an individual might belong to more than one group, each characterized by different social typology. Still we might characterize larger social units—as well as individuals—as tending to one or another type. We would typically characterize American society as high grid and low group.[9] There are strong social conventions marking successful roles and life—college education, professional or profitable business vocations, comfortable homes, and cars – but weak or optional kinds of relationships. American pluralism challenges the society to find symbols and rituals and cultural distinctives with which to unite the nation. Similarly, we

---

[9] For example, Malina, pp. 45ff.

might regard the Soviet Union, with all its nationalistic, ideological and bureaucratic qualities, as high grid and high group.

To measure the characteristics of a social group we ask certain questions of it and develop a profile of that social group and its members from those questions.[10] First, it is important to ask about the way a society views roles. Berger and Luckmann remind us that roles represent themselves *and* to a certain extent "an entire institutional nexus of conduct."[11] A policeman acts not on his personal authority but in his office as policeman. Moreover, a policeman represents an entire framework of legal and financial institutions. When we speed by the policeman parked behind an overpass on the highway, we suddenly think not just of his flashing lights behind us, but of fines, courts and increased insurance rates. In analyzing Jewish wisdom, then, it is important to ask how the sages view their own role and its integration into a larger framework of specialized social roles.

The second focus of this study concerns the way in which an individual or society confronts crises—crises of either personal identity or social stability. For example, the way in which a society answers the challenge of death will reveal important information about the social experience and expectation of its members. The keening in some cultures, for instance, suggests a communal experience of death quite foreign to the more private, hidden experience of death in individualized America. Furthermore, how a society defines immortality will indicate something of its social tendencies. For example, a focus on personal immortality of the soul, such as in found in *Sirach* and *Pseudo-Solomon*, suggests more individuation than Gordis and others have noted. In this essay I ask what is the sage's personal response to his mortality and, specifically, where does he find a permanent identity in the face of his mortality?

---

[10] Malina, for example, pp. 20ff., calls these features of social groups and their typology, "cultural scripts," including the following: purity, rite, personal identity, body (the way people regard or emphasize their physical selves), sin, suffering and misfortune, and cosmology.

[11] Berger and Luckmann, pp. 75ff. A somewhat simplified statement with a focus on the role of religion in the social construction of reality is P. Berger, *The Sacred Canopy: Elements of a Sociological Theory of Religion* (Garden City: Doubleday/Anchor, 1969), hereafter Berger. The sociology of knowledge provides real insights into the way social worlds are constructed and maintained. Wisdom scholarship has not utilized the sociology of knowledge to any great extent except to point to Berger's theories of legitimation, for example, Brueggemann (see above, fn. 6) and more recently A. A. di Lella, *The Wisdom of Ben Sira*, Anchor Bible 39, with Patrick W. Skehan (New York: Doubleday, 1987), pp. 33ff. I will be using Berger's description of social construction and maintenance to supplement my use of Mary Douglas.

Threats to the society may elicit different responses, either of securing one's own status and position or of concern for the social fabric as a whole. I will ask how wisdom's sages respond to threats, internal or external, to the society. This question is related to the last, for one of the crises facing societies is the increased specialization of roles that leads to fragmentation of the society. As roles become specialized, so does the knowledge necessary to those roles, and as the knowledge become specialized the common knowledge which cements the society is undermined. Social stability requires the integration of a fragmented society into a cohesive whole—a goal that may be achieved by rituals or theoretical frames of reference (see below). But certain roles also can serve this integrative function. For example, lawyers seem omnipresent in American society, involved in every significant activity; they seem to represent the litigious nature of our society and to be indispensable for a safe sojourn through modern social life. Similarly, medical doctors, psychiatrists and, somewhat less so, scholars and politicians play important roles in uniting the society. The preacher who once stood at the nexus of community activity and concerns is now less central in American society.

A third measure of social type is ritual. If rituals are just means to personal advancement, they indicate a high grid, weak group social type. Even church rituals may be merely the means of advancement for an ambitious young minister who performs them with flair. This is especially true of secular rituals or regular activities that serve to define the culture; for example, legal and bureaucratic procedures and school activities. Rituals furthermore define community boundaries. Those who can or want to participate in the rituals of a community belong to that community, while those who do not are excluded by the community (excommunication). The pledge of allegiance to the flag is one such ritual which has been used to define who is truly American. If the ritual has no further role than community identity, it suggests that the community is strong group but weak grid. But if the ritual represents the power of the community to order life generally, and if it is conducted by a recognized official priesthood, then it is likely to indicate a high grid, strong group social world. Thus rituals can be a powerful means to integration of the society and its maintenance in the face of crises. We will ask concerning the sage's view of ritual and to what degree it integrates or maintains social experience for him.

A fourth measurement of social relations is the social use of language. Laws making English the official language of a state, for example, seek to impose a cultural uniformity on the society that excludes some from participation in the community and from advancement in the hierarchy of roles that define success. But social control is also seen in the way the common language is used. Certain kinds of language identify social groups. Fraternities may have certain phrases and codes to identify members. Churches expect certain patterns of thought or code words of their members and are suspicious of those who do not use the same phrases as they do. Technical jargon and acronyms may identify an individual with a particular scientific community or governmental bureaucracy or profession and ensure that their knowledge remains a mystery to other people. Politicians make certain phrases a litmus test of American character and legitimacy. In the present study, I will ask how the sage uses language. Does he use a traditional vocabulary which reinforces national and religious identity or does he use a cosmopolitan vocabulary which frees him from dependance upon the shared meaning of a traditional community and encourages greater individuation?

The fifth and final question concerns the way in which the social world of the individual is legitimated or the way social and personal crises are answered with theoretical or symbolic systems. Again, Berger and Luckmann note that both "the totality of institutional order should make sense" and "the totality of the individual's life, the successive passing through various orders of the institutional order, must be made subjectively meaningful."[12] The creation and maintenance of this meaningful social order is realized through the use of language, rituals and even roles. But these may fail to comprehend the totality of social and personal experience, especially when that experience is threatened. So explicit theories and, in particular, theories that provide an all encompassing explanation for the totality of life, are necessary. Ideally

> ...all the sectors of the institutional order are integrated in an all-embracing frame of reference, which now constitutes a universe in the literal sense of the word, because *all* human experience can now be conceived of as taking place *within* it.[13]

For example, pluralism and specialization in American society threaten the cultural unity and stability of the society. Various theories and ideologies are said to be representative of the American way of life or of the American mainstream. For example, one may seek to define American culture in terms of Democracy, Liberalism, Capitalism or the Judaic-Christian tradition, and the Soviet system in terms of Authoritarianism, Communism or Secular Humanism. If those theories can be couched in quasi-religious terms and rituals (civil

---

[12] Berger and Luckmann, pp. 92ff.

[13] *Ibid.*, p. 96.

religion), the legitimation of the society is even stronger, and if the enmity between nations can be couched in terms of a cosmic dualism of good and evil, the legitimation is stronger still.   In this case the legitimation of the society is realized through a cosmology—or the way "social groups perceive their universe or world to be outfitted and to function."[14]

The social aspects are not the only concern, however; there are also issues of cosmology. Indeed, Douglas' major work, *Natural Symbols*, is subtitled "Explorations in Cosmology" and the thrust of her argument is to find a correlation between social type (on her grid-group paradigm) and cosmology. The basic distinction between individualism and group identity correlates with a distinction between cosmologies that perceive the universe to run like a machine and cosmologies that believe that some being runs the universe. Individualistic societies and persons (weak group) tend to view the universe as essentially benign, governed by impersonal forces and objects which, in the high grid profile, can be manipulated to achieve the goal of success. The group oriented person or society views the universe as dominated by personal forces. For the low grid, strong group type, the cosmic dualism of good and evil forces reflects the boundaries between the group and the hostile outside world. For the high grid, strong group type, rituals, institutional structure and personalities govern and moderate the potential conflict in the cosmos, rendering it essentially harmonious.

Scholars have long noted that the distinctive theology of the wisdom tradition is creation theology rather than covenantal theology. That is, whereas many Old Testament writers concentrate on the peculiar relationship between Yahweh and the people of Israel—as reflected in their history, their rituals and their prophetic voices—the wisdom tradition appears to concentrate on God's relationship to the whole of creation and to utilize the understanding of that world that is available to humanity generally.   While that distinction cannot be maintained without serious qualifications, the sages nonetheless have a keen interest in locating covenantal history in the context of creation. In the wisdom tradition, God oversees the creation through Wisdom or Dame Wisdom or Sophia. And the way in which humanity can know God's intentions and understand the universe is through Sophia. When the sages instruct and socialize their students to the existing order or when they seek to answer the threats to the social order, they look to Dame Wisdom and a person's relation to her.[15] In

---

[14] Malina, p. 26.

[15] W. Zimmerli has been the chief proponent of this distinction between the covenantal theology of the Old Testament generally and the creation theology

examining the sages' view of Dame Wisdom as an intellectual or cosmological frame of reference for ordering the society, I wish to ask if there is a uniform view of Wisdom among the sages or does their view of Wisdom vary according to their social type.

To conclude these opening remarks, the ancient sages of Israel and early Judaism are obviously concerned with maintaining the social worlds they represent and passing those social worlds on to succeeding generations. What is not so obvious is whether there is a single social world that can be understood as simply upper class, as Gordis and others have suggested. The evidence which Gordis marshals for the sages' upper class world view may be better understood as representing the perspective of a person who defines himself by what he does and the status he holds rather than by the community to which he belongs and to which he is responsible. That is, Gordis' portrayal of the sage suggests Douglas' profile of the high grid, weak group person: satisfaction with social hierarchy, individualism, role-centered identity, success orientation, preoccupation with technique (the skills necessary to prosper), the linkage of right action with prosperity and wrong activity with failure and poverty and therefore the reduction of morality to the issue of success or failure, a generalized but non-activist concern or *Angst* over social injustice and personal meaninglessness, finally a wisdom cosmology that secures personal fortune more than the good fortune of the society or nation as a whole.

Gordis' attempt to identify a single world view for the wisdom tradition, even allowing for a rephrasing of that profile in terms of Mary Douglas' high grid and weak group person, does not present the whole picture. Gordis draws this picture of the sages in large part from the evidence in Sirach and he excludes the evidence of Wisdom of Solomon. By employing the Douglas paradigm to study these two particular cases of wisdom writers and their world views, we can see whether the class analysis is valid or even precise enough to explain

---

of the wisdom literature in "Concerning the Structure of Old Testament Wisdom," tr. by B. W. Kovacs, *Studies in Ancient Israelite Wisdom*, ed. by J. L. Crenshaw, 175ff. (New York: KTAV, 1976) and "The Place and Limit of the Wisdom in the Framework of the Old Testament Theology," *Scottish Journal of Theology* 17 (1964), pp. 146ff. His position has been seriously and effectively challenged by R.E. Murphy, "Wisdom and Yahwism," in *No Famine in the Land*, fs. for J. L. McKenzie, ed. by J. W. Flanagan and A. W. Robinson, 117-126 (Missoula: Scholar's Press, 1975). Nevertheless, the wisdom tendency is to place Israel's covenantal history in the frame of reference of the whole of creation. See for example, J. L. Crenshaw, "Prolegomena," in *Studies in Ancient Israelite Wisdom*, pp. 27ff.

the particularity of each writer. By rephrasing the picture drawn by Gordis in terms of Douglas' model, we can see if the high grid, weak group profile (i.e., "upper class") of the sage is always valid and whether the wisdom cosmology always legitimates this social structure or even represents a unified idea.

II

"The Wisdom of the Son of Sirach," usually called "Sirach," "Ben Sira" or "Ecclesiasticus," was written in Hebrew between 198 and 175 B.C.E. in Palestine by Jesus, son of Eleazar, son of Sirach (50:27). It was translated into Greek by Sirach's grandson sometime after he arrived in Egypt in 132 B.C.E.[16] The dating of this book allows for a clear picture of its historical setting, which I will consider below.

J. T. Sanders argues that Sirach's principle innovation is organizational and not conceptual.[17] Sirach tends to be expansive where previous, similar proverbs were simple. He also clusters sayings of similar subjects where in the earlier Proverbs, by comparison, they were isolated and scattered. Furthermore, he includes fuller discourses or panegyrics, prayers and hymns. And, perhaps most importantly, he organizes the whole work into a literary unity that builds to a climax.

But Sirach's innovations extend even further. When we consider the organizationally novel units, we find that Sirach moves beyond traditional proverbial wisdom. For example, he has distinctive responses to the problem of evil, a keener interest in the cultus of Israel than is typical of the wisdom tradition generally, and a greater concern for the fate of the nation as a whole than we expect to find in the sages. In this analysis, I will focus on the organizationally distinctive material noted in R.B.Y. Scott's outline of Sirach, because it is in these sections that Sirach moves beyond the received tradition of sayings material and addresses questions of personal and corporate identity

---

[16] The approximate date of translation is indicated by preface in which the translator states that he arrived in Egypt in the 38th year of the reign of Ptolemy VII, Physkon Euergetes II, about 132 B.C.E. The general date for the original Hebrew writing is indicated by the fact that it is written by the grandfather of the translator. The death of the High Priest Simon the Just, who is the chief hero of Sirach but is described as someone in the past, suggests the earliest possible date of 198 B.C.E., and the later date is determined by the hellenistic reform of Jerusalem begun by Antiochus IV Epiphanes in 175, an event of which Sirach seems unaware.

[17] Jack T. Sanders, *Ben Sira and Demotic Wisdom* (Chico: Scholars Press, 1983), pp. 12ff.

reflecting his particular social context.[18] This outline, with its identification of special sections and subjects, indicates the way in which Sirach integrates covenantal concerns with creation theology and personal concerns with community concerns.

Outline of Innovative Sections of Sirach

Part One: 1:1-24:29
  Opening Panegyric to Wisdom (1:1-20)
    Three essays on Wisdom (4:11-19; 6:26:31; 14:20-15:8)
    Essay on God (16:26-18:31)
    Prayer for the Sage himself (22:27-23:6)
    Closing Panegyric to Wisdom (24:1-29)
Part Two: 25:1-39:11
  Meditation on Creation (33:7-15)
  Prayer for Israel (36:1-17)
  Praise of the Sage's vocation (38:24-39:11)
Part Three: 39:12-50:24
  Call to Praise God (39:12-35)
  Hymn to God (42:15-43:33)
  Hymn to Israel's Heroes (44:1-50:21)
Conclusion and Epilogue: 50:22-51:30

A. The Profile of the Sage

The middle section of the book concludes with Sirach's praise for his own vocation and shows the degree to which his role has been objectified (38:24-39:11). It is an acknowledged role alongside those of farmer, engraver and designer, blacksmith and potter (vss. 25-29), judge (vs. 33, perhaps he indicates that the sage may serve as judge) and physician (38:1ff.). The objectification of these various roles indicates the extent of division of labor and knowledge in Sirach's social world and the degree to which Sirach can speak on his authority as a sage.

While Sirach does not disparage the skill and importance of these other roles (cf. 38:34), it is clear that he regards the role of sage[19] as

---

[18] Cf. R.B.Y. Scott, *The Way of Wisdom in the Old Testament* (New York: MacMillan, 1971), pp. 205ff. Except when noted, quotations from Sirach and Pseudo-Solomon are taken from the translation by members of the Catholic Biblical Association of America and sponsored by the Confraternity of Christian Doctrine, Vol. 3 (Paterson, N.J.: St. Anthony Guild Press, 1955).

[19] Cf. Berger and Luckmann, pp. 72ff. Berger and Luckmann remind us that roles represent institutional order at two levels. First, "the performance of the role represents itself" (p. 74). Second, the "role represents an entire institutional nexus of conduct" (p. 75). Scholars who argue for the existence of a special role of sage in the ancient Jewish community usually start with Jer.

more honorable and important. The sage's praise of his own vocation (38:24-39:11) reveals the traditional advantages of the sage— extensive travel, cosmopolitan learning, association with the elite, counselor to kings. Skill and craftsmanship are the means to success in one's vocation. The primary qualification for the role of sage is the freedom from toil necessary to devote oneself to study—study of the law, the wisdom of ancients, prophecies, famous discourses, riddles and other difficult matters.[20]   On a scale of values and prestige, Sirach believes that the wise man's position ranks higher than that of other roles. From this position of authority, on the one hand, the sage may

---

18:18. See, for example, R. B. Y. Scott, "Priesthood, Prophecy, Wisdom and the Knowledge of God," *Journal of Biblical Literature* 80 (1961), pp. 1-15. He is challenged by R. N. Whybray, *The Intellectual Tradition in the Old Testament* (Berlin: Walter de Gruyter, 1979), who argues that at most there was a small educated class of people who were prosperous and accustomed to reading, pp. 69-70. Many draw analogies to the Egyptian and Babylonian courts where professional sages instructed the royal courts and bureaucrats; cf. Ronald J. Williams, "Scribal Training in Ancient Egypt," *Journal of the American Oriental Society* 92 (1972), pp. 214-21, but the Egyptian and Babylonian court life and culture was more complex than was the Israelite court and culture, so it is difficult to assume a parallel development in the Hebrew court. For example, see J. L. Crenshaw, *Old Testament Wisdom: An Introduction* (Atlanta: John Knox, 1981), pp. 28ff. For specific Jewish evidence for an identifiable role of professional sage, scholars turn to the late text of Sirach 38:24-39:11 (also 51:23) where the sage argues for distinctive responsibilities and privileges for the sage relative to other vocations. The issue of whether Sirach's society shares his sense of the sage's distinct vocation depends somewhat on whether the wisdom tradition as a body of literature is the product of a distinct sapiential viewpoint and whether it is likely that the "royal court would need the particular talents which the sages possessed" (Crenshaw, p. 28). I would agree with Crenshaw, pp. 28ff., that there is a general probability that the sages were regarded by the rest of society as having a distinct role.

[20] Sirach's learning is broad, including both Hebrew and hellenistic sources. He knows and uses Theognis, cf. T. Middendorp, *Die Stellung Jesu ben Siras zwischen Judentum und Hellenismus* (Leiden: E. J. Brill, 1975), pp. 7-34; there are in Sirach reflections of Cynic-Stoic popular philosophy, cf. R. Pautrel, "Ben Sira et le stoicisme," *Recherches de science religieuse* 51(1963), pp. 535-549; J. Marbock, *Weisheit im Wandel: Untersuchungen zur Weisheitstheologie bei Ben Sira*, BBB 37 (Bonn: Peter Hanstein Verlag, 1971), pp. 143-45; M. Hengel, *Judaism and Hellenism*, tr. by John Bowden (Philadelphia: Fortress, 1974), vol. I, pp. 146-150, 159-162, who remarks that Sirach shows a new development under hellenistic influences, pp. 78-83. Even the organizational unity shows hellenistic influence. For example, cf. T. R. Lee, *Studies in the Form of Sirach 44-50* (Decatur: Scholars Press, 1986), who argues that Sirach 44ff is modeled after the encomium, a category of the rhetorical genre of epideictic. Cf. also B. L. Mack, *Wisdom and the Hebrew Epic:* Ben Sira's Hymn in Praise of the Fathers (Chicago: University of Chicago Press, 1985), pp. 89ff.

speak concerning the whole range of roles and relationships in early Jewish society (from parent to king and from lender to table guest) and, on the other, he may teach his special students at his school for future sages (51:23ff.).

The differentiation of roles and institutions leads to the problem of binding the society together in a cohesive whole.[21]   While legitimating cosmologies normally accomplish this integration, it may also be accomplished through certain roles.[22]   In much of Israelite history, the integrating roles were played by religious and political figures, but in pre-Maccabean Jerusalem the political and priestly leaders of Jerusalem polarized, rather than integrated, Jewish society. These leaders bought their offices and gained power and wealth by aligning themselves with either the Ptolemies or the Seleucids. In Sirach's time, Coele-Palestine had been ceded to the Seleucids after the victory of Antiochus III over the Ptolemies at Panium, near the Jordan. Still there were factions in Jerusalem allied to old Ptolemaic power and these included Onias III, the successor to Simon as High Priest.   Political and religious leaders, regardless of political allegiances, were associated with Hellenization and thus the wealthy establishment. Neither political nor priestly roles could integrate institutional order for the majority of poorer Jews who were excluded from that establishment. Something of the distress of those times can be seen in Sirach's measured, restrained concern for the disparity between wealth and poverty (see 13:2-15; 31:5; 34:24-27; also 4:1, 9, 10; 21:5).

Into this crisis of a fragmented society steps the sage. The role of the sage is the central integrating role in society, for he addresses all other roles and places them in the general framework of society. Specifically, Sirach studies the law and the *prophets* , and promotes the cultus which the *priest* administers (39:1).   Because Sirach represents Wisdom in a special way in his role as sage, and because Wisdom, as we shall see, provides the integrating cosmology for his society, he has authority to challenge and counsel all other roles. In post-exilic Jerusalem, the study of the Scriptures was the key to survival and the scribe was becoming the chief representative of that

---

[21] Berger and Luckmann, p. 76. See above.

[22] *Ibid.* "Some roles, however, symbolically represent that order in its totality more than others. 3Such roles are of great strategic importance in a society, since they represent not only this or that institution, but the integration of all institutions in a meaningful world."

study.[23] Sirach, therefore, sees himself as counselor to kings (39:4) and advises the priests not to become entangled in political intrigue and with the wrong parties (45:26ff.; 50:23f. and perhaps 7:4-7). He speaks to the whole spectrum of early Jewish society where the current political and religious leaders cannot. While his focus on the temple cultus and upon the priesthood leads him to affirm the ideal centrality of the priest,[24] Sirach sees his own role as spokesman for Dame Wisdom as especially necessary to that ordering of society: "...but the ruler of his people is the skilled sage" (9:17). This can be seen as he addresses the crises confronting himself and his society.

B. The Problems of the Sage

We begin to see Sirach's concern for the whole community, however, when we consider three areas of crisis which he addresses.

1. The problem of personal mortality

Sirach, like Job and Qoheleth before him, is troubled by the fact of death (Sir. 10:17; 11:19-28; 14:11-19; 17:2, 22; 18:7ff., 22ff.; 38:16ff; 40:1ff.; 41:1ff.). He is skeptical of speculative answers generally (17:4ff.; 39:16; 42:17ff.; 43:27ff. and others) and does not resort to images of the afterlife (14:11-19 and 40:1-11), but he is nonetheless optimistic in his response to personal mortality. He acknowledges with Qoheleth (e.g., Qoh. 2:13-17) that whatever advantages come with wisdom and wealth they do not forestall death (e.g., 14:3, 12ff.; 40:1-11; 41:1-2). But unlike Qoheleth, who predicts rather gloomily that the wise man will be forgotten, Sirach is convinced that the wise man who serves his people will be remembered:

> Limited are the days of one man's life,
>> but the life of Israel is days without number.
> One wise for himself has full enjoyment,
>> and all who see him praise him;
> One wise for his people wins an heritage of glory,

---

[23] M. Hengel, *Judaism and Hellenism*, tr. by J. Bowden (Philadelphia: Fortress Press, 1974): I, 132, quotes A. Schlatter, "Here for the first time appear in Jerusalem scribes who are nothing but scribes."

[24] The degree to which office and one's call to office is important for Sirach has been examined by Mack, pp. 11-36. In studying the heroes of the hymn, he notes the pattern of characterization that focuses on office and in particular on those like Moses, Phineas, the Judges, Samuel, David and Simon, in Sirach's own time, all of whom held multiple offices. 4The hymn focuses on Simon, so that Mack concludes "...the attribution of the functions of the kings to Simon strongly suggests that the high priesthood is understood as the contemporary and sufficient locus of all of Israel's religious offices" (p. 36).

and his name endures forever (37:23-25).

His own mortality will be transcended in the on-going life of the community. Wisdom, like wealth, brings advantage, for through it one can ingratiate oneself to the community.[25]

At this first level of concern, Sirach finds meaning in his identification with his people. Individualistic egotism is modified if not indeed replaced by concern for and identity with the community. The typical, wisdom concern for prudence is here affirmed not so much with an eye toward private gain as toward a lasting name.[26] Shame is more distasteful to Sirach than is poverty, but wealth rightly used may bring honor and a lasting name in the community (10:29f.; 14:11ff.; 22:23f.; 29:1f.; 31:8-11). For Sirach, then, the sage's identity is bound up with that of the community of which he is a part, and the ongoing life of the community provides a response to the problem of individual mortality.

2. The problem of community identity

The Israelite community, with which Sirach identified, was challenged by social and economic differentiation and the rise of hellenistic ideas and institutions (such as the gymnasium and governing structures associated with the *polis*). Given his concern for the ongoing life of the community,[27] it is necessary for Sirach to reaffirm traditional language, symbols and rituals, and history.

---

[25] Sirach may reflect early Greek views of immortality where heroes live on in the songs of poets or the memory of the communities. %This view of "immortality" is associated with a high view of the polis, and seems to give way to the Orphic and mystery religion and to Platonic views of the immortality of the soul that follows the increasing individualism of the hellenistic cosmo-polis. See the brief discussion by W. Jaeger, "The Greek Ideas of Immortality," in *Immortality and Resurrection,* ed. by K. Stendahl (New York: MacMillan, 1969), pp. 97ff. In discussing theodicies, P. Berger, in *The Sacred Canopy,* points out that every society requires a certain self-denial that may take the form of masochism. The individual "cannot accept aloneness and he cannot accept meaninglessness" and so he is willing to be absorbed "in an other," or into the "collectivity of others, and finally, to the *nomoi* represented by these" (p. 55). This basic tendency may be maintained in more sophisticated theodicies and Berger goes on to describe, at the "irrational" pole of the continuum, "the simple, theoretically unelaborated transcendence of self brought about by a complete identification with the collectivity." (p.60)

[26] Cf. J.T. Sanders, "Ben Sira's Ethics of Caution," *Hebrew Union College Annual* 50(1978), pp. 73-106.

[27] Consider the beautiful prayer for Israel in 36:1-17 that balances his praise for his vocation as sage in 38:24-39:12.

His most beautiful contribution to Hebrew literature is his praise of Israel's heroes (44:1-49:24). He introduces his hymn with reference to their enduring fame because they were godly and were recipients of God's covenant. While this hymn to heroes may not be salvation history in the obvious sense,[28] it is concerned with the example of those who have transcended their individual mortality through their identity with the history of Israel and the covenants of God.

The sage is also concerned with the cultic center of Israel. It is enough to note the disproportionate attention given to the heroic priests of his catalog: Aaron, Phineas, Samuel and Simon. Repeatedly in chapter 50 he glories in the temple service. It is true that he shares the prophets' concern for genuine piety (1:26; 3:20; 19:20; 21:11; 32:14-17; 32:24; 33:3; 34:19; 35:1-2; 35:17) and he seems more interested in the cultic paraphernalia than in the sacrifices themselves. Still the temple is glorious because it is there that the people "receive from him the blessing of the Most High" (50:12). It is because of the centrality of the temple cultus to the life of the community and its future that Sirach lavishes such extensive praise upon Simon "in whose time the temple was reinforced" (50:1).

Similarly, Sirach devotes unique (for the wisdom literature) attention to the place of torah. Von Rad has discussed at length the importance of torah to Sirach,[29] arguing that torah does not replace wisdom precepts as a norm for behavior, but that torah is legitimized in connection to Wisdom.[30] He notes that Sirach never appeals to particular laws but speaks only of torah *sui generis*, and that specific conduct is guided by traditional sagacity. But torah does play a highly significant role in Sirach (e.g., 9:15; 14:20-15:10, esp. 15:1; 17:9-12; 19:17, 20; 21:11; 28:7; 32:15; 32:23-33:3; 34:8; 35:1; 42:2). Two passages are most important. In Sir. 24:1-31 and 39:1-8 he identifies Wisdom and the Law. Perhaps the law does not play as large a practical role as does sagacity in guiding the conduct of an individual, but it is central to the life and continuity of the community as a whole (16:22-17:18; 24:1-31), and the life and continuity of the community is paramount to the sage. The law

---

[28] Cf. for example, G. von Rad, *Wisdom in Israel*, tr. by J.H. Martin (Nashville: Abingdon, 1972), pp. 257f.; Gordis, p. 116; J.T. Sanders, *Ben Sira and Demotic Wisdom*, p. 12; Mack, *Wisdom and the Hebrew Epic*, pp. 49ff., who remarks, "...Ben Sira proposes a hymn in praise of the great leaders, not a history of the people" (p. 49). Nevertheless, the hymn does seem to presuppose it.

[29] Von Rad, pp. 244ff.

[30] He argues against J. Fichtner's use of the term "nomistic wisdom" in *Die altorientialische Weisheit in ihrer israelitisch-judischen Auspragung*, BZAW (Geissen: A. Topelmann, 1933), p. 97. Cf. also E.G. Bauckmann, "Die Proverbien und die Spruche des Jesus Sirach," *ZAW* 72 (1960), pp. 33-63.

is not just legitimated by reference to a more fundamental wisdom. Rather, wisdom points to the need for the individual to relate to the community which in turn is defined in large part by the law and cultus. In this sense, torah and cultus play similar roles and are even interconnected in a prophetic manner (35:1ff.). And the fear of the Lord, leading primarily to observance of torah or the commandments, is also associated with reverence for the temple service (2:15ff.; 10:19; 15:1; 19:17, 20; 21:11; 32:14ff. and 7:29f.).

Sirach's focus on the chief institutions that symbolize Israel's historic identity is unique in the wisdom literature. But it is very understandable to one whose personal solution to the problem of mortality and meaninglessness is in fact the ongoing life of the people. Rituals and symbols reinforce the boundaries and stability of the community and of one's identity within the community.[31] Those rituals and symbols are like B. Bernstein's "restricted" language code, for they presuppose unexpressed but shared meanings that reinforce the boundaries of the community.[32] Thus, not only does Sirach focus on the rituals and symbols that mark off and hold the community together, but there is a notable lack of vocabulary that belongs to the larger cosmopolitan world (a world which he enjoys and from which he

---

[31] Cf. Douglas, *Natural Symbols*, pp. 37-53. Berger, p. 40, remarks: "Indeed, it may be argued that one of the oldest and most important prerequisites for the establishment of culture is the institution of such 'reminders,'...Religious ritual has been a crucial instrument of this process of 'reminding.' Again and again it 'makes present' to those who participate in it the fundamental reality-definitions and their appropriate legitimations... It has been rightly said that society, in its essence, is a memory. It may be added that, through most of human history, this memory has been a religious one."

[32] Basil Bernstein, in his works *A Socio-Linguistic Approach to Social Learning*, Penguin Survey of the Social Sciences, ed. by J. Gould (London: Penguin, 1965) and *A Socio-Linguistic Approach to Socialization*, in "Directions in Socio-Linguistics," ed. by J. Gumperz and D. Hymes (New York: Holt, Rinehart and Winston, 1970), distinguishes a "restricted code" from a "elaborated code." The first has limited syntactical possibilities but, due to its familiarity within a given community, it allows for shades of meaning that can be understood only within a given social framework. The "elaborated code" by being more complex in syntax and vocabulary allows for more precise and "elaborate" speech that can be understood in a broader social context. Its primary function is communication, even outside given social structures. Thus while the "restricted code" of speech reinforces community boundaries, the elaborated code does not reinforce those narrow boundaries and in fact frees the individual from those boundaries. Cf. Douglas, *Natural Symbols*, for her appropriation of these models to her own "grid-group" model, pp. 20ff.

learns). He uses the time-honored and traditional vocabulary.[33] He expands upon previously simple proverbs, suggesting the extent to which the language is time-worn.[34] Whatever innovations may be attributed to Sirach, his primary concern is to preserve the boundaries and identity of his community and he does so by recalling Israel's rituals and symbols and history.

3. *The problem of social evil*

Sirach is conscious of social evils that threaten his beloved community. While he values riches that are honestly acquired and hates poverty and begging (10:27; 13:24; 25:3; 40:18; 18:31-19:1; 26:28; 25:2f.; 40:28-30), he nonetheless warns against the evils that riches can bring and he urges that the rich treat the poor with respect and mercy (3:29-4:10; 5:1ff.; 14:3ff.; 29:1ff.; 31:1ff. and others). Hengel notes that Sirach's "social preaching" is considerably different from the inactive pessimism of Qoheleth.[35] In strong language, Sirach deplores the growing social polarity between rich and poor (13:2-20). He is critical of the *status quo* (13:22ff.; 5:1ff.; 8:14) and he berates the rich who offer "sacrifice from the property of the poor" (34:24ff).

Given his concern for the socially destructive evils of injustice and abuse of wealth, Sirach returns to the wisdom theme of retribution.[36] But the old wisdom connection between action and consequences can no longer be maintained, since the evil do seem to prosper and the righteous suffer. Recognizing this, Sirach holds up God as the sovereign agent of retribution: "For the Lord is the one who repays" (35:10ff.; 12:6b; 17:23).[37]

---

[33] Cf. A. A. di Lella, "Conservative and Progressive Theology: Sirach and Wisdom," *Catholic Biblical Quarterly* 38 (1966), p. 143.

[34] Von Rad, p. 143, explaining Sirach's description of Wisdom, writes: "Sirach no longer has at his disposal the basic compactness and clarity of language which was the prerogative of earlier periods. Words are more hackneyed and must, therefore, be multiplied."

[35] M. Hengel, *Judaism and Hellenism*, I, pp.136f. This difference in social consciousness within the wisdom tradition undermines the conclusions of, for example, Gordis, regarding the upper class individualism and relative passivity of the sages when confronted with social ills.

[36] For example, 2:8; 3:14; 3:31; 4:10, 13, 20; 5:7f.; 6:16; 7:1-3; 9:11f.; 10:13f.; 11:17, 21f., 26; 12:2, 6; 15:13; 16:11-13; 17:23; 18:24; 20:18, 26; 21:10; 23:8, 11, 14, 25-27; 26:28; 27:24-29; 28:1; 33:1; 38:15; 39:25-30; 40:10; 41:6f.; 46:6-10.

[37] Hengel, p. 143, remarks: "This firm connection between human action and divine retribution runs through the work of Ben Sira like a scarlet thread, and gave [sic] it to a large degree its polemic force. While in Proverbs action and consequence are still for the most part directly related, in Sirach God himself

But the righteousness of God itself was questioned (e.g., 15:11f.) and Sirach responds by praising the perfection of creation:

The works of God are all good,

and they are appropriate for each purpose (39:16).

In a remarkable series of passages (33:11-15; 39:25-35; 40:1ff.; 42:24-25), Sirach speaks of the ultimate balance of all things in creation. Nowhere is this clearer than in 33:11-15 which concludes:

As Evil contrasts with Good, and death with life,

So are sinners in contrast with the just;

See now all the works of the Most High;

They come in pairs, the one opposite of the other.

The "efficient" cause of evil is not God's failure but the failure of humanity (15:11ff.), but ultimately evil is accounted for in creation and will be dealt with by a sovereign and purposeful creator God.[38]

Sirach's response to evil[39] may not appear as profound as the investigations of Job and Qoheleth because he resorts to explanations that are "free from empirical verification."[40] But he does, as Hengel notes, provide a more effective means of control against the threat of hellenism by connecting human responsibility (or irresponsibility) to

---

appears much more strongly as the author and guarantor of righteous retribution."

[38] Although Sirach sees evil and good as "pairs," his theodicy is not dualistic because the duality within human society and the creation generally is still under the sovereignty of God. Sirach is not negative about the material world or about history. He is not, to use Berger's description of dualistic theodicies, "acosmic, ascetic, and ahistorical" (p. 72).

[39] O. S. Rankin, *Israel's Wisdom Literature: Its bearing on Theology and the History of Religions* (New York: Schocken, 1936), p. 35: "The thought which he develops upon the perfect harmony and adjustment of creation would seem to be his own contribution to Theodicy."

[40] Von Rad, p. 254: "This attempt to tackle the problem of theodicy is new...it is released from the unpleasant task with which Job's friends still felt themselves faced, of interpreting God's power in comprehensive terms on the basis of a definite, fixed norm." On von Rad's point, Crenshaw remarks: "If this is where Sirach takes his stand, however, it is a slippery one" in J. Crenshaw, "The Problem of Theodicy in Sirach: Of Human Bondage," in *Theodicy in the Old Testament*, ed. by Crenshaw (Philadelphia: Fortress, 1983), p. 129. Crenshaw continues (pp. 129f.): "In his flight to areas *free from empirical verification*, I Sirach has ceased to walk in the steps of former sages for whom experience was the ground of all knowledge. Instead, he has allied himself with the dogmatic tradition of prophet, priest and historian (both deuteronomistic and chronistic) [my emphasis]."

the retribution of God and to the very nature of the created order.[41] The force of Sirach's theodicy may be seen by citing Berger's description of the self-transcending theodicy:

> ...in primitive religion...there is typically not only a continuity between individual and collectivity, but also between society and nature. The life of the individual is embedded in the life of the collectivity, as the latter is in turn embedded in the totality of being, human as well as non-human. The entire universe is pervaded by the same sacred forces.[42]

In Sirach, it is not merely prudence but community norms and the order of universe which control the actions of individuals.

Sirach, then, responds to three levels of problems: that of personal mortality, that of continued community identity and that of social evil. Sirach finds the answer to the question of personal mortality and meaninglessness in his ongoing identity with the community. The community endures as long as it is centered around the temple cultus and the law. Social evils which would jeopardize community unity and faith in God are interpreted as part of the balance in the cosmos.

Sirach's response to these problems confounds the image drawn of the sage by Gordis, which I have rephrased in terms of Mary Douglas' paradigm. Granted that Sirach is very conscious of the importance and status of his role as sage and granted that he enjoys the privileges and opportunities which this role provides him; the fact remains that he finds his security not in his own success and self-transcendence but in his relationship to the community and in its social stability and continuity. That is, he is role conscious *and* group conscious. We would suspect, therefore, that his interpretation of the wisdom cosmology would correlate with this social profile and that he would on the one hand personalize the cosmology and on the other hand see it as legitimating not just his own experience but that of the society at large.

C. The Picture of Sophia

Where traditional wisdom begins with the human search for understanding, the transmission of proverbs and folk wisdom, and thus the assumption of the goodness of the given order, wisdom mythology begins with Wisdom in the creation and moves to human wisdom in the

---

[41] Hengel, pp. 143f. Sirach's views, if novel for a sage, are not entirely alien to Israel's faith in an avenging god, although the specific ways he formulates his response seem to reflect more Stoic conceptions of cosmic harmony. See Hengel, pp. 147ff.

[42] Berger, p. 61. This kind of theodicy is not limited to primitive religions but "continues,...wherever the microcosm/macrocosm scheme prevails" (p. 62).

social and personal world.[43] The order of the world must be affirmed rather than assumed.

Israelite Wisdom literature has a reputation for being incomplete and episodic. In fact, scholars have assumed an Egyptian background for the Wisdom "mythology" in an attempt to impose a certain order on Proverbs 1-9.[44] In Sirach that fragmented and not entirely coherent picture of Sophia remains. Nonetheless, Sirach fleshes out the picture of Sophia with greater narrative detail and more specific connection of Sophia to Israelite religious life than is clear in Proverbs.

In the first place, Sirach expands on Sophia's cosmic role. In Prov. 8, Wisdom is begotten by God as the firstborn of God's ways (8:22-26) and was present at the creation "playing before him" as God's "delight" (8:27-31).[45] The ambiguity of this imagery in Proverbs 8 gives way in Sirach to quite a concrete "personal" history for Sophia. Wisdom's relationship with God is spelled out in Sir. 1:7-8 in terms similar to those of Proverbs 8:23ff. But Sirach's description is in the objective third person and links the pouring out of Wisdom upon creation with her being given to the friends of God (Sir.1:7f.). In her own self-presentation (24:3ff.), Wisdom speaks of her emergence from the mouth of God, of her dwelling in heaven upon "a pillar of cloud," and of her "circling" the heavens and wandering the depths, restlessly seeking a home over sea and land and among every nation. This first

---

[43] B.L. Mack, *Wisdom and the Hebrew Epic: Ben Sira's Hymn in Praise of the Fathers* (Chicago: University of Chicago Press, 1985): 148.

[44] *Ibid.*, p. 149. Rather than assume that Wisdom/Sophia is a full blown or developing mythology (as in, among many others, J.T. Sanders, *The New Testament Christological Hymns: Their Historical Religious Background* [Cambridge: Cambridge University Press, 1971]) or on the other hand mere personification or hypostatization (as in H. Ringgren, *Word and Wisdom: Studies in the Hypostatization of Divine Qualities in the Ancient Near East* [Lund: Ohlssons, 1947]), I prefer the notion that in Israelite wisdom, the figure of Sophia is shaped from mythological images—"reflective mythology" (Conzelmann) or "mytho-logy" (Mack). See H. Conzelmann, "The Mother of Wisdom," tr. by C.E.Carston and R.P. Scharlemann in *The Future of Our Religious Past*, fs. for R. Bultmann, ed. by J. M. Robinson (New York: Harper and Row, 1971), pp. 230-43; B. Mack, "Wisdom Myth and Mythology," *Interpretation* 24 (1970): pp. 46-60; E. Schussler Fiorenza, "Wisdom Mythology and the Christological Hymns of the New Testament," in *Aspects of Wisdom in Judaism and Early Christianity*, ed. by R.L. Wilkens (Notre Dame: University of Notre Dame, 1975), pp. 17-41.

[45] The major question in this passage concerns the meaning of the hebrew *'amon* in vs. 30: does this refer to Wisdom as "master craftsman" or "nursed child" or something general, like R. B. Y. Scott's "living link" or "vital bond"? Cf. Scott's "Wisdom in Creation: The *'AMON* of Proverbs VIII 30," *Vetus Testamentum* 10(1960), pp. 213-123.

strophe (24:3-7) with its mythological or cosmic narrative of Sophia's sojourn is striking for two reasons. It goes beyond previous descriptions of Dame Wisdom in laying out her personal story and it concludes with the open-ended search for a resting place. For Sophia's personal story takes a striking turn when, in 24:8ff., it is historicized. The mythological language is rationalized by linking the cosmic Sophia to Israel's history in very specific ways. Sophia is commanded by God to cease her wandering and dwell in Jacob, minister in the holy tent, rest in the chosen city and take root among the glorious people. She concludes her speech with a rhapsodic description of the benefits of wisdom. Sirach (vs. 22) remarks "All this is true of the book of the Most High's covenant, the law which Moses commanded us as an inheritance for the community of Jacob." Thus Sophia's personal story intersects with that of the covenant people.

In the second place, the individual's encounter with Sophia is no less personalized. Dramatization of one's encounter with wisdom may be seen in Proverbs 1, where Wisdom wanders the street calling out for those who would accept her counsel.[46] But there is nothing in Proverbs to compare with Sirach's vision of the wise man's encounter with Sophia. Where in Proverbs 7 Dame Folly ambushes the fool, in Sirach the happy wise man ambushes Dame Wisdom (14:20ff.): "Happy the man ... who pursues her like a scout, and lies in wait at her entry way; Who peeps through her windows, and listens at her doors; Who encamps near her house and fastens his tent pegs next to her walls..." Bondage to her brings rest and joy and a crown (6:24-31). The one who fears the Lord "builds his nest in her leafage, and lodges in her branches; ...and dwells in her home" (14:26f.). "Motherlike she will meet him, like a young bride she will embrace him" (15:2).

Moreover, the centrality of Sophia in Sirach's thought can be seen in a number of ways. She functions to legitimate individual and community identity at the three points of concern mentioned above.

First, Sirach seeks to ground his own identity in the ongoing life of the community and thus to respond to the crisis of mortality with a theodicy of self-transcendence. This is accomplished through courting and dwelling with Sophia, who herself dwells in the Holy City, in the

---

[46] She is described as a choice possession who brings happiness, long life and riches (2:13-18) and the children are urged to "forsake her not" (4:6ff.) and she is presented as the ideal hostess (9:1-6). In contrasting Wisdom with the whore Folly the text of Proverbs becomes more concrete. The seduction of the fool by Dame Folly (who is dressed in alluring robes, who pulls the fool into dark corners to kiss him and who promises that her husband is not home, 7:10, 12f., 18) is described in more graphic terms than is Wisdom's invitation to the wise in chapter 8.

holy Tent and in the law. For both the community as a whole (24:22) and for the individual (15:1), therefore, Dame Wisdom is incarnated in the law and is appropriated through religious piety.[47] So also the role of sage is legitimated through acquisition of Wisdom (38:24-39:11) and the scribe becomes the ideal figure,[48] mediating God's wisdom to Israel because of his special relationship with Wisdom, who herself communicates God's blessing and will to Israel.[49]

Second, Sirach affirms the community's historic identity by holding up Israel's history, cultus and law. These symbols and rituals remind the people that the order which Sirach seeks to construct and maintain has existed since their beginning as a people. But he goes beyond that basic conservatism by saying that the rituals and the law and even Israel's history manifest Divine Wisdom herself. The singular contribution of Sirach is his identification of law and cultus with Sophia in chapter 24.

Third, Sirach affirms the continuity between human society and the universe. Social anomalies are ultimately absorbed into the eurhythmy of the creation. No one will succeed in uncovering the unfathomable secrets of this mysterious balance. Nonetheless, the wise man has some access to God's creation purposes through Wisdom (16:22ff.) even as it is through Wisdom that God's covenantal purposes are understood (17:6ff.). Sirach's great hymn to the mystery of God's sovereign, creative purposes concludes:

> It is the Lord who has made all things,
>> and to those who fear him he gives Wisdom.(43:35)

In providing a symbol that integrates various aspects of the individual's life as well as the totality of the community's insti-

---

[47] The Fear of the Lord is connected primarily to observance of Torah or the commandments (cf. 2:15ff.; 10:19; 15:1; 19:17, 20; 21:11; 32:14ff.) and also to reverence for the Temple service (7:29f.). Sir. 24:8 describes God's command that Wisdom "tabernacle" in Jerusalem.

[48] Cf. D. J. Harrington, "The Wisdom of the Scribe According to Ben Sira," in *Ideal Figures in Ancient Judaism*, ed. by G.W.E. Nickelsburg and J.J. Collins (Chico: Scholars Press, 1980), pp. 181-188, who with Mack understands Sirach to be holding up the scribe as the ideal figure rather than following the model already established by Aaron. For the latter view see E. Rivkin, "Ben Sira-The Bridge between the Aaronide and Pharisaic Revolutions," *Nelson Glueck Memorial Volume*, ed. by B. Mazar (Jerusalem: Israel Exploration Society, 1975), pp. 95-103 in the english edition.

[49] Compare the conclusion of Berger and Luckmann, pp. 96ff.: "The symbolic universe is conceived of as a matrix of all socially objectivated and subjectively real meanings; the entire historic society and the entire biography of an individual are seen as events taking place within that universe."

tutional life, Sophia functions as the most comprehensive type of legitimation.[50] Sophia represents the "sacred canopy" that covers all the objectivated order of the nation as well as the subjective experience of that order. With respect to Douglas' paradigm, the picture of Sophia in Sirach conforms to what we would expect from someone who is both role conscious and group conscious; namely, a view of the universe and the society that is governed by personal forces—in this case a personalized Sophia—who is known by qualified leaders and who is present in the rituals, law and history of the nation.

Conclusion

The mythological, personalized figure of Wisdom, therefore, pulls together the various strands of Sirach's concerns: the Eternal Cosmic order established and maintained by the Lord, mysterious though it may be; the connection between this eternal order and the community order of the people of Israel; the connection between the community life, with its history and rituals and laws, and the individual. This picture of Sophia fits the social identity of Sirach who takes his relationship to the group seriously; it represents a highly personalized cosmology.

Sirach's social world, in terms of Mary Douglas' classification, is a world of marked group boundaries, identified by central rituals, laws and history, and seen in Sirach's own self-transcending commitment to his community. *But* it is also a world where roles are carefully defined and related hierarchically, although in Sirach's case his role as sage is integrative of the whole of society and not merely indicative of personal success. As such it is a world with an anthropomorphic cosmology where the dualism is mitigated by the intervention of personal powers, so that ultimately there is an essential harmony in the cosmos and the universe may be regarded as just and reasonable. Sophia plays an integral role in this order and reveals it to the faithful community and its members. In short, Sirach's social world is both high grid *and* high group.

---

[50] Berger and Luckmann, pp. 95ff.

III

The Wisdom of Solomon, or Pseudo-Solomon

Pseudo-Solomon, composed in Greek, was written in Egypt, presumably Alexandria,[51] at the beginning of the Common Era.[52] As wisdom literature it is notable for three related characteristics. First, it is rich in Greek stylistic features and vocabulary.[53] Second, the work is written in the genre of a "protreptic," which is "an appeal to follow a meaningful philosophy as a way of life,"[54] and is carefully organized in three interconnected sections.[55] That is, it has a unified structure

---

[51] The overwhelming majority of scholars consider Pseudo-Solomon to have been written in Egypt. Cf. B.J. Lillie, "A History of the Scholarship of the Wisdom of Solomon from the 19th Century to our Time," unpublished dissertation, Hebrew Union College, Jewish Institute of Religion, 1981, pp. 87-101, for an exhaustive survey of this scholarship.

[52] The date of Pseudo-Solomon's writing is much less certain than in the place of its origin; cf. Lillie, pp. 149ff. The *terminus a quo* is the completion of the Septuagint (285-246 B.C.E.) and the *terminus ad quem* is the writing of the New Testament. Two other considerations have generally been made in attempts to date the book: first, its reference to persecution of the Jews (cf. Ps.-Sol. 3:1-12; 5:1ff.; 65-9; 12:22-33); second, its relationship to Philo. Although the range of suggested dates runs from 217 B.C.E. to 66 C.E., the majority taking note of the persecution of Jews suggest dates from 100 B.C.E. to 40 C.E. I have found most convincing the date of 40 C.E., suggested by D. Winston, *The Wisdom of Solomon, The Anchor Bible*, vol. 43 (New York: Doubleday & Company, 1979), pp. 20ff. He argues that: (1) Ps.Sol. 14:16-20, referring to the distant king, refers not to the Ptolemies, but to the Roman Emperors after Augustus; (2) that the vocabulary belongs to the early Christian Era; (3) that the nature of the persecution fits that under Caligula (37-41 C.E.). We shall consider the nature of that situation in our argument below which confirms Winston's dating.

[53] Winston, pp. 14ff., points out 17 or 18 features of Greek style. It is full of Greek words found nowhere else in the biblical tradition. In one short passage, 7:22-23, there are 10 words appearing only in Wisdom and 5 more appearing only here and in 3 and 4 Maccabees.

[54] J. M. Reese, *Hellenistic Influence on the Book of Wisdom and its Consequences* (Rome: Biblical Institute Press, 1970), pp. 117-121.

[55] Cf. B.J. Lillie, pp. 5ff. Many have adopted a two-fold division of Pseudo-Solomon, dividing the book at about chapter 11 with a first section on speculative wisdom and a second on historical illustrations. Reese offers a variation on this division, dividing each of those two sections into two further divisions: (1) Book of Eschatology (roughly 1-6); (2) Book of Wisdom proper (roughly 6-10); (3) Book of Divine Justice and Human Folly (roughly 11-15); and (4) Book of History (16-19). Reese defends this unique division of the book on the basis of the rhetorical device of *inclusio* so that he sees the sections overlapping each other at the seams; cf. Reese, pp. 91ff. and 122ff. However,

patterned after a recognizable Greek rhetorical genre and thus is unique to the wisdom literature. Third, as Winston argues, the author's thought is permeated by mystical Middle Platonism. The vocabulary and structure reflect the assimilation of contemporary hellenistic thought, as do the ideas in Pseudo-Solomon, including the author's presentation of Sophia itself.[56] In short, Pseudo-Solomon is linked more with the Alexandrian tradition of Aristobulus and Philo than with the biblical tradition.[57]

The Wisdom of Solomon may be outlined as followed:

I.   The Book of Eschatology: 1:1-6:11
II.   The Book of Wisdom: 6:12-9:18
III. The Book of History: 10:1-19:22 (including excurses on God's mercy (11:15-12:22) and idolatry (13:1-15:19).[58]

The first and last sections are devoted to a contrast between the foolish and the wise (the wicked and the just). In the first section the

---

the majority of modern scholars follow the more obvious three-fold division: (1) Book of Eschatology (as it is frequently called; 1-6); (2) Book of Wisdom (7-10); (3) Book of History (11-19). I have assumed this structure which may be maintained even though the precise demarcation of each version has been seen differently by various scholars. The unity of the book as the work of a single author is generally accepted today. My analysis supports the unity of the work since the first and third sections do not necessarily represent subjects that conflict with the central section.

[56] Winston, p. 3. On pp. 25-62, he provides an exhaustive analysis of the way Pseudo-Solomon has appropriated ideas from Middle Platonism, Stoicism, neo-pythagoreanism and Zoroastrianism, among others. His notions of pre-existence and immortality are optimistic modifications of Plato's conceptions of the soul, siding with the view of some Middle Platonists that the incarnation of the soul was not so much the result of a fall but was intended to bring life to the body (pp. 25ff.). In other regards—ideas concerning the origin of death, the emanation of Wisdom from God (7:24ff.), creation of earth from formless matter (11:17), etc.—his notions reflect a synthesis of ideas drawn from different sources. It is an "eclecticism" which was common in Middle Platonism and which Pseudo-Solomon shares with Philo (see below on Sophia).

[57] A.A. di Lella, "Conservative and Progressive Theology: Sirach and Wisdom," C.B.Q. 38(1966), p. 147, who describes Pseudo-Solomon as "progressive," relative to the "conservative" Sirach, nonetheless argues that Pseudo-Solomon does not seek "to reconcile Judaism with hellenism—a task that Philo attempted a few years later—but rather to prevent the hellenization of Judaism." (This view is disingenuous, since Pseudo-Solomon has already so thoroughly assimilated hellenistic ideas and thought forms.) Reese also insists on the Jewishness of its ideas, pp. 38, 41.

[58] Cf. G. W. E. Nickelsburg, *Jewish Literature Between the Bible and the Mishnah* (Philadelphia: Fortress Press, 1981), pp. 175ff. and above, footnote 122.

issue is couched in terms of the after-life, or personal immortality of the soul, which the fools reject and in which the just are vindicated.[59] In the last section the issue is couched in terms of the example of the Exodus in which the Egyptians and Israelites (never expressly named but described in veiled, abstract terms) are types for the wicked and the just. Both of these sections revolve around the central, pivotal section in chapters 7-9, where Pseudo-Solomon describes his own experience and the nature and role of Wisdom. It is in this middle section that we must begin.

A. The Profile of the Sage

The author's identity is concealed behind the fiction that he is Solomon, the chief exemplar of a wise man. He speaks as a king to kings and rulers (e.g., 1:1-15; 6:1-11). In spite of this fiction it is possible to uncover something of his social identity.

In the pivotal, middle section, Pseudo-Solomon sets out to describe Sophia (compare 6:12ff.) but he ends up by describing himself. He devotes attention to the normality of his birth and even his pre-natal state (7:1ff.) and he speaks of the pre-existence of his noble soul.[60] He tells of his own search for Sophia in the romantic manner that Sirach, in 14:21ff., describes the wise person's desire for wisdom,[61] but he considers Wisdom a treasure he may possess (7:8, 11, 14). Possession of wisdom is a means to the end of power and glory, the prerogatives that belong to a ruler (8:10-15). Pseudo-Solomon's desire, prayer and search for Wisdom is self-centered, if not actually selfish (8:18; 9:4, 6, 10). While Pseudo-Solomon is not jealous with Wisdom and invites others to possess her (6:1ff.), he is addressing those who have a similar desire to rule. He identifies with an elite class of individuals who are well-

---

[59] Cf. the discussion in G.W.E. Nickelsburg, *Resurrection, Immortality and Eternal Life in Intertestamental Judaism*, Harvard Theological Series XXVI (Cambridge: Harvard University Press, 1977). He identifies three forms of these concerns: (1) the apocalyptic in which an end time judgment is central; (2) the vindication of the Righteous Man; (3) The Two-Way Theology where afterlife is the culmination of walking in either death or life. Of course, Nickelsburg notes how confusing all this is as themes are borrowed from one genre and used in another and thus transformed.

[60] Cf. 8:19f: "Now I was a well-favored child, and I came by a noble nature; Or rather, being noble, I attained an unsullied body." (Cf. Winston, pp. 198-199 and pp. 25-32 for the philosophical background to this idea.)

[61] Although Sirach speaks of the search in the third person – "Happy the man who...," Pseudo-Solomon speaks in the first person (8:2, 18): "Her I loved and sought after from my youth; I sought to take her for my bride and was enamored of her beauty...I went about seeking to take her for my own."

versed in the ways of the hellenistic world and who assume leadership status.

Pseudo-Solomon desires Wisdom for specialized reasons and wants special kinds of wisdom. When he describes the kind of wisdom given him, he speaks of a knowledge requiring broad learning and familiarity with the intellectual currents of his day (7:17-21).[62] Pseudo-Solomon's desire for Wisdom reflects special interests. Although Wisdom is more valuable to him than throne or riches (7:9ff.), he desires it *because* "all good things together come to me in her company, and countless riches at her hands" (7:11). Riches may be desirable, but Wisdom is more so because it produces all things (8:5): wisdom in prosperity and comfort in grief; glory and fame; the ability to govern people and the appearance of nobility and courage (8:9ff.). Through Wisdom one may become privy to the thoughts of God (9:10). In short, Pseudo-Solomon desires Wisdom because it enables him to master his physical and social world.

The language the author employs is at once specialized language with a philosophical and oriental-religious history familiar to a special class or type of person *and* at the same time a language that belongs to no single community. That is, he uses the language of a social class of people who are capable of moving across cultural and national boundaries. Compared to Sirach's use of traditional language, Pseudo-Solomon's language is very cosmopolitan and philosophical.[63] Pseudo-Solomon's language is "elaborated code," to use Bernstein's classification, indicating that he operates beyond the shared meanings and nuances of a closed community.[64]

What Pseudo-Solomon claims for wisdom and thus for himself is not entirely different from what Sirach claims for himself in chapter 39. Both are high-grid. Both operate in a world that is structured

---

[62] Consider also 8:8f. The passage in 7:17ff. is loaded with technical, philosophical terms and collocations ("the beginning and the end and the mid-point of times," found in Orphic and Pythagorean literature and commonly during this period). Cf. Winston, pp. 172-77 for bibliography and discussion of the passage.

[63] See for example, Winston, pp. 14f.

[64] Winston, p. 64, speaking especially of part three says: "The writing is...highly allusive, allowing those possessed of a wider range of learning to enjoy the full thrust of its intent. The audience addressed was thus considerably wider than could be reached by a narrow technical treatise, although it must have comprised a somewhat restricted and highly literate group of readers." Similarly, Reese, p. 88, citing Di Lella, p. 147: "He not only interprets but makes a personal elaboration in order to 'present a new synthesis in a language that the new age would understand.'"

hierarchically.   Both are familiar with the hellenistic world.   But Sirach, who avoids almost all technical language and uses traditional language, affirms the rituals and symbols of traditional, corporate Judaism.   Pseudo-Solomon, on the other hand, employs an elaborate vocabulary and does little to affirm the particularist, nationalistic symbols of cultus, law and history except in abstract terms (see below). The evidence points to the fact that Pseudo-Solomon fits Gordis' stereotype of the sage more than does Sirach and that he is very much preoccupied with his own fortune and success by comparison to Sirach's genuine concern for the community.

B. The Problems of the Sage

The first and third sections of the Wisdom of Solomon address the problems facing the sage.   I want to look at the third section first because at first glance it would seem to be reaffirming the history of Israel in a way comparable to Sirach's account and thus to reflect a commitment to the community at large.

1. The Book of History: 11:1-19:22

In his analysis of the genre of this section of Pseudo-Solomon, Reese notes the tendency of some scholars to identify it as a "midrash" or at least as "midrashic,"[65] despite the cautions of others.[66]   Instead,

---

[65] Among them: K. Kohler, "Wisdom of Solomon," *Jewish Encyclopedia* (New York: 1906), vol. 12, p. 539; E. Gartner, *Komposition und Wortwahl des Buches der Weisheit* (Berlin: Mayer & Muller, 1912), p. 84; S. Holmes, "Introduction to Wisdom of Solomon," in *The Apocrypha and Pseudepigrapha*, ed. by. R.H. Charles (Oxford: 1913), vol. 1, pp. 518-563; F. Feldmann, "Die literarische Art von Weisheit, Kap. 10-19," *Theologie und Glaube*, I (1909), pp. 178-84; E. Osty, *Le Livre de la Sagesse* (Paris, Editions du cerf, 1957), pp. 19, 95; J. Reider, *The Book of Wisdom* (New York: Harper and Brothers, 1957), pp. 3, 40, who is ambivalent; R. T. Siebeneck, "The Midrash of Wisdom 10-19," *Catholic Biblical Quarterly* 22(1960), pp. 176-82; R.E. Murphy, *Seven Books of Wisdom* (Milwaukee: Bruce, 1960), p. 130; R.H. Pfeiffer, *History of New Testament Times* (New York: Harper, 1949), p. 24; A.G. Wright, *The Literary Genre Midrash* (Staten Island: Alba House, 1967), pp. 106-110. See Reese, pp. 92ff.

[66] Reese, pp. 93, 95ff. Cf. J. A. Gregg, *The Wisdom of Solomon* (Cambridge: The University Press, 1909), pp. xiii and 95, who called Pseudo-Solomon a philosophy of Israelite history; see also A. Causse, "La propaganda juive et l'hellenisme," *Revue d'histoire et de philosophie religieuses* 3(1923), pp. 408-414, who, "attempted to 'denationalize the Old Testament' as Causse expressed it. And so he departed from the literary forms of the Bible in order to make a bridge between the biblical ideal of wisdom and the Greek philosophical ideal" (Reese, p. 93). Reese himself notes that there are general similarities between the Jewish midrash and the hellenistic literature that retells ancient myths so that the category of "midrash" is not helpful in this case for delineating a genre of literature.   Furthermore, Pseudo-Solomon

Reese[67] classifies this section of Pseudo-Solomon as a *sugkrisis* or "comparison," a genre of literature widely used for didactic and polemical purposes.[68] This third section is dominated by seven "antitheses" contrasting the "Egyptians" misfortunes with the blessings of "Israel." It recalls the biblical account of the Exodus and is an especially appropriate word of encouragement to Jews in Egypt who were suffering misfortune in the time of Pseudo-Solomon. There are numerous allusions to the hand of God acting generously to vindicate Israel (16:12, 21, 26; 18:4, etc.) and Pseudo-Solomon concludes with a stereotypical doxology: "For in every way, O Lord! you exalted and glorified your people, and did not neglect to assist them in every time and place" (19:22, Winston's translation). For all that, its form indicates its purpose is not so much a fond retelling of Israel's history but a polemical attack on those who would threaten the sage's world.

Even though it is an identifiable recounting of the Exodus, Pseudo-Solomon's account is abstracted and intellectualized. It is thin on historical concreteness. Not once are the Egyptians named by name. They are the "unjust" or the "wicked" or the "enemies" or the "lawless," etc. This might be explained by the author's need to be

---

assumes a view of nature foreign to that of the Old Testament, one in which the historical acts of God are seen as unexpected intrusions into the cosmic harmony. "Such a scientific view of a perfectly ordered universe subject to physical laws...lies outside the scope of the genre of midrash" (*Ibid.*, pp. 96-97). But above all, the (a) arrangement of "biblical events in the artificial form of comparison" and (b) the difficulty of identifying specific biblical texts for some of Pseudo-Solomon's details argue against classifying chapters 11-19 as midrash (*Ibid.*, p. 98).

[67] *Ibid.*, p. 98. Cf. F. Focke, *Die Entstehung der Weisheit Salomos* (Gottingen: Vandenhoeck & Ruprecht, 1913), pp. 12-16; J. Fichtner, *Weisheit Salomos* (Tubingen: Mohr, 1938), pp. 6, 42-43; I. Heinemann, *Philons griechische und judische Bildung* (Breslau: M. & H. Marcus, 1932), pp. 376-377.

[68] Reese, pp. 99ff., supplements his argument for the hellenistic influence on this re-telling of Israelite history by pointing to its treatment of the harmony of the elements (16:16-17:1; 19:18ff) and the psychology of fear and darkness of sinners (17:2-21). He sees parallels between Pseudo-Solomon and Alexandrian commentators on Homer who sought to make his poems acceptable to the contemporary mind; cf. p. 100. "(Pseudo-Solomon) does not follow the popular moralizing of the Palestinian midrash but employs the highly developed rhetorical and scholastic techniques of the sophisticated pagan culture of Alexandria. He places Greek rationalism at the service of eschatology, as both G. Kuhn and J. Fichtner have demonstrated. In so doing the Sage mobilized the material of Jewish tradition into a new lesson, namely, that God was preparing his chosen people so that they could give the "incorruptible light of the law" to mankind (18:4)." *Ibid.*, p. 102.

careful and cryptic when describing his competitors in the Alexandrian society. But neither are the Israelites, as a nation or as individuals (alluded to in chapter ten), mentioned by name. The people involved lose their distinct identities to become types to learn from and illustrations of the general principle stated in the introduction of 11:1, "(Wisdom) made their affairs prosper through the holy prophet."[69] The negative and positive experiences of Egypt and Israel during the Exodus shows that wisdom is the key to success and prosperity.

The retelling of the Passover incident in the Exodus illustrates the degree to which the historical narrative has been abstracted, philosophized and "de-nationalized." Pseudo-Solomon 18:5-25 recalls the passage of the angel of the Lord through Egypt to kill their first-born:

> ...your all-powerful Logos, out of heaven, from the royal throne, leaped like a relentless warrior into the midst of the land marked for destruction, bringing your unambiguous decree as a sharp stone. Standing it filled all things with death; it touched the heavens, yet stood poised upon the earth...(vss. 15f.)

Between this "destroyer" and the people of Israel stood the "blameless man" who "overcame the divine anger" and "by Logos he subdued the chastiser." He was dressed in a full-length robe on which "there was a representation of the entire cosmos, and the glories of the fathers upon his four rows of carved stones and your splendor on the diadem upon this head. To these the destroyer gave way..." (vss. 21ff). As Winston points out, the picture of the Logos here is "strikingly similar to that of Sophia" (see 7:23; 9:4, 10, 17; 7:21; 8:4). There are numerous literary and philosophical allusions to Greco-Roman myths.[70] Reese speaks of the hellenistic psychology of fear that is

---

[69] Winston, p. 226, and Reese, "Plan and Structure in the Book of Wisdom," *Catholic Biblical Quarterly* 27(1965), p. 392, argue persuasively that 11:1 introduces section 3 rather than concludes chapter 10 and the middle section. For the opposing opinion, see A. G. Wright, "The Structure of the Book of Wisdom," *Biblica* 48(1967), p. 176.

[70] The dress of the "blameless man," with its "representation of the entire cosmos" (18:24), makes allusion to the Stoic and Cynic idea that the "true temple is the Universe itself." Winston, pp. 321: "We read, for example, in the fourth epistle of Ps-Heraclitus: You ignorant men, don't you know that God is not wrought by hands and has not from the beginning had a pedestal, and does not have a single enclosure! Rather the whole world is his temple, decorated with animals, plants, and stars" (Attridge 1976:59; cf. 13-23, where the same idea is quoted from an Egyptian shard...Cf. Euripides Frag. 968; Seneca *Ep.* 90. 28; *Beneficiis* 7.7.3; Plutarch *Moralia* 477c; Chrysippus, ap. Cicero *ND* 3.10.26; *De Republica* 3.14; 6.15.15. An exact parallel, however, to our author's allusion may be found in Philo *Spec.* 1.66-97, where we are told that the truest temple of God

used in 18:17.[71] In short, the Exodus accounts have been probed for all manner of lessons and symbolism appropriate to Pseudo-Solomon's particular interests and those of the wider hellenistic audience.

The two major excurses on God's Mercy (11:15-12:22) and Idolatry (13:1-15:19)[72] reinforce the impression that the "Egyptians" (and "Canaanites") suffer punishment fitting their own foolishness. The plagues are sent "that they might *know* that by those things through which a man sins, through them he is punished" (11:16). God's mercy is seen in that by these various calamities "he jogs (the Egyptians') *memory*" (12:1) and thereby "*taught* your people that the righteous man must be humane" (12:19; emphasis added).

The excursus on idolatry is similar to that of Paul in Romans 1:18ff. and analogous to passages in Philo,[73] although here the worship of natural elements[74] is due to ignorance and error.[75] The idolaters are distracted by natural beauty and power and fail to see the Divine Creator. Such nature worship, foolish and dead-end as it may be, is understandable and less reprehensible than idol worship, which is truly "wretched" (13:10), shameless (13:17) and hateful (14:9). Idol worship is a "snare for the feet of fools" (14:11). "Not content to err concerning the knowledge of God," in their ignorance "they call such monstrous evils peace" (14:22). The result is "madness" and "confusion" (14:25, 28) and thinking "wrongly about God" (14:30). And from all this Israel is saved because she is "cognizant of your might,... knowing that we are reckoned yours" (15:2) and because "to know you is the sum of righteousness, and to recognize your power is the root of immortality" (15:3).

In sum, Pseudo-Solomon reviews the history of his people—a history relevant to the current struggle in Egypt—but is more interested in illustrating the principle that Wisdom enables people to prosper (11:1). He defends his people's heritage as glorious and the status of his community as worthy of respect, but he philosophizes and abstracts

---

is the whole universe, with heaven for its sanctuary, the stars for its votive ornaments, and the angels for its priests.)

[71] Reese, pp. 100-102.

[72] Reese isolates these chapters as a section distinct from the Book of History rather than as excurses within that final section. His case is made on the fact that it represents a different genre, that of "diatribe," pp. 114ff.

[73] *Decal.* 52ff.; *Spec.* 1:13ff.; *Cont.* 3ff.; *Congr.* 133.

[74] Winston, p. 248, referring to Philo, *Decal.* 54. According to Winston, the author refers to Stoicism.

[75] Pseudo-Solomon 13:1; 15:14; Cf. Philo, *Spec.* 1, 15; *Decal.* 52, 59, 69.

that history to emphasize universal principles. All this is compatible with the person for whom success comes with learning and who is able to cross social and cultural boundaries easily. This book of history does not, as in Sirach's praise of Israel's historic heroes, indicate a high group consciousness, but rather it merely illustrates mastery of the means to personal success, means available to Jew and non-Jew alike.

2. *The Book of Eschatology: 1:1-6:11 (+ 6:17-20)*

Reese disputes the common designation of this section as "The Book of Eschatology."[76] His distinction between the concerns of Pseudo-Solomon regarding immortality and those of the more typical eschatological texts may be clarified by reference to G. W. E. Nickelsburg's study of these themes in post-biblical Judaism.[77] Nickelsburg identifies the material in this section as representative of the Isaianic Servant motif of the individual righteous man vindicated by God. Where Pseudo-Solomon differs from Isaiah is that the wise man actually dies so that his vindication is after death.[78] For both Reese and Nickelsburg there is a distinction drawn between the afterlife fortunes and vindication of an individual (in Pseudo-Solomon) and the vindication in a final judgment of God's people (more typically apocalyptic).

This distinction is relevant for the difficulty of finding "eschatology" in the wisdom tradition. For example, one of Gordis' firm assertions is that the wisdom school is upper class because it resolutely refuses to resort to the afterlife to answer life's injustices. Only lower classes need the compensation of future bliss to answer their

---

[76] J.M. Reese, *Hellenistic Influence*, pp.109-110, who calls it instead, an example of the "hellenistic diatribe," defining the diatribe as "an informal, flexible ethical exposition in lively and colorful language to defend a position and to win others to it" (p. 110). E. Kent Stowers, *The Diatribe and Paul's Letter to the Romans*, SBL Dissertation Series 57 (Chico, Calif.: Scholars Press, 1981, points out, however, that: "No two literary or subliterary genres, or even styles, can be satisfactorily compared by a mere listing of parallel characteristics. This is because a single characteristic is rarely, if ever, unique to one literary type" (p. 39), and he criticizes Reese's imprecise use of the term diatribe, citing Reese's definition, given above, as an example of that imprecision (p. 40).

[77] G.W.E. Nickelsburg, Jr., *Resurrection, Immortality and Eternal Life.* Nickelsburg identifies three "forms" of these concerns: (a) the apocalyptic, in which an end time judgment is central; (b) the vindication of the Righteous Man; (c) the Two-Way Theology where afterlife is the culmination of walking in either death or life. These themes may be borrowed from one genre and used in another and thus transformed.

[78] *Ibid.*, pp. 48-92 and pp. 170f.

present misery.[79] Perhaps it is for this reason that Gordis omits all mention of the *Wisdom of Solomon* in his essay; its futurism does not fit his model. But Pseudo-Solomon's emphasis on individual immortality is not so strange in the context. The sage couches his concern in terms of the immortality of the individual soul, a concern common to the philosophical thought of his day.[80] Greek notions of personal immortality of the soul gained currency in the hellenistic and Greco-Roman world. Older notions of immortality through the memory of the community (as found, for example, in Sirach) had given way as communities were more and more integrated into the "cosmopolitan" world and lost some of their power to define individual identity. Belief in personal immortality of the soul, then, accompanies the growing individualism and fragmentation of the hellenistic world.[81]

Berger's analysis of theodicies[82] confirms this. The theodicy of self-transcendence (such as that of Sirach) may be modified by projected compensation into a this worldly future, for example in messianism or millenarianism. But this theodicy is "highly vulnerable to empirical disconfirmation" and so "compensation is promised in *other-worldly* terms... In its simplest form, this type of theodicy maintains a reversal of present sufferings and evils in a life after death." Berger concludes:

> This transposition is probably more likely to the extent that the prototypical theodicy by self-transcendent participation weakens in plausibility, a process related to progressive individuation.... It will be evident that, unlike the this-worldly theodicy of the messianic-millenarian complex, the other-worldly type of theodicy is more likely to be conservative than revolutionary in its effect.[83]

Pseudo-Solomon's emphasis upon immortality fits precisely our description of the sage here as high grid and weak group. In Douglas' classification of the high grid, weak group person, there are those who fall into futurism. This is not the dualistic apocalypticism of the low

---

[79] Gordis, pp. 102ff.

[80] Cf. Winston, pp. 25ff.

[81] Sirach's view of "immortality" is associated with a high view of the polis or community, and seems to give way to the Orphic and mystery religion and to Platonic views of the immortality of the soul that follows the increasing individualism of the hellenistic "cosmo-polis." In this sense, Sirach no less than Pseudo-Solomon reflects hellenistic influences. The difference has much to do with socio-cultural changes in their world and the shift from the polis culture to the cosmopolitan culture. Again see W. Jaeger, "The Greek Ideas of Immortality," pp. 97ff.

[82] Berger, pp. 60ff.

[83] *Ibid.*, p.70.

grid, strong group sectarian community, whose high boundaries against the outside world reflect the cosmic conflict between good and evil powers which will come to a head in the near future. Rather, an individual may accept the standards of the world in which he or she lives and may believe that success and prosperity will result from acquiring and using the right skills with which to master and "manipulate" the rules or impersonal forces which govern the universe. But when external circumstances challenge that working assumption, and one's position on the hierarchy of prosperity and power is, at best, ambiguous, then that person looks to the future for vindication.[84] Pseudo-Solomon affirms the traditional wisdom perspective that Wisdom will help the individual to gain success. But due to external circumstances or the injustice of others, that success may be postponed to the afterlife and transformed into incorruptibility.

This socio-cultural analysis confirms Winston's dating for the Wisdom of Solomon at about 40 C.E. and his reading of the crisis facing Pseudo-Solomon. In 38 C.E., riots broke out in the Jewish quarters of Alexandria. Jewish synagogues were damaged and defiled with portraits of Gaius Caligula. The Roman prefect, A. Avillius Flaccus, declared Jews in Alexandria to be "aliens and foreigners," downgrading their status from "resident aliens." Although this decree was revoked in 41 by Claudius, the new decree forbade Jewish participation in gymnasium activities and education, thus excluding Jews from the rights of citizenship.[85] This trouble most affected those Jews who had successfully mastered the rules of hellenistic Alexandrian society, that is, the "upper classes of the Jewish population of the city (who) were profoundly imbued with Greek culture."[86] The sudden reversal of

---

[84] Douglas, pp. 104f. "The world is (for the high-grid, low-group individual) a potentially benign place. But a sudden dislocation of their channels to prestige and success, and the realization that they never win, are likely to spark off an always incipient millenialism."

[85] Cf. Winston, pp. 24-25; Also see V. Tcherikover, *Hellenistic Civilization and the Jews*, tr. by S. Applebaum (New York: Atheneum, 1959), pp. 311ff. for fuller details. Claudius further threatened vengeance upon Jews who caused trouble in this new status. See Philo, *Legatatio ad Gajum*, 133-134; *In Flaccum*, 54. In *Corpus Papyrorum Judaicarum*, 150, known as the "Papyrus of the Boule," an anonymous person petitions for a council that excludes, presumably, Egyptians and Jews as uncultured people seeking citizenship; also *C.P. Jud.*, 153, 156, and other literature cited by Tcherikover, p. 313.

[86] Tcherikover, p. 311, who points out that the external symbol of this problem was the imposition of the poll tax which constituted a severe financial burden on prosperous Jews but also a cultural degradation to the level of the native Egyptian *fellahin*. Tcherikover cites the "Papyrus of the Boule," in which a citizen of Alexandria petitions the Emperor Augustus to permit Alexandrians to

fortunes challenged the conviction that skill and wisdom led to prosperity. The prosperity of Jews relative to rival groups in Alexandria (native Egyptian and the hellenized citizens) and their access to the various resources of the city were thus compromised.

The degree to which Pseudo-Solomon addresses this competition can be seen in the vigor of his comparison of Jewish virtues and fortunes with those of the hated Egyptians in chapters 10-19. The veiled references to the Exodus in these chapters and the long excursus on idolatry suggest the intensity of the contemporary struggle with hellenized citizens in 40 C.E., and the theodicy of afterlife vindication in chapters 1-6 suggests the failure to succeed in this life. Thus, the author's response to the crisis in the life of his particular community, or sector of Alexandrian society, confirms our analysis that he is high grid and weak group. He reflects a hitherto privileged sector of society where individuals have been able in the past to escape the boundaries of their ethnic community and enter into the life of the cosmopolitan community at large. Despite his mastery of the normal means of success in a large, cultured Hellenistic city, his opportunities have been lost due to powers beyond his control.

C. The Picture of Sophia

In a high grid, weak group society we should expect, according to Douglas, a cosmology of an essentially benign universe, dominated by abstracted or impersonal forces. These forces may be manipulated or acquired by the individual who would be successful and they have less to do with moral principle than with principles for success. The means to success, then, are available to any and all who are sufficiently endowed to seize the opportunities and principles. Rituals are means to manipulate the abstracted forces to one's own benefit. If the world of Pseudo-Solomon is high grid and weak group, we would expect Sophia to be presented less personally and more as a means or universal principle of success.

---

have their own council, thus exempting themselves from the poll tax imposed on non-citizens while also excluding undesirables from citizen rights. Tcherikover describes these undesirables as "people without culture and education" who might contaminate "the purity of the city of Alexandria by entering the list of citizens. Although the Jews are not alluded to explicitly, it is clear that it is they and the Egyptians who are meant, since these are the people 'without culture and education' who, against the will of the Alexandrians, are unscrupulously daring to penetrate the ranks of the citizens, for this purpose registering themselves or their sons as pupils of the gymnasia..." (p. 312-13).

In the first place, the Sophia of Pseudo-Solomon generally fits the description found in Sirach. Wisdom was with God in intimate companionship from the beginning (Ps.-Sol. 8:3; 9:4, 9, 10) and is the agent of creation and the preservation of the creation (7:21, 27; 8:1-5; 10:1ff.; 9:1ff.). Wisdom is also the agent of "salvation" (7:11, 14f.; 7:27-28; 8:9ff.; 9:4f.; 9:10f., 18) that comes from God (9:4, 6, 10), and actively seeks out those who would love wisdom (e.g. 6:13f., 16f.; 7:27). Therefore, those who would know Wisdom seek it as a lover would seek his loved one (6:21; 7:7-10; 8:2, 9, 18, 21).

But this now traditional view of Sophia, gives way, in Pseudo-Solomon, to very abstract terms. Nowhere is this more apparent than in his description of Wisdom in 7:22-27. In the first half of this passage, Wisdom is described in a series of terms, which for the most part have parallels in Greek philosophy.[87] More important than specific verbal parallels[88] is the conventional use[89] of the series terms, here twenty-one, to describe Wisdom.[90]

Winston's views reflect the majority opinion concerning the hellenistic influences on Pseudo-Solomon's picture of Sophia.[91]

---

[87] For example, Winston, pp. 180ff., identifies parallels for the following terms: "unique," "manifold," "subtle," "agile," "loving goodness," "unhindered," "beneficent," "more mobile," "penetrating and pervading all things." This language may be traced to the range of Greek religion and philosophy, but most particularly to Stoic texts. Beyond these terms there are several with parallels in Philo, with whom Winston identifies the Wisdom of Solomon, and a few words that are first attested in the Wisdom of Solomon.

[88] Lillie criticizes Winston for indiscriminate use of parallels; cf. pp. 29f.

[89] Winston identifies parallels in Mithraism (from the 4th century CE), ancient Zoroastrianism, the Stoic philosopher Cleanthes (who listed 26 divine attributes), Indian literature (describing "Perfect Wisdom" [Prajnaparamita] with 32 attributes), and the Isis cult (e.g., in the *Oxyrhynchus* papyrus # 1380, where a list of 20 some qualities are attributed to her, along with various names of goddesses identified with her). Similar lists may be found in Philo and in the Rabbinic literature. Cf. Winston, pp. 178-79. Even granting that some of these parallels are later and inexact, it is clear that such lists of abstract qualities were common in the Greco-Roman era.

[90] Winston, pp. 184-85. On the second section, verses 25ff., Winston remarks: "This is very bold language indeed for someone who is writing within the biblical tradition. Even the more philosophically ambitious Philo backs off from such explicit terms...for his description of the origin of the Divine Logos..."

[91] Cf. B.J. Lillie's survey of opinions on this matter, pp. 180ff. Among those emphasizing hellenistic, philosophical origins for the images of Sophia are Grimm (1860), Gregg (1909), L. H. Brockington (1961), Ch. Harris (1929), M. Stein (1936), B. Metzger (1957), and J. Geyer (1963). However, some older scholars see Pseudo-Solomon's Sophia as scarcely more developed than the biblical Wisdom; cf. Farrar (1888) and C.H. Toy (1903).

Moreover, the older issue of whether Sophia is here personified or not,[92] may largely be laid to rest; in Pseudo-Solomon the earlier personality of Sophia, portrayed by Sirach, is lost in abstractions. Even Ringgren, who argues for the *progressive* hypostatization of *Sophia*, admits that here in Pseudo-Solomon "Wisdom has an obscure position between personal being and principle. She is both, and she is neither the one nor the other."[93]

In the middle portion of the book, then, Pseudo-Solomon's Sophia is hardly personal, in the sense that one could relate to her, and is more of a means to an end—whether God's means to the end of creating or maintaining the universe, or an individual's means to the end of successful living. In this work, Sophia is, to borrow Reese's description of the book, a "philosophical way of life" to which the "protreptic" of Pseudo-Solomon would invite the reader.

Sophia is the means to success and to a body of knowledge through which one can achieve certain goals—status, riches, knowledge, virtues, and the capacity to rule (7:11f.; 8:5ff.; 8:10ff.; 9:10ff.). Above all, Sophia brings the ultimate success of immortality, which is equated with a relationship with God (see esp. 6:17ff. and also 7:27; 8:3; 8:13; 8:17). In the final analysis (he concludes in 9:15ff.) it is corruptibility associated with the material world that weighs down the individual who would soar free and it is Wisdom that opens the cage and allows the individual to escape corruptibility and ascend to God.

Pseudo-Solomon, of course, sees Wisdom as associated with Jewish tradition and thought. He belongs to the Jewish tradition and chooses Solomon as his persona. However abstract, he contrasts the fortunes of the Jews to those of the Egyptians with reference to the Exodus. But Wisdom imagery in Pseudo-Solomon is largely free of any allusions to the covenant, to the cultus and to the Mosaic law. The invitation is extended to all who would be successful (e.g. 1:1ff; 6:1ff.; 6:22ff.; 7:3f.). Some of that which our author hopes for at the hands of Wisdom sounds surprisingly ephemeral, the fantasy of one who has failed to achieve the expected success (cf. 8:10f.).

---

[92] *Ibid.* For example, C.H. Toy (1903) argued that in the Wisdom of Solomon, Sophia was hypostatized and personalized, while E. C. Bissell (1886) argued that "she" was not personalized. Samuel Holmes (1913) maintained that this question could not be answered.

[93] Ringgren, p. 119. That is, Ringgren admits that in this most significant testimony to Sophia, the progressive hypostatization theory (and therefore the developing myth theory), cannot be maintained.

This description of Sophia in the Wisdom of Solomon, then, conforms to the type of cosmology that we would expect from a high grid, weak group social framework. It, Wisdom, reflects an essentially benign universe, one that can be manipulated in order to achieve success. It is more a way of life, or a principle of life to be followed than a moral agent or personality. It is not historicized in terms of specific community rituals or laws or boundaries, but is abstracted and available to all who have the learning and ability to accept it. Ultimately, Wisdom even provides comfort to the one who does not succeed in this life, namely, by promising success and vindication in the afterlife.

Just as Sophia is central to Sirach's thought, so also it is central to Pseudo-Solomon's thought. This can be seen in a number of ways, beginning with the fact that his description of Sophia and his desire for her constitutes the central, pivotal section of the work. For the author, as for Sirach, Wisdom functions to legitimate his individual identity and role.

First, Wisdom legitimates the essential value system of this individual who is thoroughly integrated into the cosmopolitan world of first century Alexandria. His success orientation and his good fortune in being born into this privileged society, with all its possibilities, is legitimated through reference to Sophia who is the means to success. There is no indication that one must belong to a particular religious or national community to gain these privileges. It is only necessary to acquire this Wisdom, which is described in terms that are accessible to all searching folks. Hengel describes the "higher wisdom through revelation" as characteristic of religion in late antiquity in responding to earlier waves of skepticism.[94] The cosmopolitan tendency was to gain individual, personal relationship with particular deities— Asclepius, Serapis, Isis. Against this background, it is not surprising that Sophia seems a great deal like Isis, and that Pseudo-Solomon held Sophia up to individuals for their consideration.

Second, it is clear from Pseudo-Solomon's first and third sections that he belongs to a particular sector of this broader cosmopolitan world that has experienced dislocation and anomie. While this sector of society is not defined in national, religious terms, it is made up of educated and prosperous Jews who sought to distinguish themselves from the Egyptians and gain access to citizenship in cultured Alexandria. Sophia is central to the author's legitimation of his own specialized class of knowledgeable and successful Jewish elite, and therefore functions more as a "third-level legitimation." That is, the

---

[94] Hengel, pp. 169ff.

wisdom cosmology provides a theoretical frame of reference for a particular sector of society—*not the whole of a society*—and due to its complexity is "entrusted to specialized personnel."[95] Sophia is described in the highly technical language of hellenistic philosophy and religion, combining elements of Pythagoreanism, Stoicism and neo-Platonism with Jewish ideas after the manner of Aristobulus, who addressed Ptolemy VI Philometer (181-145 B.C.E.).[96] Pseudo-Solomon's description of Sophia fits the later hellenistic concern of oriental intellectuals to demonstrate the priority, and also the compatibility with and contribution of, oriental ideas and religion to Greek thought. Thus, Sophia loses the earlier contours of personality and assumes a shape approximating "pure theory," known in terms familiar to a cosmopolitan intellectual class but not necessarily to the traditional Jewish worshipper. Pseudo-Solomon uses Sophia as a powerful tool in the legitimation of a "sub-universe" that is competing with other sub-universes in Alexandria, and not as a "sacred canopy" covering the whole of Jewish society.

Finally, Sophia is central to the author's theodicy of personal immortality. This response to evil is unique among the wisdom books, as was Sirach's emphasis on community cultus and history. But it is predictable given the high grid, weak group profile of the author's community and its experience of disenfranchisement in Alexandria. Moreover, it reflects the intellectual currents of a cosmopolitan world where the old security of corporate identity in the *polis* gives way to increased individualism. In Pseudo-Solomon, the Wisdom cosmology that legitimates the personal values of success and the claims of a class of potentially successful Jews, also provides the promise of deferred success in the afterlife.

Despite the continuities in the Wisdom mytho-logical language, then, there are significant differences in the functions of the Wisdom cosmology and the social values represented in large part because of changes in the socio-historical context.

Conclusion

Analyses of the social context for wisdom sayings have helped us to read between the lines and to understand the world view that informs the text. They have also helped us to understand the world to which the disciple is being socialized and to understand the way in which that social world is being legitimated by the theological arguments of

---

[95] Berger and Luckmann, pp. 94f.
[96] Cf. Hengel, pp. 163ff.

the sage. But class analyses have tended to impose an artificial unity on the various texts in the wisdom tradition. They have tended to force false notions of the origin of the tradition or of its relationship to the Egyptian background. Class analysis, such as that of Gordis, has been unable to address all of the data—the cultic or social concerns of Sirach or the preoccupation with the afterlife in Wisdom of Solomon. In short, class analysis has proved fruitful but a bit heavy handed; more nuanced investigation requires a more refined and flexible model.

The grid-group model allows for more nuance and variety than does the simple class analysis. My use of the grid-group model confirms the sage's privileged status, his hierarchical world, his closeness to power and the status quo. But it also allows us to see significant departures from this stereotype, depending upon the historical and social context. And it allows for a more subtle reading of the affinity between the ideology of the sage and his social values.

Specifically, I conclude that Sirach is high grid *and* strong group (valuing social structure as well as community) whereas Pseudo-Solomon is high grid *but* weak group (more individualistic). Accordingly, in Sirach, Sophia is a personalized power who mediates in the crises facing the nation and is defined in terms of national and traditional symbols. For the group-oriented Sirach, who thinks in terms of his many relationships, the universe is personalized in Sophia. For the writer of the Wisdom of Solomon, who thinks more in terms of his personal success and mastery of the riddles of life, Sophia is more abstracted, more the means to personal success. Sirach affirms the boundaries and religious history of the society of pre-Maccabean Jerusalem as a whole, whereas Pseudo-Solomon responds to a crisis in Roman Alexandria in which his particular sector of society is being disenfranchised. While both authors are being hellenized, Sirach reflects the more traditional values of corporate identity of national, if not also *polis*, life, while Pseudo-Solomon reflects the tendency of the increasingly cosmopolitan Greco-Roman world toward individuation and personal salvation.

One of the interesting implications of this conclusion is that with respect to the traditional world of the Sage (for example, in Prov. 1-9) Sirach is actually *less* traditional than is Wisdom of Solomon, at least in social terms.[97] Sirach may be more conservative than Pseudo-Solomon with respect to biblical language and cultic concerns, but by focusing on parochial community identity he thereby departs more

---

[97] Consider di Lella's case for the reverse—that Sirach presents a conservative theology incompatible to Pseudo-Solomon's progressive theology—and the continued debate of di Lella's thesis at the 1987 SBL meeting in Boston.

dramatically from the cosmopolitan wisdom tradition itself (with its apparent elitism and success orientation). Pseudo-Solomon's social values and even his use of the Sophia material are more like that of Proverbs than are Sirach's. Moreover, Pseudo-Solomon's focus on afterlife vindication is a socially more conservative theodicy and more consistent with the intellectualist and individualist tendencies of the wisdom tradition than is Sirach's focus on stability and justice in his society. When comparing these two writers with each other and with the previous tradition, it is necessary to analyze not merely the ideas they present but the social world they represent.

Chapter Two

Interpreting the Gospel of Mark as a Jewish Document in a Graeco-Roman World

Vernon K. Robbins
Emory University

The New Testament gospels feature a disciple-gathering sage from Nazareth who is considered to be the Messiah as a result of his words and deeds. Jesus himself was a Jew and probably spoke a northern Galilean dialect of Aramaic.[1] Yet the gospels that present the earliest accounts of his life and activity are written in Greek and contain various features in common with Graeco-Roman βίοι and *vitae*.[2] In this literary form, the stories and sayings of Jesus function interculturally. Jewish heritage merges with Graeco-Roman forms of thought and

---

[1] Geza Vermes, *Jesus the Jew* (Philadelphia: Fortress Press, 1981).

[2] Moses Hadas and Morton Smith, *Heroes and Gods: Spiritual Biographies in Antiquity* (New York: Harper & Row, 1965); Dieter Georgi, "The Records of Jesus in the Light of Ancient Accounts of Revered Men," *Seminar Papers II*, edited by Lane C. McGaughy (Missoula, Mont.: Scholars Press, 1972) 527-42, Charles H. Talbert, *What is a Gospel? The Genre of the Canonical Gospels.* (Philadelphia: Fortress Press, 1977); *idem*, "Biographies of Philosophers and Rulers as Instruments of Religious Propaganda in Mediterranean Antiquity," in *ANRW* II.2 (Berlin and New York: Walter de Gruyter, 1978) 1619-51; *idem.*, "Prophecies of Future Greatness: The Contribution of Greco-Roman Biographies to an Understanding of Luke 1:5-4:14," in *The Divine Helmsman: Studies on God's Control of Human Events, Presented to Lou H. Silberman*, edited by James L. Crenshaw and Samuel Sandmel (New York: KTAV, 1980) 129-41; Philip Shuler, *The Genre of the Gospels* (Philadelphia: Fortress Press, 1982); *idem.*, "The Griesbach Hypothesis and the Gospel Genre," *Perkins Journal* 33 (1980) 41-90; Vernon K. Robbins, *Jesus the Teacher: A Socio-Rhetorical Interpretation of Mark* (Philadelphia: Fortress Press, 1984).

action in literature to evoke a separate identity for Christianity. The Judaism in the gospels, then, is a particular kind of Judaism—an intercultural one in which Jesus speaks and acts in roles that combine Jewish and Graeco-Roman modes of thought and activity.

The gospel of Mark, which is thought by many interpreters to be the first gospel written, provides this essay's focus of analysis. Like the other New Testament gospels, the heritage of the gospel of Mark is Jewish. The stories and sayings in it refer specifically to Jewish figures—Abraham, Isaac, Jacob, Moses, David, Elijah—and social categories—scribes, Pharisees, Sadducees, priests, chief priests, elders, and the High Priest of the Jerusalem temple.[3] Also, quotations and allusions to passages in the Torah, the prophets, and the writings in the Jewish Bible occur in Mark.[4] In addition, the author includes transliterated Aramaic words for: "sons of thunder" (3:17); "little girl, arise" (5:41); "given [to God]" (7:11); "be opened" (7:34); "rabbi" (9:5, 10:51, 11:21, 14:45); "Father" (14:36); "skull" (15:22); and "My God, my God, why hast thou forsaken me?" (15:34).[5] In contrast, the Markan gospel also contains data that shows it was written in a Graeco-Roman world. The author writes in Greek and translates Aramaic words into Greek meanings but leaves Latin loanwords untranslated, presupposing that the reader knows the meaning of these words.[6] Also, in one instance the author explains Jewish customs to the reader.[7] In addition, the author features Greek and Roman people in some of the scenes.[8] The author, therefore, writes in the *lingua franca* of Graeco-Roman culture

---

[3] Abraham, Isaac, and Jacob: Mark 12:26. Moses: Mark 1:44; 7:10; 9:4, 5; 10:3, 4; 12:19, 26. David: Mark 2:25; 10:47, 48; 11:10; 12:35, 36, 37. Elijah: Mark 6:15; 8:28; 9:4, 5, 11, 12, 13; 15:35, 36. Scribes: Mark 1:22; 2:6, 16; 3:22; 7:1, 5; 8:31; 9:11, 14; 10:33; 11:18, 27; 12:28, 35, 38; 14:43, 53; 15:1, 31. Pharisees: Mark 2:18, 24; 3:6; 7:3; 8:11, 15; 10:2; 12:13. Sadducees: Mark 12:18. Priests: Mark 1:44; 2:26. Chief priests or the High Priest: Mark 2:26; 8:31; 10:33; 11:18, 27; 14:1, 10, 43, 47, 53, 54, 55, 60, 61, 63, 66; 15:1, 3, 11, 31. Elders: Mark 7:3, 5; 8:31; 11:27; 14:43, 53; 15:1.

[4] Torah: Mark 1:2, 44; 7:10; 10:4, 7, 19; 12:19, 26, 29-31, 32-33. Prophets: Mark 1:2-3, 11; 4:12; 7:6-7; 11:17; 13:26; 14:27, 62. Writings: Mark 1:11; 2:25-26; 11:9; 12:10-11; 12:36; 15:24, 34.

[5] Translations of Aramaic: βοανηργές, Mark 3:17; ταλιθα κουμ, 5:41; κορβᾶν, 7:11; εφφαθα, 7:34; αββα, 14:36; γολγοθᾶν, 15:22; ελωι ελωι λεμα σαβαχθανι, 15:34. Only ῥαββί (9:5; 11:21; 14:45) is not translated, although manuscripts D and it translate ῥαββί with κύριε in 10:51 instead of printing ῥαββουνί.

[6] Latin loanwords: δηναρίων, Mark 6:37; 12:15; 14:5; κεντυρίων, Mark 15:39, 44, 45; κῆνσος Mark 12:14; κράβαττος, Mark 2:4, 9, 11, 12; 6:55; λεγιών, Mark 5:9, 15; ξέστης, Mark 7:4; σπεκουλάτωρ, Mark 6:27. In one instance (12:42), the author explains the meaning of a Greek term (λεπτόν) with a Latin loanword (κοδράντης).

[7] Mark 7:3-4.

[8] Mark 7:24-30; 12:16-17; 15:1-15, 16-20, 21, 39, 43-44.

and consciously addresses the readers as members of Graeco-Roman society who know Latin loanwords and Greek but do not know Aramaic or certain Jewish customs. The transmission of Jewish heritage in this cultural mode makes the gospel of Mark an explicitly intercultural document.

To analyze how the author of Mark uses these two cultures, I propose to employ the comparative method of "socio-rhetorical criticism."[9] The way this method reveals Mark's intercultural nature can be briefly explained by delineating its terms. First, the "socio" part of the method centers on interaction among people and groups. This social analysis focuses on the intermingling of individuals, how individuals are unified into groups, and how the boundaries between different groups are established and identified.[10] Thus the particular characteristics of individuals are viewed as features that identify not their personalities, but their relationships to other people, particularly those in the same group. Similarities indicate the factors that unify people into groups, while differences reveal the boundaries that divide people and groups.

Second, the term "rhetorical" in "socio-rhetorical criticism" refers to modes of communication used when individuals and groups interact. That is, the clues that identify groups and the boundaries between them stem from the language, actions, gestures and communication (i.e., rhetoric) recorded in the text. The gospel of Mark, for example, presents individuals and groups in "role-sets"—pairs of individuals or groups portrayed as mutually supporting or as conflicting—such as teacher/disciple(s), teacher/scribe(s)-and-Pharisee(s), healer/afflicted, and teacher/political leader(s).[11] The document establishes these sets by interweaving repetitive and progressive

---

[9] For applications of this method, see Robbins, *Jesus the Teacher; idem.,* "Picking Up the Fragments," *Foundations and Facets Forum* 1.2 (1985) 31-64; *idem.,* "Pragmatic Relations as a Criterion for Authentic Sayings," *Foundations and Facets Forum* 1.3 (1985) 35-63; *idem.,* "The Woman who Touched Jesus' Garment: Socio-Rhetorical Analysis of the Synoptic Accounts," *New Testament Studies* 33 (1987) 502-515; *idem.,* "Rhetorical Argument about Lamps and Light in Early Christian Gospels," in *Context: Essays in Honour of Peder Johan Borgen,* edited by P. W. Bockman and R. E. Kristiansen (University of Trondheim: Tapir, 1987) 177-195; *idem.,* "The Crucifixion and the Speech of Jesus," *Foundations and Facets Forum* 4.1 (1988) 33-46.

[10] Wayne A. Meeks, *The First Urban Christians: The Social World of the Apostle Paul* (New Haven: Yale University Press, 1983); Bruce J. Malina, *The New Testament World: Insights from Cultural Anthropology* (Atlanta: John Knox Press, 1981); M. A. K. Halliday, *Language as Social Semiotic: The Social Interpretation of Language and Meaning* (Baltimore University Park Press, 1978); Roger Fowler, *Literature as Social Discourse* (Bloomington: Indiana University Press, 1981).

[11] Robbins, *Jesus the Teacher,* pp. 109-119.

rhetorical patterns—two of the primary forms of rhetorical discourse.[12] These forms make use of different scenes where groups and individuals interact through speech and action, which in turn reveal how people deliberate together, evaluate one another, and establish common values, attitudes, and goals through commendation and censure.[13] Rhetorical analysis in Mark, therefore, seeks the patterns of communication that identify allied and opposed individuals and groups in successive stages of Mark's story.

Third, the term "criticism" reflects the Greek term "κριτικός" referring to judgment. A critical form of interpretation calls for the interpreter to make judgments, to clarify through rigorous examination, to weigh sets of statements against other sets within a system of testing, and to establish forms of perception rich in discernment, purpose, and articulation.[14] A form of criticism adduces evidence that warrants conclusions in some social arena. Socio-rhetorical criticism assumes that a wide variety of readings are possible and natural, because people read from different perspectives and because language and meaning continually refuse "closure."[15] Since the readings occur among communities of critical discourse, however, some readings are judged to be more satisfactory than others. The criteria for satisfactory readings will vary considerably among interpreters and groups of interpreters, but a basic criterion will be readings supported by warranted evidence and argumentation. The dynamics within the warranting will be closely related to social location and postures within interpretive communities.[16]

Comparative analysis is a natural form of interpretative activity within the framework of socio-rhetorical criticism, since social analysis regularly seeks to identify phenomena that are similar and phenomena that are different. Comparative analysis shows that socio-rhetorical patterns in Mark merge patterns that are present in the Hebrew scriptures and in Graeco-Roman literature. Certain social and rhetorical features of Mark follow patterns present in prophetic

---

[12] Kenneth Burke, *Counter-Statement* (Berkeley, Los Angeles, and London: University of California Press, 1931) 124-126; Robbins, *Jesus the Teacher*, pp. 9-10.

[13] George A. Kennedy, *New Testament Interpretation through Rhetorical Criticism* (Chapel Hill and London: University of North Carolina Press, 1984); Burton L. Mack and Vernon K. Robbins, *Patterns of Persuasion in the Gospels* (Sonoma: Polebridge Press, 1989).

[14] Wayne C. Booth, *Critical Understanding: The Powers and Limits of Pluralism* (Chicago and London: University of Chicago Press, 1979).

[15] David Tracy, *Plurality and Ambiguity: Hermeneutics, Religion, Hope* (San Francisco: Harper & Row, 1987).

[16] Stanley Fish, *Is There a Text in This Class? The Authority of Interpretive Communities* (Cambridge, MA and London: Harvard University, 1980).

biblical literature. Where those patterns diverge from biblical prophecy, Mark uses Graeco-Roman patterns. The reverse also holds true. When Mark follows Graeco-Roman patterns and then diverges from them, the difference can be explained by reference to biblical patterns. Knowledge of the merger of these patterns helps to explain the intercultural nature of the genre of Mark and the particular Markan characterizations of Jesus' action and speech, Jesus' special relation to his disciples, and Jesus' interaction with various Jewish and Graeco-Roman individuals and groups.

It will be obvious to the reader that it is not possible to pursue the entire agenda of a socio-rhetorical analysis of Mark in this paper.[17] Since the narrator of Mark refers to the prophet Isaiah in the second verse of the document, the paper begins by comparing Mark with prophetic biblical literature. First, there is a presentation of the socio-rhetorical pattern through which prophetic biblical literature portrays the transmission of the word of the Lord. Second, the prophetic pattern is compared with the pattern Mark uses to portray the transmission of God's gospel through the messianic teacher. This comparison shows that, although the Markan Jesus perpetuates certain prophetic patterns, significant features in the pattern are replaced by features from some other socio-cultural arena. Third, analysis of the socio-rhetorical pattern through which Xenophon, in his *Memorabilia*, portrays the transmission of the philosopher-teacher's system of thought and action to his disciple-companions reveals a pattern that is also in Mark. At this point, then, the reader will see that Mark, by combining a conventional Hellenistic pattern with a conventional biblical pattern, has created an intercultural pattern in which Jesus uses authoritative prophetic speech and action within an autonomous mode (a mode not dependent on an outside source) characteristic of a Hellenistic disciple-gathering philosopher-teacher. Fourth, the paper reveals that the pattern common to both Xenophon's *Memorabilia* and Mark emphasizes that the teacher himself manifests the central, paradoxical part of his system of thought and action. Again, however, Mark's portrayal of this feature is intercultural. The paradoxical feature of Socrates' system in the *Memorabilia* is "self-control" (ἐγκράτεια); in Mark the paradoxical feature is "losing one's life in order to save it." The fifth part of the paper, then, shows the pervasive intercultural thinking that goes into Mark's portrayal of Jesus' argumentation that losing one's life is a means of saving it. The overall purpose of the paper, therefore, is to reveal the considerable interaction of biblical and Graeco-Roman patterns and conventions with one another in Mark. At the end of the paper, we will present a few reflections on the significance of the intercultural nature of the Markan portrayal of Jesus.

---

[17] See Robbins, *Jesus the Teacher*, for a more extensive analysis.

The Socio-Rhetorical Pattern for the Prophetic Word of God

We will begin by comparing some basic features of Mark with some basic features of prophetic biblical literature. The first verse of Mark presents us with ἀρχὴ τοῦ εὐαγγελίου Ἰησοῦ Χριστοῦ, "the beginning of the gospel of Jesus Christ." If our interest is to compare Mark with the prophetic literature, we find an important similarity in Hosea 1:2, which reads in the LXX version: ἀρχὴ λόγου κυρίου..., "the beginning of the word of the Lord...." The reader will notice that the Old Testament is being quoted here in the Greek Septuagint version (LXX) rather than the Hebrew Masoretic version (MT). The reason is that the author of Mark reads the scriptures in Greek rather than Hebrew. The Markan gospel transmits biblical heritage in the widespread Greek speaking and reading Jewish environment that had resulted from the conquests of Alexander the Great toward the end of the fourth century B.C.E.[18]

In the environment of Greek speaking, reading, and writing Jewish culture, both Mark 1:1 and Hosea 1:2 begin with ἀρχή and are followed by genitive nouns. We notice, however, a change from λόγος in Hosea to εὐαγγέλιον in Mark. What is the significance of this change in wording? The term דָּבָר/λόγος word, is part of a pattern in prophetic biblical literature. The pattern is as follows:

1.   the דְּבַר־יהוה/λόγος κυρίου, word of the Lord, comes to a prophet;

2.   the prophet announces the דְּבַר־יהוה/λόγος κυρίου;

3.   events occur according to the דְּבַר־יהוה/λόγος κυρίου that the prophet announces.

This pattern is established by means of repetitive phrases throughout the prophetic books.[19] The book of Jeremiah is an excellent place to see how repetition establishes the pattern. In the MT of Jeremiah, three variant word strings establish the first part of the pattern where the word of the Lord comes to Jeremiah:

(a)   [20](אֲשֶׁר הָיָה/וַיְהִי) דְּבַר־יהוה אֶל יִרְמְיָה(וּ) (לֵאמֹר)

---

[18] Saul Lieberman, *Greek in Jewish Palestine* (New York: Jewish Theological Seminary of America, 1942); *idem., Hellenism in Jewish Palestine* (New York: Jewish Theological Seminary of America, 1950); Moses Hadas, *Hellenistic Culture: Fusion and Diffusion* (New York: Columbia University Press, 1959); Martin Hengel, *Judaism and Hellenism*, 2 vols. (Philadelphia: Fortress Press, 1974); *idem, Jews, Greeks, and Barbarians* (Philadelphia: Fortress Press, 1980).

[19] For the importance of repetition in Hebrew Bible tradition, see Robert Alter, *The Art of Biblical Narrative* (New York: Basic Books, 1981) 88-113.

[20] Jer. (1:2); 14:1; 28:12; 29:30; 32:26; 33:1, 19, 23; 34:12; 35:12; 36:27; 37:6; (39:15); 42:7; 43:8; 46:1; 47:1; 49:34.

^{21}הַדָּבָר אֲשֶׁר הָיָה אֶל יִרְמְיָהוּ מֵאֵת יהוה (לֵאמֹר) (b)

^{22}הָיָה הַדָּבָר הַזֶּה אֶל יִרְמְיָה (וּ) מֵאֵת יהוה לֵאמֹר (c)

In the LXX, the word strings become:

(a) (καὶ ἐγένετο/ἐγενήθη) λόγος κυρίου πρὸς Ιερεμιαν (λέγων);^{23}

(b) ὁ λόγος ὁ γενόμενος παρὰ κυρίου πρὸς Ιερεμιαν (λέγων);^{24}

(c) ἐγένετο/ἐγενήθη ὁ λόγος οὗτος (παρὰ κυρίου).^{25}

Twelve times in the MT of this book this assertion is put in first-person form as Jeremiah tells the reader that the word of the Lord came to him: וַיְהִי דְבַר־יהוה אֵלַי לֵאמֹר.^{26} In the LXX the assertion occurs in the following form: καὶ ἐγένετο/ἐγενήθη λόγος κυρίου πρός με λέγων.^{27} The first part of the pattern, therefore, occurs in first and third person narration. In the second part of the pattern, when Jeremiah goes out to speak the word of the Lord, he regularly begins with "thus says the Lord (of hosts/God of Israel)." In the MT this appears as:

כֹּה אָמַר יהוה (צְבָאוֹת/אֱלֹהֵי יִשְׂרָאֵל)

In the LXX, the pattern is:

τάδε/οὕτως λέγει/εἶπεν κύριος (ὁ θεὸς Ισραηλ/παντοκράτωρ).

This is so much a part of the speech of Jeremiah that the word-string occurs in one of these forms approximately 150 times in the document. Also, Jeremiah says, "hear the word of the Lord." In the MT, this appears as שִׁמְעוּ דְבַר־יהוה,^{28} and in the LXX as ἀκούσατε/ἄκουσον/ἄκουε (τὸν) λόγον κυρίου.^{29} To this pattern is added הִנֵּה יָמִים בָּאִים נְאֻם־יהוה in the MT^{30} and ἰδοὺ ἡμέραι ἔρχονται, λέγει/φησίν κύριος in the LXX,^{31} meaning "behold the days are coming says the Lord." Through these phrases, the "word" of the Lord is transmitted through a prophet to the people of Israel. The prophet repeatedly refers to God as the source of his speech and the cause of his action during the process of

---

^{21} Jer. 7:11; 11:1; 18:1; 21:1; (25:1); 30:1; 32:1; 34:1, 8; 35:1; 40:1; (44:1).

^{22} Jer. 26:1; 27:1; 36:1.

^{23} Jer. 14:1; 35:12; 36:30; 39:6; 40:1; 41:12; 43:27; 44:6; (46:15); 49:7; 50:8.

^{24} Jer. 11:1; 18:1; 21:1; (25:1); 37:1; 39:1; 41:1, 8; 42:1; 47:1; (51:1).

^{25} Jer. 26:1; 33:1.

^{26} Jer. 1:4, 11, 13; 2:1; 13:3, 8; 16:1; 18:5; (20:8); 24:4; (25:3; 32:6).

^{27} Jer. 1:4, 11, 13; 13:3, 8; 18:5; (20:8); 24:4; 39:26; 42:12; 43:1.

^{28} Jer. 2:4; 7:2; 17:20; 19:3; 21:11; (22:2); 29:20; 31:10; 42:15; 44:24, 26.

^{29} Jer. 2:4, 31; 7:2; (9:19); 10:1; 17:20; 19:3; 21:11; 22:2, 29; 35:7; 38:10; 41:4; 45:20; 49:15; 51:24, 26.

^{30} Jer. 7:32; 9:24; 16:14; 19:6; 23:5, 7; 30:3; 31:31; (38); 33:14; 48:12; 49:2; 51:52.

^{31} Jer. 7:32; 9:24; 16:14; 19:6; 23:5, 7; 28:52; 31:12; 37:3; 38:27, 31, 38.

transmitting the word. The third part of the pattern is fulfilled as Jeremiah does what the Lord tells him to do and events occur as the Lord said they would. In this way, "the word of the Lord" comes through the prophet and becomes historical reality for the people of Israel.

The Socio-Rhetorical Pattern for the Gospel of God in Mark

In the Gospel of Mark, Jesus presents τὸ εὐαγγέλιον τοῦ θεοῦ, the gospel of God (Mark 1:14), and this message is called ὁ λόγος, the word.[32] These phrases are similar to λόγος τοῦ θεοῦ and ῥῆμα τοῦ θεοῦ in the LXX of Jeremiah 1:1-2, but the phrasing in Jeremiah differs by asserting that the word "came (ἐγένετο/ἐγενήθη) to Jeremiah" (LXX Jer. 1:1-2). In contrast, the gospel of Mark does not contain repetitive statements emphasizing that the gospel or the word "came from God." The phrases and the terminology in Mark shift the emphasis from the Lord God to Jesus. In Mark, Jesus never says, "thus says the Lord." Nor does Jesus say "hear the word of the Lord," "the Lord said to me," or "behold the days are coming says the Lord," as does Jeremiah. Since some of the conventions of prophetic biblical speech have influenced the Markan portrayal, phrases that perpetuate the authority of prophetic speech do appear. But none of the repetitive phrases in Jesus' speech claim authority for his speech by reference to "the Lord." Rather, the phrases perpetuate the authority of Jesus' speech and action in a manner that points to Jesus himself. Instead of "thus says the Lord" or "the Lord said to me," Jesus says ἀμὴν λέγω ὑμῖν, "truly, I say to you."[33] Instead of "hear the word of the Lord," he says ἀκούετε/ ἀκούσατε, "hear," or ὃς ἔξει ὦτα ἀκούειν "he who has ears to hear, let him hear."[34] Instead of "behold the days are coming says the Lord," he says βλέπετε, "take heed" or γρηγορεῖτε, "watch."[35] The prophetic speech of Jesus does not perpetuate a repetitive reference to the Lord God as the source of the speech. Rather, the speech of Jesus reflects a pattern that emphasizes his own embodiment of the system of thought and action he teaches.

A modification in the pattern of transmission of God's message to the people accompanies the change in terminology and phrasing. In Mark, the reader does not hear or see God transmit his gospel to Jesus. Through all of Mark, a heavenly voice speaks directly to Jesus only once, namely, at the baptism when it says, "you are my beloved Son in whom I am well pleased" (Mk 1:11). Jesus speaks to God twice: (1) in Gethsemane when he prays, "Abba, Father, all things are possible to

---

[32] Mark 1:45; 2:2; 4:14, 15, 16, 17, 18, 19, 20, 33; 8:32.

[33] Mark 3:28; 8:12; 9:1, 41; 10:15, 29; 11:23; 12:43; 13:30; 14:9, 18, 25, 30.

[34] Mark 4:3, 9, 23; 7:14, (16).

[35] Mark 4:24; 8:15; 12:38; 13:5, 9, 23, 33, 35, 37; 14:34, 38.

thee; remove this cup from me; yet not what I will, but what thou wilt" (Mk 14:32); and (2) on the cross when he cries, "My God, My God, why hast thou forsaken me" (Mk 15:34). But God never answers Jesus, as he answers the prophets in the Hebrew Bible. A heavenly voice speaks to the disciples once: on the Mount of Transfiguration when it tells them, "This is my beloved Son, listen to him" (Mk 9:7). But God never is portrayed in dialogue with Jesus or the disciples as he is with the prophets of Israel. As a result, the gospel of God resides in Jesus in a manner that does not emphasize either an initial transmission of the gospel from God to Jesus or dialogue between Jesus and God that clarifies the meaning of the gospel.

Since the message Jesus teaches is the gospel of God (Mk 1:14), the reader never doubts that God has transmitted the gospel to Jesus. But the reader never sees God tell the gospel to Jesus, and God never tells Jesus to go and tell the gospel to others. This creates a pattern in which Jesus' speech and action are the central content of the gospel. The "gospel of God" becomes both Jesus Christ's gospel to the people ("gospel *of Jesus Christ*" as subjective genitive) and the gospel about Jesus Christ ("gospel *of Jesus Christ*" as objective genitive). The central content of the gospel is the action and speech of Jesus himself. Indeed, in Mk 8:35 and 10:29 Jesus and the gospel are nearly identical as Jesus refers to action "for my sake and the sake of the gospel."[36] The book of Jeremiah, in contrast, does not allow "the word of the Lord" to become a complete system of thought and action which Jeremiah has mastered. The Lord God must unfold his "word" progressively to Jeremiah so that he knows what to say and do next. For this reason, the MT does not refer to the book of Jeremiah as "the word of Jeremiah" (דְּבַר־יִרְמְיָהוּ) but as "the *words* of Jeremiah...to whom the word of the Lord came" (דִּבְרֵי יִרְמְיָהוּ...אֲשֶׁר הָיָה דְבַר־יהוה אֵלָיו) (1:1-2; cf. 11:1-2; 43:1). Jeremiah can be the subject, but only in a setting which clarifies that God made him the subject for that specific occasion. The LXX follows a similar pattern by referring to the contents of the book of Jeremiah as "the word of God" (τό ῥῆμα τοῦ Θεοῦ/ὁ λόγος τοῦ θεοῦ, 1:1-2) and immediately indicating that the word came "to" (ἐπί/πρός) Jeremiah (1:1-2). In the book of Jeremiah, therefore, there is never the possibility of an objective genitive which could mean "the word about Jeremiah," like "the gospel of Jesus Christ" can mean "the gospel about Jesus Christ." The book of Jeremiah does not purport to tell "the word about Jeremiah." The "word" in the book of Jeremiah is constituted by "words" from God that Jeremiah transmits to the people. In contrast, the "gospel" in Mark is not constituted by "good messages" that God progressively transmits to Jesus. The "gospel of God" is a system of thought and action that Jesus knows and enacts. For this reason, Jesus

---

[36] Willi Marxsen, *Mark the Evangelist* (Nashville: Abingdon Press, 1969) 117-119, 126-38.

says, "*my words* will not pass away" (Mark 13:31) and "whoever is ashamed *of me and my words...*, of him will the Son of man also be ashamed" (Mark 8:38). The gospel of Mark emphasizes Jesus' own words and actions. Moreover, God's only two statements in Mark praise Jesus (1:11) and tell the disciples to listen to Jesus (9:7). God's statements do not transfer words to Jesus which determine Jesus' speech and action. In the book of Jeremiah, in contrast, the phrases dissuade the reader from concluding that the prophet embodies the word of the Lord apart from the transmission of new words to the prophet in the new situations that emerge.

In Mark, then, the first part of the prophetic pattern is missing, where God tells the word to the prophet. Instead, the pattern is as follows: Jesus goes to new places on his own initiative, people interact with his action and speech, then Jesus summons his disciples and others to a life that manifests the principles he has spoken and enacted. The absence of God's continual transmission of words for Jesus to preach, and the absence of continual reference by Jesus to God as the source of the words he speaks, suggests that the gospel resides in Jesus as a system of thought and action he himself has mastered. He is therefore a messianic teacher whose action is consistent with his speech, and the most frequent term used to address Jesus is in fact διδάσκαλος, teacher.[37] His authority is from God, but it has been transferred to him in a form that does not need continually to be supplemented by God. The narrator points to this attribute of Jesus when he says that Jesus "taught them as one who had authority, and not as the scribes" (Mk 1:22). Moreover, the narrator tells us that when Jesus summoned twelve disciples, προσκαλεῖται οὓς ἤθελεν αὐτός, "he summoned those whom *he himself* wanted" (Mark 3:13). In other words, Jesus is a sage who possesses special wisdom and autonomy within himself. This causes the people in his homeland to remark, after he teaches them in the synagogue:

> Where did this man get all this? What is the wisdom given to him?
> (Mark 6:2).

Jesus has the knowledge within himself to deal with each new situation that arises. He is not portrayed as waiting for God to reveal a new word to him before he engages in speech or action.

The change from prophetic agent to messianic teacher in Mark includes the transmission of the system of thought and action to a group of disciple-companions. This change is auspicious in a Jewish document written during the first century, especially when the disciple-companions play such an important role that their interaction with

---

[37] Mark 4:38; 9:17, 38; 10:17, 20, 35; 12:14, 19, 32; 13:1.

Jesus forms a subsidiary plot within the action.[38] Disciples play no similar role in the Hebrew Bible. Moses had a successor in Joshua, Elijah had a successor in Elisha, and Jeremiah had a scribal successor in Baruch, but none of the biblical narratives portrays an attempt by these prophets to teach a select group of successors a system of thought and action which they themselves embody. The closest comparison resides in the Elijah-Elisha narrative, since Elisha continues the work of Elijah after Elijah is taken into heaven by God. Still, the biblical account presents Elisha as a servant-successor of Elijah whom God told Elijah to anoint, not a disciple whom Elijah selected and systematically taught.[39] In contrast, Jesus attempts to transmit a system of thought he authoritatively embodies to a group of disciple-companions whom he himself has chosen, and this attempt gives Mark a special, dramatic quality.

Xenophon's *Memorabilia* and the Intercultural Pattern for the Disciple-Gathering Teacher in Mark

As we attempt to explain the changes in emphasis from prophetic literature to the gospel of Mark, it is important to explore another realm of influence—namely antecedent Greek literature that does not transmit Jewish traditions. Since antecedent Greek literature outside the sphere of Jewish culture exhibits aspects of the broader Hellenistic social and cultural milieu in which Jewish literature was functioning during the first century, it would be natural for any Jewish document written during the first century C.E. to combine conventional biblical patterns with conventional patterns in Graeco-Roman culture.

As the interpreter searches through non-Jewish Greek literature for patterns of thought and action exhibited in Mark, he or she comes to literature that features teachers who gathered disciple-companions around them and systematically attempted to teach them a system of thought and action. Xenophon's *Memorabilia* about Socrates is an excellent place to begin for comparison with Mark. In this book, written during the fourth century B.C.E., the narrator tells us:

πάντας δὲ τοὺς διδάσκοντας ὁρῶ αὐτοὺς δεικνύντας τε τοῖς μανθάνουσιν, ᾗπερ αὐτοὶ ποιοῦσιν ἃ διδάσκουσι, καί τῷ λόγῳ προσβιβάζοντας.

I find that all teachers themselves show their disciples how they themselves do what they teach, and lead them on by speech.
(Mem. 1.2.17)

---

[38] Theodore J. Weeden, *Mark —Traditions in Conflict* (Philadelphia: Fortress Press, 1971) 26-51.

[39] Martin Hengel, *The Charismatic Leader and His Followers*, trans. J. Greig (New York: Crossroad, 1981) 16-18; Robbins, "Mark 1.14-20," pp. 223-25, 228-31; *idem., Jesus the Teacher*, pp. 54-56, 84-85, 98-101.

This pattern, in contrast to the prophetic pattern we analyzed earlier, contains three essential elements:

1. the teacher himself does what he teaches others to do;
2. the teacher interacts with others through speech to teach the system of thought and action he embodies;
3. the teacher transmits a religio-ethical system of thought and action to later generations through his disciple-companions.

The teacher/disciple pattern in Xenophon's *Memorabilia* is perpetuated by phrases that are repeated with variation, rather than by verbatim repetitive phrases like the reader encounters in prophetic biblical literature. The rationale for this variation appears to be expressed in the *Rhetorica ad Herennium* when it says:

> *Eandem rem dicemus non eodem modo—nam id quidem obtundere auditorem est, non rem expolire—sed commutate,*
>
> We shall not repeat the same thing precisely—for that, to be sure would weary the hearer and not elaborate the idea——but with changes.
>
> (*Rhet. ad Her.* 4.42.54)

A writer influenced by Graeco-Roman style repeats a phrase with variation throughout the document, saying the same thing again and again with slight modifications.

Through varied repetitive phrases, Xenophon's *Memorabilia* perpetuates the pattern of the disciple-gathering teacher. These phrases focus on Socrates "himself" (αὐτος/ἑαυτόν) and what he himself did and said (ἐποίει/πράττων/τὰ ἔργα; λέγων).[40] By his action and speech, he exerted his influence on others especially through conversation (διαλέγεσθαι),[41] exhorting (προτρέπειν) his companions and others toward good actions and thoughts,[42] and discouraging (ἀποτρέπειν) them from bad actions and thoughts.[43] The opportunity for these conversations often emerged "when seeing (someone or something)...he said" (ἰδων/ὁρῶν...ἔφη/ἤρετο) or "when learning that (someone had said or done something)...he said" (αἰσθανόμενος...ἔφη).[44] Frequently the conversation begins with

---

[40] *Memorabilia* 1.1.16; 1.2.2, 4, 8, 18, 28, 29, (52), 55, 59; 1.3.1, 4, 14; 1.5.6; 1.6.14, (15); 3.8.1; (3.10.15); 4.2.1; 4.3.18; 4.5.1, 2; 4.6.15; 4.7.1, 8.

[41] Cf. *Memorabilia* 1.1.16; 1.2.9; 1.5.6; 1.6.1; 1.7.5; 2.4.1; 2.6.1; 2.10.1; 3.3.1; 3.5.1; 3.10.1; 4.4.5; 4.5.1-2, 12; 4.6.15.

[42] *Memorabilia* 1.2.64; 1.4.1; 1.7.1; 2.1.1; 2.5.1; 4.5.1; 4.8.11.

[43] *Memorabilia* 1.1.4; 1.2.29, 30; 1.7.1, 5; 4.7.6.

[44] Cf. *Memorabilia* 1.2.29; 2.2.1; 2.3.1; 2.5.1; 2.7.1; 2.8.1; 3.1.1; 3.4.1; 3.5.1; 3.7.1; 3.12.1; 3.14.5; 4.1.3; 4.2.1, 8.

Socrates' statement, "tell me" (εἰπέ μοι).[45] Through this activity Socrates was able (ἱκανός) to make his companions do what he directed them (ποιεῖν plus infinitive), making them better (βελτίων).[46]

The gospel of Mark manifests a pattern of interaction similar to the pattern implicit throughout Xenophon's *Memorabilia*. On his own initiative, Jesus goes to places, engages people in conversation, and exhorts people to accept the system of thought and action he embodies. The narrator presents the occasions for interaction with comments that "Jesus saw...and said,"[47] people "asked...and he said,"[48] or Jesus "asked."[49] In the midst of this activity the disciples of Jesus receive special attention. Much as Xenophon's *Memorabilia* repeatedly refers to Socrates' conversations with and exhortations to his disciple-companions, so the Gospel of Mark persistently reminds the reader that Jesus is accompanied by disciples whom he summons to participate in the system of thought and action he manifests in their presence.[50] Thus, while the gospel of Mark has a heritage that lies within prophetic biblical literature, it exhibits a pattern of interaction present in a Hellenistic document like Xenophon's *Memorabilia*.

The Teacher's Enactment of the Central Paradox of His Teaching

It might be tempting to suggest that the similar pattern in Mark and Xenophon's *Memorabilia* is a universal pattern common to teachers who gather disciple-companions, and, therefore, nothing more should be made of the pattern. But there is another dimension of Mark that suggests the importance of further comparison with Graeco-Roman literature. Once Jesus begins his companionship with a group of disciples, he takes them through phases of interaction that have important relationships to Graeco-Roman literature featuring disciple-gathering teachers. These phases represent the cycle of relationships between disciple-companions and their teachers in the social and cultural milieu of the Hellenistic and Roman world. The first phase (Mark 1:14-3:6) features the gathering of disciple-companions, the second phase (3:7-12:44) contains stages of teaching and learning, and the third phase (13:1-16:8) presents the farewell and death of the teacher.[51]

---

[45] *Memorabilia* 1.3.9; 1.4.2; 2.1.1; 2.2.1; 2.3.1; 2.6.1; 2.9.1; 2.10.1; 3.7.1; 4.2.8; 4.3.3; 4.5.2; 4.6.2.

[46] Cf. *Memorabilia* 1.2.2, 3, 9, 27, 29, 61; 1.4.1, 19; 2.9.3; 3.2.3; 4.2.6, 37, 38; 4.4.25; 4.5.1, 3; 4.6.1; 4.7.3; 4.8.3, 10.

[47] Mark 1:16-17, 19; 2:5, 14; 6:34; 8:33; 9:25; 10:14; 11:13-14; 12:(15), 34.

[48] Mark 4:10; 7:5, 17, 26; 9:11, 28; 10:2, 10, 17; 12:18; 13:3; 14:60-61; 15:2, 4.

[49] Mark 5:9; 8:5, 23, 27, 28; 9:16, 21, 33; 11:29.

[50] Mark 3:13; 6:7; 8:1, 34; 10:42; 12:43.

[51] Robbins, *Jesus the Teacher*, pp. 82-196.

The teaching/learning phase in Mark is especially revealing when compared with the teaching/learning phase in Xenophon's *Memorabilia* IV, since each document depicts four stages in this phase. The first stage contains a basic introduction to the teacher's system of thought and action (Mark 3:7-5:43; *Memorabilia* 4.3.1-18). The second stage builds the complexity of the teacher's system (Mark 6:1-8:26; *Memorabilia* 4.4.1-25). The third stage features the center of the teacher's system of understanding and reveals an underlying paradox within it (Mark 8:27-10:45; *Memorabilia* 4.5.1-12). The fourth stage portrays a public form of the teacher's system which communicates basic ideas to a broad public and sets the stage for his official indictment (Mark 10:46-12:44; *Memorabilia* 4.6.1-15).[52]

The third stage in the teaching/learning phase is especially important, since it introduces the paradox which the teacher enacts to establish his integrity as a person who does what he teaches. In Xenophon's *Memorabilia* 4.5.1-12, which presents the third stage of the teaching/learning phase in Book IV, Socrates discusses ἐγκράτεια (self-control) and exhorts his companions to cultivate ἐγκράτεια above all things. Socrates explains that a paradox lies at the center of ἐγκράτεια. The goal is to achieve that which is pleasurable (τὸ ἥδος), and it would appear that lack of self-control (ἡ ἀκρασία) produces the greatest pleasure (4.5.9). With ἀκρασία there is no deprivation which causes a person to suffer. If one has sexual desire or is hungry, thirsty, or tired, he or she can indulge in sex or drink, eat, or sleep. Thus, pleasures are continually produced and displeasure is avoided. Paradoxically, however, this approach

κωλύει τοῖς ἀναγκαιοτάτοις τε καί συνεχεστάτοις ἀξιολόγως ἥδεσθαι.

prevents a person from experiencing any pleasure worthy to be mentioned in the most elementary and recurrent forms of enjoyment.

(*Mem.* 4.5.9)

In contrast, ἐγκράτεια alone causes people to endure displeasure and to experience pleasure that is truly worth mentioning. Socrates concludes the dialogue with the statement:

τοῖς ἐγκρατέσι μόνοις ἔξεστι σκοπεῖν τὰ κράτιστα τῶν πραγμάτων καὶ λόγῳ καὶ ἔργῳ διαλέγοντας κατὰ γένη τὰ μὲν ἀγαθὰ προαιρεῖσθαι, τῶν δὲ κακῶν ἀπέχεσθαι,

only the self-controlled have power to consider the things that matter most, and sorting them out after their kind, by word and deed alike to prefer the good and reject the evil.

(*Mem.* 4.5.11)

---

[52] See *ibid.*, pp. 125-69.

Having introduced this paradox in the third stage of the teaching/learning phase, the author returns to it in the setting of Socrates' death. After Meletus had formulated his indictment, Socrates' disciple-companion Hermogenes tried to persuade Socrates to prepare a defense. Socrates replied that he had been preparing his defense all his life:

οὐδὲν ἄλλο ποιῶν διαγεγένηται ἢ διασκοπῶν μὲν τά τε δίκαια καὶ τὰ ἄδικα, πράττων δέ τὰ δίκαια καὶ τῶν ἀδίκων ἀπεχόμενος.

he had been constantly occupied in doing nothing other than considering right and wrong, and in doing what was right and avoiding what was wrong.

(*Mem.* 4.8.4)

The constant activity of "considering" (διασκοπῶν) right and wrong so that he could do (πράττων) what was right and avoid (ἀπεχόμενος) what was wrong is the exercise of ἐγκράτεια. Especially when confronted with the prospect of fleeing from death or accepting it, he consulted his δαιμόνιον, "divine guide," and decided that he must accept death according to their decision. For this reason, he goes on to assert:

τὸν δέ, θαυμάζεις, φάναι, εἰ τῷ θεῷ δοκεῖ βέλτιον εἶναι ἐμὲ τελευτᾶν τὸν βίον ἤδη; οὐκ οἶσθ', ὅτι μέχρι μὲν τοῦδε τοῦ χρόνου ἐγὼ οὐδένι ἀνθρώπων ὑφείμην ἂν οὔτε βέλτιον δυθ' ἥδιον ἐμοῦ βεβιωκέναι; ἄριστα μὲν γὰρ οἶμαι ζῆν τοὺς ἄριστα ἐπιμελομένους τοῦ ὡς βελτίστους γίγνεσθαι, ἥδιστα δὲ τοὺς μάλιστα αἰθανομένους, ὅτι βελτίους γίγνονται,

Do you think it strange, if it seems better to the god that I should die now? Don't you see that to this day I never would suggest that any man had lived a better or a pleasanter life than I? For they live best, I think, who strive best to become as good as possible; and the pleasantest life is theirs who are conscious that they are growing in goodness.

(*Mem.* 4.8.6)

With these words, Socrates manifests the central, paradoxical part of the system he has taught. Following the principle he introduced earlier, he has exercised ἐγκράτεια when he has perceived that consciously accepting death, according to the god's wish, produces the pleasure of growing in goodness. What appears, therefore, to be unpleasant will actually produce a pleasure well worth attaining.

Socrates realizes, however, that his acceptance of death can be seen in the public sphere as a discrediting of his reputation. For this reason he explains that those who kill him must bear the shame rather than he himself:

ἀλλὰ μὴν εἴ γε ἀδίκως ἀποθανοῦμαι, τοῖς μὲν ἀδίκως ἐμὲ
ἀποκτείνασιν αἰσχρὸν ἂν εἴη τοῦτο εἰ γὰρ τὸ ἀδικεῖν
αἰσχρόν ἐστι, πῶς οὐκ αἰσχρὸν καὶ τὸ ἀδίκως ὁτιοῦν
ποιεῖν; ἐμοὶ δὲ τί αἰσχρὸν τὸ ἑτέρους μὴ δύνασθαι περὶ
ἐμοῦ τὰ δίκαια μήτε γνῶναι μήτε ποιῆσαι;...οἶδα γὰρ ἀεὶ
μαρτυρήσεσθαί μοι, ὅτι ἐγὼ ἠδίκησα μὲν οὐδένα πώποτε
ἀνθρώπων οὐδὲ χείρω ἐποίησα, βελτίους δὲ ποιεῖν ἐπειρώμην
ἀεὶ τοὺς ἐμοὶ συνόντας.

But now, if I am to die unjustly, they who unjustly kill me bear the
shame of it. For if to do injustice is shameful, whatever is unjustly done
must surely bring shame. But to me what shame is it that others fail to
decide and act justly concerning me?... For I know that they will ever
testify of me that I wronged no man at any time, nor corrupted any
man, but strove ever to make my companions better.

(*Mem.* 4.8.9-10).

As Socrates explains his position, he removes his case from the official
jury at Athens and places it before public judgment throughout
posterity. Anyone who looks closely at Socrates' words and deeds will
know that there was no shame in what he did. Rather, those who
unjustly put him to trial and killed him brought shame upon
themselves. In this way Xenophon's Socrates maintains ἐγκράτεια to
the end, enacts the central principle he has taught, and asks the reader
to be the final judge of his words and deeds.

The gospel of Mark also portrays Jesus enacting at death the
central, paradoxical principle he taught his disciples. During the
third stage of his teaching (Mark 8:27-10:45), Jesus tells his disciples
that:

whoever would save his life will lose it; and whoever loses his life for my
sake and the gospel's will save it.

(Mark 8:35)

This principle, which is as paradoxical as ἐγκράτεια, is enacted by
Jesus at his death. While Jesus is on the cross, those who pass by deride
him, wagging their heads and saying:

Aha! You who would destroy the temple and build it in three days, save
yourself and come down from the cross.

(Mark 15:30)

Then chief priests and scribes mock him saying:

He saved others; he cannot save himself. Let the Messiah, the King of
Israel, come down from the cross, that we may see and believe.

(Mark 15:31-32)

In both instances, those who mock Jesus correlate his death on the cross
with his inability to "save himself." With this formulation of the
statements, the reader knows that Jesus is enacting the paradoxical

principle he attempted to explain to his disciples in the central section of his teaching (Mark 8:27-10:45). As Jesus dies (Mark 15:37), the reader knows that Jesus has taken up his cross and lost his life, unable to save himself (Mark 8:34-35). Yet in the final scene of the gospel, the message is announced that Jesus has risen (Mark 16:6-7). By losing his life, therefore, Jesus has saved it. In this way, Jesus has enacted the central, paradoxical principle in his teaching. Thus, Jesus is portrayed according to the same Greek conventions used to depict the death of Socrates.

The Intercultural Nature of Losing One's Life in Order to Save It

The preceding evidence suggests that Xenophon's *Memorabilia* and Mark's gospel share in common the portrayal of a disciple-gathering sage who shows his integrity at death by enacting what he has taught, but it still does not show the thoroughgoing intercultural portrayal in the gospel of Mark. For this evidence, the interpreter must look at the argument Jesus presents to show that accepting the cross is an enactment of ultimate self-denial that saves life. In Mark 8:34-38, Jesus presents an argument with a proposition followed by four statements of rationale. The proposition is as follows:

> If any one would come after me, let him deny himself and take up his cross and follow me.
>
> (Mark 8:34)

This proposition asserts that a person must be willing to identify with Jesus' crucifixion in order truly to follow Jesus' system of thought and action. The proposition is set up by Peter's unwillingness to accept Jesus' assertion that the Son of man must be rejected, killed, and rise up (Mark 8:31), but it takes the assertion one step further by introducing crucifixion as the mode by which he is killed. This is an important step, since even if one accepts that the Messiah must die, it is still another thing for the Messiah to die by the shameful mode of crucifixion. Indeed, as Paul asserted, the crucifixion of Jesus seemed to the Greeks to be μωρία, "foolishness," rather than σοφία, "wisdom" (1 Cor. 1:23). The skillful part of the proposition is its association of "taking up one's cross" with "denying oneself." The latter is a milder form of negating one's life than the former and provides a means of strengthening the possibility of accepting it. In fact, the reader may hear within Mark 8:34 dimensions of Socrates' discussion of denial within ἐγκράτεια, self-control. Once the proposition has been asserted in this form, however, Jesus must provide an argument that suggests how accepting the cross can be understood as an act of self-denial rather than an event that signifies dishonor and shame.

The argument for accepting the crucifixion as an act of self-denial is presented in four steps, each in the form of a rationale introduced with γάρ. The first rationale is as follows:

For whoever wishes to save his life will lose it; and whoever loses his life
for my sake and the gospel's will save it.
(Mark 8:35)

There are two parts to this rationale. The first part presents the
principle that attempting to save one's life causes one to lose it. This
principle may be presupposed in Jesus' announcement that the Son of
man must die and rise up (Mark 8:31), but it appears that the emphasis
lies on the eschatological necessity (δεῖ) of the death and resurrection
in that announcement. In Mark 8:35, however, the emphasis shifts to
the saving of life through the loss of life, and this principle, as
William A. Beardslee has shown, was a motif in Greek culture prior to
the first century.[53] The earliest setting in which the motif functioned
appears to be exhortations during wars between communities. After
Socrates' life and death, Socrates became the classic example of the one
who had enacted the principle.[54] This tradition is summed up in
Epictetus' *Discourses* 4.1.162-65. According to Epictetus, Socrates did
not wish to save his paltry body (οὐ ἤθελεν σῶσαι τὸ σωμάτιον,
Discourses 1.162). Instead, he chose to accept the verdict of the jury,
and was saved by death (ἀποθνῄσκων σῴζεται, *Discourses* 1.165). In
the first half of Mark 8:35, Jesus presents the view that anyone who
wishes to save his life (ὃς ἐὰν θέλῃ τὴν ψυχὴν αὐτοῦ σῶσαι) will
lose it. This part of the initial rationale for accepting an identification
with Jesus' cross, then, reflects a basic principle associated with
Socrates' death in Graeco-Roman society and culture. A Greek-reading
person would probably see something familiar in this part of the
rationale, especially when it is part of the teaching and action of a
disciple-gathering sage. This familiar dimension would strengthen the
possibility that the reader could accept its logic. The last part of the
saying puts the principle into a thoroughly Christian framework by
associating the saving of life through the loss of life with Jesus and the
gospel ("for my sake and the gospel's"). In this way, the first and
primary rationale for "taking up one's cross" is based on a familiar
principle in Mediterranean society and culture that proposed a
paradoxical way of saving one's life through losing it.

While the first rationale refers to the attempt to save life itself,
the second rationale refers to an attempt to save life through the
attainment of wealth and power:

For what does it profit (ὠφελεῖ) a man, to gain (κερδῆσαι) the whole
world and forfeit his life (τὴν ψυχὴν αὐτοῦ)? (Mark 8:36).

---

[53] William A. Beardslee, "Saving One's Life By Losing It," *Journal of the
American Academy of Religion* 47 (1979) 57-72.
[54] *Ibid.*, pp. 61-63.

This saying also is based on a motif in Graeco-Roman society. The motif was developed especially within Cynic tradition. An excellent paraphrase of the statement exists in Dio Chrysostom, *Discourses* 10.15, where Diogenes the Cynic is talking with a man who is travelling to Delphi to seek an oracle:

> Are you going to try to secure first, not that other thing, which will enable you to derive profit (ὠφελεῖσθαι) from everything and to order all your affairs well, but in preference to wisdom are you going to seek riches or lands or teams of horses or ships or houses? You will become their slave and will suffer through them and perform a great deal of useless labour, and will spend all your life worrying over them without getting any benefit whatsoever from them.[55]

With this motif, the emphasis lies on worldly possessions and power, and it asserts that acquiring possessions and power can become a forfeiture of life, because a person will spend all of life worrying over them without getting any benefit. This motif also is found in Dio Chrysostom, *Discourses* 4.6, where Alexander the Great is characterized as one who perceived that other men "had all been well-nigh ruined in soul (διεφθαρμένοι...τὰς ψυχάς) by luxury and idleness and were slaves to making gain (τοῦ κερδαίνειν) and pleasure." Denying oneself possessions and power, then, may result in the true attainment of life. Once this principle emerges in Mark 8:36, it recurs in Mark 10:17-31, where Jesus discusses wealth and possessions with the disciples,[56] and in Mark 10:42-44, where he discusses prestige and power.[57] Since these motifs also are well-established in Graeco-Roman tradition, the argumentation would appear to stay within a sphere of understanding familiar to a Greek reader.

The third rationale supports the two previous ones by emphasizing that life has a unique value:

> For what can a man give in return (ἀντάλλαγμα) for his life (τῆς ψυξῆς αὐτοῦ)?

> (Mark 8:37)

---

[55] This passage continues with a fascinating parallel to Matthew 6:26: "Consider the beasts yonder and the birds, how much freer from trouble they live than men,...they have one very great blessing—hey own no property" (Dio Chrysostom, *Discourses* 10.16).

[56] Cf. the list of possessions in Mark 10:28-31 and Dio Chrysostom, *Discourses* 10.15.

[57] For an extended exploration of the implications of Mark 10:42-45 in a Graeco-Roman environment, see David Seeley, *The Noble Death: Greco-Roman Martyrology and Paul's Concept of Salvation.* JSNT Supplement Series 18. Sheffield: Sheffield Academic Press, 1989.

This rationale uses the imagery of exchange to suggest that nothing has a value equal to life. Again, this statement reflects a point of view in Graeco-Roman tradition. In the *Sentences of Menander*, we read:

ψυχῆς γὰρ οὐδέν ἐστι τιμιώτερον,

There is nothing more valuable than (one's) life.[58]

Graeco-Roman tradition encouraged a person to think seriously about one's life and to improve it, because it was a person's most valuable possession. This point of view was emphasized also by Jews who valued the Hellenistic system of *paideia*, as can be seen in Sirach 26:14:

οὐκ ἔστιν ἀνατάλλαγμα πεπαιδευμένης ψυχῆς

nothing is an exchange for a well-instructed life.

With these three rationales, the Greek reader has encountered familiar concepts and motifs. If accepting the cross means refusing to be infatuated with saving one's life and attaining possessions and power in order to place supreme value on life itself, then the cross is not just a shameful, foolish thing. Perhaps instead it can be, much as Socrates' death, an event that illuminates a paradoxical truth about the things that are and are not worth attaining. This kind of argument, it would seem, is at home in a Graeco-Roman environment.

If the first three rationales gather motifs from the Graeco-Roman world of thought, the final rationale breaks sharply with that tradition as it refers to a public trial over which the Son of man will preside:

> For whoever is ashamed (ἐπαισχυνθῇ) of me and of my words in this adulterous and sinful generation, of him will the Son of man also be ashamed (ἐπαισχυνθήσεται), when he comes in the glory of his Father with the holy angels.
>
> (Mark 8:38)

We recall that Xenophon's *Memorabilia* establishes a future trial for Socrates by asking the readers to function as judge and jury over his words and deeds. In contrast, the Markan Jesus evokes a future trial over which the Son of man will preside. In other words, the future public trial in which Xenophon asks the reader to participate as judge and jury is replaced by a public trial to be held by the Son of Man with the complete power of God the Father. But a major phenomenon in common between the two accounts is shame.[59] Thus we must look carefully at the function of shame in both accounts.

---

[58] 843: Siegfried Jaekel, *Menandri Sententiae* (Leipzig: Teubner, 1964); Beardslee, "Saving One's Life By Losing It," p. 63.

[59] For the importance of "shame vs. honor" in Mediterranean culture, see Malina, *The New Testament World*, pp. 25-50; *Honour and Shame: The Values*

In *Memorabilia* 4.8.9, Socrates asserts: "If I die unjustly, they who unjustly kill me will bear the shame (αἰσχρόν) of it." This assertion is based on a premise intrinsic to justice as a social system: justice is honorable; injustice is shameful. Socrates' proposition extends the principle to its social effect. A public jury led by one or more judges has the social responsibility to decide whether a person should be brought to complete shame through physical annihilation, be required to pay a penalty that may restore honor, or be exonerated publicly by an acquittal. Since a jury under the leadership of one or more judges has this social responsibility, if an accused person dies unjustly, those who unjustly kill him will bear the shame rather than he.

As Socrates continues the argument, he interweaves assertions containing personal pronouns with generalized statements containing no personal pronouns. Thus, he continues with:

> For if to do injustice is shameful, whatever is unjustly done must surely bring shame.

This statement moves the argument from the personal arena of Socrates vs. the jury to a social arena governed by generalized principles that correlate justice and injustice with honor and shame. Immediately after this, however, Xenophon's Socrates returns to a personalized form of argument:

> But to me what shame is it that others fail to decide and act justly concerning me?

With this personalized assertion Socrates dissociates himself and his actions from shame. Any judgement that he is guilty will be a verdict based on injustice. Therefore, the jurors will bear the shame, not he.

As Socrates interweaves personal and impersonal statements, he appeals to a future jury:

> I see that posterity judges differently of the dead according as they did injustice (τῶν ἀδικησάντων) or suffered injustice (τῶν ἀδικηθέντων).

This statement summarizes the situation in terms of an active/passive correlative: He who does injustice (active) will bear the shame of it; he who suffers injustice (passive) will bear no shame in posterity. Therefore, whatever injustice exists at present, the future will correct.

After Socrates introduces the injustice/shame correlative, he adds the concept of memory to the concept of posterity in the future. In this context the act of memory develops into an act of testimony:

---

of Mediterranean Society, edited by Jean G. Peristiany (London: Weidenfeld and Nicolson, 1965; *Honor and Shame and the Unity of the Mediterranean*, edited by David D. Gilmore (Washington, DC: American Anthropological Association, 1987). For the biblical use of αἰσχύνειν, see, e.g., LXX Isaiah 41:11; 42:17; 44:10, 11; 45:16, 17, 25; 49:23; 50:7; 65:13; 66:5.

I know that men will remember me too, and, if I die now, not as they
will remember those who took my life. For I know that they will ever
testify of me (ἀεὶ μαρτυρήσεσθαί μοι) that I wronged no man at any
time, nor corrupted any man, but strove ever to make my companions
better.

(Mem. 4.8.10).

At this point, Xenophon's Socrates ends his speaking, and the
narrator's voice takes the argument to the end of the document. At the
end, the narrator returns to the reader as a member of the public jury:

> To me then he seemed to be all that a truly good and happy man must
> be. But if there is any doubter, let him set the character of other men
> beside these things; then let him judge (κρινέτω).

As the document ends, the final verdict is left to the reader who is to
function as judge and jury over Socrates' action and speech as presented
in the Memorabilia.

It will be obvious to the reader that the argument in Xenophon's
Memorabilia calls forth a future public trial that puts shame upon
certain people without any shades of Jewish eschatology or
apocalypticism. The Markan account, in contrast, uses biblical
tradition that was articulated in Daniel 7 and 11 as Jesus appeals to
the Son of man who will come with the honor of his Father and will be
ashamed of those who are ashamed of Jesus and his words.[60] We recall
that Xenophon's Socrates says that no shame comes upon him even if he
is condemned to death. Likewise, Mark dissociates Jesus from shame.
The Son of man will suffer many things and be rejected (πολλὰ παθεῖν
καὶ ἀποδοκιμασθῆναι: 8:31), *but* he will not be shamed. Rather, the
future Son of man will be ashamed of the person who is ashamed of
"Jesus and his words" (8:38).

Mark keeps shame away from Jesus by means of thoroughly
personalized argumentation. Jesus never uses social principles
concerning justice, injustice, honor, and shame, even though he does use
social principles about seeking possessions. The argument featuring the
future Son of man introduces a complex set of personal dynamics. The
reasoning appears to go like this: the person who is ashamed of Jesus
and his words is unwilling to deny him/herself; therefore that person
will be publicly shamed, and this public shame will be performed by a
judge who bears the honor (δόξα) of "his Father." The four steps here
concern: (a) the action of honoring Jesus and his words (which appear
shameful because of the rejection and crucifixion), (b) the action of
denying oneself, which is the dynamic involved in accepting Jesus and
his words; (c) the action of being shamed by the Son of man; and (d) the
action of the Son of man's coming with the honor bestowed on him by
his Father.

---

[60] δόξα; cf. *Memorabilia* 4.8.10 with Daniel 11:38-39 and Mark 8:38.

These dynamics combine biblical patterns with Graeco-Roman patterns. The action of honoring Jesus and his words is very much like the action of honoring Socrates and his words. Both experienced a shameful verdict on their words and deeds at the end of their careers, and the reader is asked to reverse the verdict. A major difference, however, is the honor God has placed upon the Son of man. God's honoring of the Son of man's rejection and death establishes a dynamic whereby the person who is ashamed of Jesus and his words will be shamed by God's representative, who is the very personage who was rejected and killed. Thus the future correlative works differently. Instead of shame being based on a generalized social principle of injustice, it is based on the personal authority of the Son of man.[61] The Son of man, then, is the judge. The reader watches as Mark's Jesus envisions the Son of man bringing shame on the person who is ashamed of Jesus and his words. That which is an internal principle in the *Memorabilia* is a matter of personal divine agency in Mark. Thus, in Mark honor and shame function within a Jewish ideological framework where the ultimate determiner of honor and shame is God.

The action of honoring the words and deeds of a person by denying oneself resonates well with both Xenophon's *Memorabilia* and Mark. As different as Mark is from the *Memorabilia,* its intercultural nature is signified by its lack of contradiction with points of view in the *Memorabilia.* Greek readers could easily take ideas from the *Memorabilia* directly into the Markan account. They could think that Jesus was unjustly crucified and that the shame really lies on those who crucified him (in fact, people regularly read Mark in this manner). Also, Socrates' forewarning by the δαιμόνιον (4.8.1) easily coheres with the Markan portrayal of Jesus' relation to God (esp. Gethsemane: 14:32-42). And a Greek reader could add the system of virtue from the *Memorabilia* to the Markan portrayal with ἐγκράτεια as one of the major emphases. Thus, the gospel of Mark is amazingly open to a Graeco-Roman reading. But more than this, it is highly intercultural in and of itself. Following Jesus' words and deeds requires denial of oneself that is closely related to denial in traditions of Hellenistic moral philosophers. The insight that one may save oneself by dying emerges from exhortations during wars in Greek society and is specifically associated with Socrates in literature written during the first and second centuries C.E. In addition, the futile nature of attempting to gain life by gaining possessions is a well-established tradition in Hellenistic culture. But the idea of a public trial to be held by the heavenly Son of man is a tradition located in certain Jewish circles during the first century C.E. The intercultural nature of the Markan presentation comes clearly to the fore as Jesus announces the Son

---

[61] Richard A. Edwards, "The Eschatological Correlative as *Gattung* in the New Testament," *Zeitschrift fur die neutestamentliche Wissenschaft* 60 (1969) 9-20.

of man's response to those who are ashamed of Jesus and his words. Then, in Mark 9:1, the Markan Jesus takes the themes one step further into the sphere of biblical culture as he announces: "Truly I say to you that there are some standing here who will not taste death until they see the kingdom of God come with power." With this statement the Markan Jesus brings the discussion to a climax within an environment of biblical temporality and cosmic power. God is the one who rules the world, and he is the one who sanctions the Son of man who was rejected and killed, but arose and will come again to shame those who are ashamed of him and his words. With this conclusion, the reader sees that the intercultural portrayal of Mark is a matter of presenting biblical heritage in a Graeco-Roman world rather than simply bringing aspects of biblical tradition into Graeco-Roman heritage. The gospel of Mark is, then, a Jewish document in a Graeco-Roman world.

Conclusion

When the Markan hypothesis emerged near the end of the 19th century and Christians began to accept Mark as the most authentic portrayal of the historical Jesus, the intercultural nature of the Markan Jesus established a congenial stage for accommodating the historical Jesus to modern culture. The paradoxical nature of Jesus' speech and action in Mark, which is an aspect of the intercultural portrayal, has supported the image of a Jesus who systematically overturned people's views of the world.

But this view of Jesus has produced major divisions among interpretive communities. One response has been for interpreters to insist that all the gospel materials have arisen through Jewish midrash.[62] Thus the gospels themselves remain thoroughly Jewish. A counter to this overemphasis soon will appear in *Patterns of Persuasion in the Gospels*,[63] which uses insights from Hellenistic rhetorical textbooks for analysis of the synoptic gospels. Thus, a debate over the place of Jewish culture within Graeco-Roman culture is alive and well today, and the debate concerns not only the gospels but Jesus of Nazareth himself. Some scholars of early Judaism want scholars of early Christianity only to think that Jesus is God, and many Christians adopt this misunderstanding of their tradition with a docetic view in which Jesus is essentially a Greek god without sexual desires. Others would like scholars of Christianity to emphasize that Jesus was a Jewish man in the tradition of a rabbi who studies the Talmud, and there are those who accommodate this misunderstanding also, by regularly adopting a view that Pharisees created a dead tradition

---

[62] See, e.g., Michael D. Goulder, *Luke: A New Paradigm* (Sheffield: Sheffield Academic Press, 1987).
[63] See above, n. 13.

that Jesus brought to life through penetrating new analysis of the Torah and the prophets.

The New Testament gospels stand in the midst of these debates, and the debates have subtle intercultural dynamics. Deep cultural commitments express themselves as interpreters debate whether the gospel of Mark is the earliest gospel or an epitome of Matthew and Luke. Approaching the gospel of Mark as a Jewish document in a Graeco-Roman world brings a perspective not usually brought to this gospel. As a result of the last century of research, there should be agreement among interpreters that early Christianity was one kind of Judaism during the first century. The gospel of Mark was a document that emerged within a particular sector of first century Judaism, and it stands alongside other Jewish literature written in Greek, like the documents of Philo of Alexandria, Josephus, the Wisdom of Solomon, Sirach, and many others. These other documents are intercultural, and all of them merge biblical tradition with Hellenistic patterns and conventions. The question is the particular kind of intercultural product any of these documents is.

An application of socio-rhetorical criticism to Mark reveals an important cultural shift as the prophetic "word of God" is transformed into both the "gospel of God" and "the gospel of Jesus Christ." This shift reveals an emphasis on the action and speech of Jesus himself which features the autonomy and integrity of the disciple-gathering sage. This autonomy and integrity stands in a tensive relationship to God's heteronomy in the biblical tradition, which is usually described as theonomy.[64] The interweaving of Jesus' autonomy with God's theonomy creates an intercultural tension that exists to this day. God's theonomy derives from biblical tradition. Jesus' autonomy opens the way for Greek tradition, since autonomous wise sages play as important a role as gods in much Greek literature. As soon as Jesus' autonomy is taken into God's theonomy, as it is in the Son of man tradition in Mark, then Hellenistic Jewish thought is challenging biblical heritage from the inside. The debate will not subside. It is built into the New Testament gospels themselves. Perhaps tension between the theonomy of God and the autonomy of sages on earth is a widespread phenomenon in Jewish literature written in the context of Graeco-Roman culture, and perhaps it also was a significant dynamic in the arena of social interaction among Jews and between Jews and non-Jews in the Graeco-Roman world.*

---

[64] See H. Wayne Merritt, "'In Word and Deed:' A Contribution to the Understanding of Moral Integrity in Paul" (Ph.D. dissertation, Emory University, 1986) 328-329.

* An earlier version of this essay was written during 1983-84 while the author was at the Religionsvitenskapelig Institutt at the University of Trondheim, Norway, under the sponsorship of a Fulbright-Hays Research-Lecture

Fellowship. During this time, substantive portions of the material were delivered in lectures at the Universities of Sheffield, Manchester, and Glasgow, and at the Metodistkirkens Seminar in Bergen, Norway. I am grateful to these institutions for their support of this research.

Chapter Three

The Mishnah's Philosophy of
Intention: Defining the Data

Jacob Neusner
Brown University

On the surface, the Mishnah—a principal holy book of Judaism written about A.D. 200—is a compilation of rules. But a deeper look reveals that these rules yield regulations on a program of a distinctively and particularly philosophical character, so that much of the the Mishnah in fact is a philosophical writing. True, the Mishnah's philosophical tractates—approximately two-thirds of the whole—present their a philosophy in an odd and peculiar idiom. But the document is a work of systematic thought on a sustaining program of issues that, in the Mishnah's authorship's time and place, other philosophers addressed and people in general recognized as philosophical. When philosophers did philosophy, these are some of the things that concerned them: the rules of classification and generalization, the issues of mixtures, the resolution of doubts, the relationship of the actual to the potential (the familiar chicken-or-egg debate), the role of attitude or intention in the assessment of an action and its consequences, and the like. These abstract issues of general intelligibility turn out to form the intellectual program of considerable portions of the Mishnah as well.

My intent when I speak of philosophy, therefore, is very specific. I mean more than that there was a rather general philosophy expressed through the law, that is, "philosophy of law." I mean, further, something more particular than that the intellects represented here thought in a manner philosophers respected, for example, in accord with rules of order and intelligibility. I mean that, in the medium and idiom of rules, the authorship of the Mishnah worked out positions on matters of distinctively philosophical interest. They were not lawyers who had a general philosophy, e.g, of society and the social order. They were *philosophers* who happened also to produce law. The bulk of their writing, though by no means all of it, is philosophy in the form of law. The Mishnah's program concerns both topics (e.g., potentiality and actuality, intention and action) and rules of philosophical thought (e.g., the correct manner of classification, that is, assessing mixtures on the one side and hierarchization on the other, or the proper rules governing resolutions of matter of doubt). These rules of thought are specific to philosophy in that they guide inquiry of a particular order into a distinctive set of questions. Once again, my claim is clearly that we deal with discourse of a peculiarly philosophical nature, if in an idiom otherwise alien to philosophy as it was carried on in the age and place under study.

The criteria for determining whether or not the Mishnah as a whole, or one of its tractates, is philosophical may be spelled out in this way:

1. Are issues "generalizable"? That is to say, are they subject to generalization—and so exemplary—with principles pertinent to a variety of other cases? In that case we can move from cases to principles encompassing a variety of cases.

2. Are the principles essentially philosophical ones or are they merely *ad hoc* or legal ones, lacking any profound philosophical character? Here too the issue is defined as exemplarity or particularity, with the added consideration that what must be exemplified is a principle applicable in wholly abstract, not merely concrete and practical, settings.

3. Is the tractate possible, as we now know it, if elements displaying its character as a philosophical discourse are omitted? This is not a question only of the extent to which philosophical principles serve to impart their character on discourse. The issue is not solely or even mainly settled by appeal to the facts of quantity. Rather, it concerns the basic structure and dynamic of a tractate.

A simple example suffices, drawn from my *The Philosophical Mishnah. The Initial Probe*, to illustrate the interaction of these three criteria. The potential modes of addressing the subject matter of the tractates Uqsin, Besah, Qiddushin, Orlah, and Meilah are surely without limit. There are many varieties of questions one can bring to those topics. But the tractates as we now have them, covering those topics, cannot have been composed without the prevailing concern for the issues of classification, mixtures, potentialities, and intentionality. In other words, there can be no Uqsin, Besah, Qiddushin, Orlah, or Meilah, without a fundamentally philosophical program of inquiry into the subject matter of those tractates. Not only so, but, in the case of Meilah at least, the philosophy is worked out in sequence and logical order dictated by the character of the philosophical theorems that are laid out.

The Mishnah's principal philosophical program deals with the classification of things: identifying the correct taxonomic indicators, forming the logical taxa, forming hierarchical classifications. Its problematic, brought to bear upon one subject after another, requires us to set into relationship several discrete taxonomic systems and then to sort out the consequent confusions or mixtures. The Mishnah's treatment of any given topic will often, though not always, draw attention to (1) the classification of the data of that problem, (2) the sorting out of sets of data that are formed by discrete taxonomic indicators, and (3) the resolution of issues of mixture, confusion, or doubt (sometimes, though not always, concerning facts). That tripartite program describes the unfolding of no fewer than forty tractates.[1]

A key element used by the Mishnah framers to accomplish this classificatory agenda is the factor of intention. Indeed, under certain circumstances, intentionality determines the classification into which something falls. Another task of intentionality is to express the relationship of the potential to the actual. For intention, or attitude, remains in the realm of potentiality, until a concrete action brings it to realization. In addition, intentionality is a critical consideration for the assessment of connection and mixture. For example, the status of a subsidiary part of an object—such as a pot's handle—may be determined by the attitude or intention of the owner or craftsman regarding its use; if it is necessary for the use of the object, it is connected, and if not, it is not. So this third category really flows out of the first two.

That fact accounts for what is to follow. When I first observed the place occupied by intentionality in sorting out issues of the potential and the actual, I was troubled to find this category particular to a few specific subjects; it is not as ubiquitous as I had anticipated it would be,

---

[1] I have shown that fact in my *The Philosophical Mishnah* (Atlanta, 1989: Scholars Press for Brown Judaic Studies) Vols. II-III. *The Tractates' Agenda*. Forty-one of the sixty-one usable tractates (excluding Avot and Eduyyot) conform to that simple pattern. My classification of tractates is philosophical, scriptural, and other. The forty-one philosophical tractates conform to the rule given here. The scriptural tractates are not philosophical but present only a reprise of information in the written Torah. Seven tractates prove anomalous, being neither philosophical nor scriptural. An example of the first kind of tractate is Terumot or Meilah; of the second, Yoma; of the third, Tamid or Taanit.

and I was not at all certain that we deal with a philosophical principle of broad interest. That observation drew my attention to a more considerable problem, which is how the philosophers of the Mishnah defined and set forth their classifications of things. For I realized that if intentionality in relationship to the considerations of the potential and the actual proved specific to a distinctive subject, then it was not a philosophical category at all. For, by definition, philosophy sets forth principles that apply to all subjects without important variation. Its task is to generalize, and its propositions must be subject to generalization (conducive to "generalizability"). An account of intentionality in the philosophy of the Mishnah restricted to the Mishnah's treatment of one subject or another bears no philosophical interest, since it does not conform to the requirement of generalizability.

I was misled in my initial impressions because I relied on the doctoral dissertation of my former student, Howard Eilberg-Schwartz, *The Human Will in Judaism. The Mishnah's Philosophy of Intention* (Atlanta: Scholars Press for Brown Judaic Studies, 1986). Eilberg-Schwartz undertook his analysis through word studies, with special attention to two words, *kavvanah* and *mahshabah*. The former refers (p. 7) to "the intention with which a person performs an action." The latter refers "to the intention an individual formulates before he or she actually begins to act." Now were Eilberg-Schwartz to have proposed an essentially lexical study, his results would, in my judgment, stand firm. And in so far as his analyses focus upon the two words in question, he has produced useful hypotheses. But, as he has shown in later work,[2] Eilberg-Schwartz generalizes on the basis of a small sample of evidence, and the sample is, moreover, not well-drawn. That is not to suggest the dissertation-work was not valuable. To the contrary, there is much to be learned from the lexical studies that Eilberg-Schwartz has completed. It is the generalizations that must be set aside for the moment, since, as I shall explain, he has missed most of the evidence relevant to an account of "the human will in Judaism: the Mishnah's philosophy of intention."

The reason is that the Mishnah's philosophers make their points not through selections of particular words, which preserve a distinctive meaning in all circumstances and which singularly express that meaning. Quite to the contrary, lexical studies mislead, because the Mishnah's philosophers work out their ideas through the study of the

---

[2] See the exchange *Journal of the American Academy of Religion* 1989, 56:4, in which I call into question his claim to have discovered a philosophy of language in what seems to me evidences of a literary genre (if that).

principles of classification, therefore also of relationship. They find it possible to express their ideas in a variety of ways, not through particular word-choices, but through diverse cases that, without appeal to specific key-words, make a single point. That fact is shown, with reference to the Mishnah's authorship's theory of intention, by the important place of intentionality in the definition of slavery. There we find fundamental data on the power of intentionality and its taxonomic authority, although such words as *kavvanah* and *mahshabah* do not appear. The theory of intentionality is fully exposed; its power of classification worked out in profoundly nuanced manner; and the key-words Eilberg-Schwartz chose for his dissertation never appear. Here is how Paul Flesher expresses the matter:

> This brings us finally to the most important aspect of slavery, a master's capacity to have his bondman perform his wishes. The master accomplishes this feat through his faculty of will—that is, his own capacity to plan his actions in advance and to act in accordance with those plans. In effect, the Mishnah's authorities imagine that the master's will replaces that of the bondman...the bondman constitutes an extension of his master's will.[3]

Flesher's discussion impinges upon the definition of intentionality, making points of fundamental importance for understanding the principles of intentionality in the taxonomic theory and taxonomic structure of the philosophy of the document. He clearly alludes to the definition of *mahshabah* that we have found in Eilberg-Schwartz's dissertation. But the word does not occur, and, conversely, in Eilberg-Schwartz's book, the passages critical to Flesher's discussion are never mentioned. Thus Flesher's analysis provides an important contribution to the discussion of the power of intentionality, namely, a broad definition of what the framers mean by the conception of "will":

> The Mishnah's framers base the householder's power of will on his capacity to reason. Reason constitutes the mind's ability to understand information and ideas. A person's will, by contrast, comprises his capacity to use reason to deliberate and to make decisions regarding his future actions. The householder's power of will thus enables him to consider possible courses of action and their ramifications so that he can arrive at a reasoned judgment about what he wants to do. (pp. 162-3)

---

[3] Paul Virgil McCracken Flesher, *Oxen, Women, or Citizens? Slaves in the System of the Mishnah* (Atlanta: Scholars Press for Brown Judaic Studies, 1988), pp. 160ff.

I look in vain in Eilberg-Schwartz's account of intentionality for
discussion of the role of reason in the formation and recognition of
affective intentionality.

The reason is now clear. It is that Eilberg-Schwartz has relied
solely upon lexical indicators for the identification of relevant
passages, and his account therefore is asymmetrical to the
philosophical medium of the Mishnah.[4] That medium of thought, as I
said, appeals to the discussion of problems of classification, on the one
side, and relationship, on the other, for the full and complete
presentation of philosophical principles. And that is a mark of the
philosophical mind, which seeks to generalize beyond cases and
therefore cannot limit itself, in the end, to the data that are generated
by cases, e.g., of a particular order. Once the criterion for a
philosophical quotient of a representation of thought is
generalizability, then the lexical approach, convenient though it is,
falls away as insufficient.[5]

How to proceed? To make possible a reconsideration of the place of
intentionality in the system of the Mishnah—or, as I now claim, in the
philosophy of the Mishnah—I have accomplished a survey of the
sixty-one tractates of the Mishnah that are subject to analysis. In the
catalogue that follows, I list all pericopae in which the issue of
intentionality plays an important role. I hasten to add that, even here,
I do not identify the passages on the principles of attitude,
intentionality, and will that Flesher has discussed, and that fact
shows the full dimensions of the analytical work that awaits
accomplishment. But here is a list that far transcends the rather
limited base selected by Eilberg-Schwartz for his dissertation.
Whether or not a survey will require us to set aside his generalizations
is not to be gainsaid. The work of describing, analyzing, and
interpreting the human will in Judaism, in the context of the Mishnah,
awaits.[6]

---

[4] When he proposed his dissertation program, I took the view that a narrowly
lexical study would be valuable, and indeed, it is valuable. It is the recasting of
matters, beyond the dissertation-stage, that has claimed more for the work
than is justified. But even here too I would commend Eilberg-Schwartz's
intellectual ambition, and I hope that his abilities will prove commensurate.

[5] That is not to suggest that Eilberg-Schwartz's results are unreliable. For the
passages of the Mishnah that he discusses, the results are insightful and
interesting. It is to say that his generalizations are, if probable, at this moment
unsubstantiated because they remain untested against the full range of
evidence.

[6] In the following discussion, when I say "I find nothing pertinent," I mean that
intentionality or attitude plays no role in the identification of problems for

1. ABODAH ZARAH

The principal consideration of M. Abodah Zarah 1:1-5 is to ensure that a Jew should not contribute to the joy of the idolator in the celebration of his rite. That consideration appeals to the concern for attitude and intention, not merely concrete deed; one cannot assist in the celebration, in however remote a manner. M. Abodah Zarah 3:5 appeals to attitude. If one makes use of an idol's property with the intent of expressing offense, then that act is permitted; if it is to express respect, the act is prohibited. The entire colloquy makes the point that the attitude with which a deed is done defines the character and consequence of the deed. M. 3:6 reverses that point; if the gentile has not treated an object as an idol, such as a mountain, then its status is unaffected, and an Israelite may make use of that object. M. Abodah Zarah 3:7 presents an absolutely standard exercise in systematic classification, by appeal to the indicative traits of the object under discussion. But the traits are imposed through differing attitudes or intentions as to the use of an object. If a house to begin with was built for purposes of idolatry, it is in one classification; if it is built for a neutral purpose and renovated for that purpose, it is in a different category; and if one's intention, vis-à-vis idolatry, has no affect upon the house, it is in yet a third category. The same differentiation applies to the *asherah*. The operative consideration at M. Abodah Zarah 4:3 is again attitude. Israelites may do nothing that may contribute to the support of idolatry, and if the Israelite assumes that his actions make no contribution to that purpose, the act is permitted. At M. Abodah Zarah 4:4-6 the gentile has power of intentionality over the idol, the Israelite does not. Hence when the gentile nullifies the idol, it is deemed null, but if an Israelite does so, his power extends only to an idol that belongs to him himself. Nullification involves deed, not merely an attitude; one must do something to express one's attitude that the thing is null and of no account. Finally, M. 4:7E-F reveal that God's actions are aimed at changing attitudes.

2. ARAKHIN

M. Arakhin 8:5 sets forth the limitation on the affects of intentionality. One cannot affect the status—e.g., by the declaration of

---

solution or in the systemic discourse around which a tractate centers (if a tractate proposes to participate in a systemic discourse at all, and some do not). I do not mean to say that no where in the tractate, e.g., in the framing of its inert facts or background information, intentionality or attitude or the heart or the will comes into play. The distinction between an inert and a systemically active fact, conception or consideration therefore has to be kept in mind throughout.

one's attitude—of something that does not fall within one's own domain. That limitation on attitude or intentionality is important here, because one can declare oneself obligated to pay the Valuation or the worth of another person. That is because one controls one's own property, which is what is at stake. But here one cannot change the status of someone else or that person's property.

3. BATRA BATRA

In M. B.B. 1:3-5, the Mishnah's framers assume that since the landowner has indicated by his action that he approves the building of the wall and wishes to take advantage of it, he has shown his intention and is required to pay the cost of the wall that he proposes to exploit. The action now bespeaks the (prior) intention. The consideration here and through the remainder of Chapter Four and half of Chapter Five (M. 4:1-9 and 5:1-5) is the definition of the intention of a person who has purchased or sold a property which is defined as a collective item. For example, the sale of a boat includes the sale of its mast, sail and anchor. If one has sold one thing, he sells everything that belongs to the classification of that thing, but nothing that does not. The remainder of the chapter spells out the same matter in various cases. At stake then is the definition of the intention of the seller and buyer. The established classifications or definitions of things are assumed to define the intentionality of individual participants in any given transaction. The Mishnah's framers do not make provision for idiosyncratic readings of a transaction. At M. Baba Batra 5:6, we see how to take account of intentionality in a transaction. If the conditions of sale turn out to be contrary to what one party has assumed—and hence the intentionality of the two parties to the transaction are not the same—the injured party may retract. If the conditions of sale are precisely as represented, there is no injury to prior intentionality, so neither party may retract. If the conditions of sale are different from the way in which they were represented but there is no clear advantage or disadvantage, both parties have the right to retract. At issue in M. Baba Batra 6:1-4, 5-7, 8 is the unstated stipulation that a person entered a transaction with a given intention in mind. In M. 6:1, for example, if one sells produce without saying whether it is for food or seed and the purchaser plants the grain and nothing sprouts, he has no recourse to the merchant, who may claim that his intention was to sell the seed for food, not for planting. There are further unstated stipulations at M. 6:2, 3, 4, 8. In all these cases, we impose the prevailing attitude or intentionality upon all transactions. M. Baba Batra 9:6 interprets a person's intentions by appeal to his actions—in this case, a seriously ill man who gives away his property.

Since the man left himself a piece of land, his intention was merely to make a valid gift. The Mishnah's framers do not consider these "gifts in contemplation of death," in which, if the man recovers, the gifts are invalidated because they were given incorrect premises. Hence, the case illustrates the interesting principle that from what one does, we reconstruct the prior and governing attitude or intentionality. Finally, the issue at M. Baba Batra 10:5 is the intent of the one who makes the statement. Yose sees the intent of the statement to carry out the stipulation, and Judah does not take seriously the statement, seeing it as merely an effort to appease the lender, not to propose to pay again what he already has paid. So here the framers of the law interpret intentionality in reference to statement, not deed, and, as is clear, it is not at all certain that, in such a case, we are prepared to impute to a party who has done nothing at all a clear intent as to what he wishes to do.

4. BABA MESIA

The important point of M. Baba Mesia 3:9 is that when the owner of a bailment expresses his intention as to the handling or disposition of the bailment, then that intention governs the transaction. The bailee is therefore culpable for any violation of that intention. But then should the intention of the owner of the bailment be observed and the bailment be damaged, the bailee bears no responsibility at all. M. B.M. 7:11 reveals that one's attitude or intention is null when in contradiction with the law of the Torah. That fundamental principle places a close limitation on the effect of intentionality. Finally, a paltry sum is not subject to litigation. Since no one would have paid attention to so minor a consideration, so M. B.M. 8:5, it cannot be subject to anyone's prior intentionality.

5. BABA QAMMA

Judah, at M. B.Q. 6:5, maintains that a person bears full responsibility for what he has done. Even though he may not have known that there were utensils in the stack of grain and therefore cannot have intended to burn them up, in point of fact he has done exactly that. What he has done defines what he wanted to do. Sages charge the man only for what he has done, but concede that a person has to exercise foresight, F-G. Moving on to M. B.Q. 10:1, we discover that one is responsible for a crime only if one has intentionally committed that crime; unwitting beneficiaries of a theft do not have to make restitution. However, a person must avoid dealing with persons who are assumed to have stolen property, D-E. That distinction forms the fine line between intentional theft, for which one is responsible, and unwitting theft via a third party, for which one is not responsible, but which one must avoid where prima facie evidence suggests that thievery is an issue. In assessing the transfer of ownership, according to M. B.Q. 10:2, we take account of the attitude of the original owner of property that has come into someone else's hands, whether legally or by theft. Once the owner has given up hope of retrieving his property, the property falls outside of his possession and is available for the acquisition of another party. This consideration is complicated by M. B.Q. 10:4, which reveals that an unspecified stipulation is null; we do not assess the attitude or intentionality of a participant to an action and impute to a person a stipulation that he has not made explicit. This limits the position of M. B.Q. 10:2; we do at some point assess the attitude of the owner of property, basing our judgment on the probabilities that the owner has given up hope of retrieving what is his. At that point, when we believe the owner's attitude has changed, the status of the object also shifts. At M. B.Q. 10:10, at stake in the division of these remnants is whether or not the owner takes account of them and deems them of value. If he is assumed to regard them as valuable, then the craftsman may not keep them. If he is assumed to regard them as null, then the craftsman may take possession of them. This is a replay of the conception of nullification of ownership through an act of will.

6. BEKHOROT

One may never enjoy a benefit that has come to him through deliberately violating the law, so M. Bekh. 5:3. "This is the general principle: Anything [done] deliberately—it is prohibited. And anything [done] unintentionally—it is permitted."

7. BERAKHOT

M. Ber. 2:1 introduces the consideration of attitude or intention to the recitation of the *Shema*. If one has had the intention of carrying out one's obligation to recite the *Shema* when in fact he did recite the *Shema*, then he has completed the obligation to do so. Otherwise, he has not. If, therefore, one recited the words for some other purpose, that act is null so far as the religious duty to recite the *Shema* is concerned. Accordingly, when assessing whether or not one has carried out his obligation, the principal consideration is that one intend to do so. At stake at M. Ber. 4:4-6, 5:1, is that the Prayer—that is, the Eighteen Benedictions—not be a matter of mere habit, and that consideration introduces the consideration of attitude. Carrying out the obligation of the Prayer requires that the opposite of doing so with the *Shema*; the *Shema* must be done in an attitude of obligation, the Prayer must be performed in a fresh way, as a supplication. Joshua provides for a supplication of an abbreviated order, congruent to the circumstance, so sustaining Eliezer's basic position. The matter of "directing the heart" toward a specific location then places yet another consideration into play when we take up the correct attitude for the Prayer. The lamp and spices, M. Ber. 8:6A-C, have been affected by the purpose of those who have already made use of them. Hence attitude or intention plays a critical role in the classification of things. The issue of M. 8:6D is congruent. We wish to ascertain that the lamp's light has served for the purpose of illumination and for no other purpose; then it falls into the classification of what may serve for the present purpose, which is to recite a blessing over the creation of light. So all things are classified by the attitude of man, who makes use of them.

8. BESAH

M. Bes. 1:2 (also M. Bes. 1:5-6) takes up the definition of the inclusionary or exclusionary character of intentionality. The House of Shammai at M. Bes. 1:2 maintain that one's intentionality is general, covering whatever is required for the accomplishment of one's basic purpose. The House of Hillel take an exclusionary view and regard as subject to one's intentionality only the specific action that one has contemplated in advance, not the ancillary actions associated therewith. Note also M. Bes. 1:3. Here the House of Hillel dissociate action from intention, and the House of Shammai regard a concrete action as required in the expression of intentionality. M. Bes. 1:4 reinforces this point.

At M. Bes. 2:3C&D, one's purpose in immersing utensils affects matters. If one has immersed utensils intending to make use of them for one purpose and then decides to use them for some other, the utensils require a second immersion.

M. Bes. 3:2 raises the issue of designation, that is, the explicit expression of intention. If one has not explicitly expressed intention concerning a particular item, that item is deemed unavailable for use on the festival day, even though one might in general have wanted that category of item. Hence intention must be specific to the item that is supposed to be affected. This same question is in play at M. Bes. 4:3, where one has not, in advance of the festival, designated wood for use on the festival in cooking food. This intervenes between the potentiality for such use and the actuality of using the wood for that purpose. At M. Bes. 4:6, 7, Eliezer regards as adequately designated for use in advance an object that can serve a variety of purposes; any of these purposes is permitted, even when not signified in advance. M.

Bes. 5:7 reiterates this point, that there should be a prior act of designation, now in connection with the transport of food. If the owner has in advance of the festival assigned ownership of food to his guests, then they may carry that food home; but if not, they may not do so.

9. BIKKURIM

I find nothing relevant.

10. DEMAI

I find nothing relevant.

11. ERUBIN

A person may establish residence for purposes of the Sabbath in some place other than one's normal abode by making provision for eating a meal at that other place. This action allows the person to measure his allotted area for travel not from one's ordinary residence but from that other place; the measure is 2,000 cubits. In order to establish a symbolic place of residence, one has to set out prior to sundown on the Sabbath or festival a symbolic meal, or accomplish that same end by a verbal declaration of one's intention and will. One's action, either through placing the meal or an act of speech, accomplishes the purpose; a mere unstated thought does not. In that sense, the provision of the symbolic meal constitutes a powerful judgment that unexpressed intention by itself is null. At M. Erub. 3:5 we deal with stipulations that may be made in forming and expressing one's intention. It is entirely acceptable to stipulate in advance a variety of prior intentions, to be worked out in terms of what actually comes about after the fact.

At stake at M. Erub. 4:1-3 is the role of intentionality. If one has not meant to violate the Sabbath limit but has done so, he is nonetheless bound by what has happened, whether to his advantage or disadvantage. But if one's intention was to save life, then that mitigates the situation. So the role of intention is dual: personal, in which it is null, and in the public interest, deemed a prior and prevailing, if unstated, stipulation.

The role of intentionality is further investigated at M. Erub. 4:4. Someone has settled down on a road not realizing that he is near a town. Meir says that one must have the prior intent to establish his Sabbath residence in a town in order to share the benefit of its Sabbath limit. If a man had no such prior intent, he stays where he is. Judah says he may enter the town; intention is no issue, for here we deal with error. M. Erub. 4:5 goes on to someone who fell asleep Friday afternoon and did not realize it had gotten dark. Yohanan b. Nuri has the man establish his Sabbath limit where he slept; intention is not an issue at all. Sages insist on a prior act of intention. M. 4:6 builds on this matter. At M. Erub. 4:7-9, 10+11, we have someone on a journey who comes near the territory of his town. He may designate his Sabbath residence by a mere verbal declaration. He refers to a given place that he knows and calls that his Sabbath residence, even though a distance from the place. A mere verbal declaration of intention, without an associated action (e.g., setting out the symbolic meal) is acceptable. The interesting question, M. Erub. 7:11, is whether or not one may prepare a meal without a person's knowledge and consent. One authority says that that is the case when the commingling of the domains of courtyards is at stake, for that serves only to benefit all concerned. But if it is a matter of setting a meal out to allow travel in a given direction beyond the limits of a town, then the one involved must give his consent, since in gaining the right to travel in one direction, he loses the right to travel in the other. Thus, intentionality is not required when a person can only benefit, without any chance of loss; we impute automatic agreement in such a case.

12. GITTIN

The writ of divorce must be prepared for a particular case and not drawn from an available stack of blank documents, M. Git. 3:1-3. The intentionality of the scribe must focus upon the particular woman for whom the writ is prepared, and the husband who requests the document must have in mind a specific wife among his several wives. The introduction of the issue of intentionality in the preparation of the document makes the action very specific. It insures that the husband's intention is fully set forth and fully carried out, since the marriage itself is formed of an act of concurring wills of the husband and the woman, or the man who controls her, at the time of betrothal and marriage. In his initial stipulation, the husband has stated his intention, and that must be followed, as specified at M. 3:5D, "for it is not the wish [of the husband] that his bailment should fall into someone else's hands."

A person who has inadvertently changed the status as to cleanness or tithes of someone's produce is not liable, M. Git. 5:4, because he has done nothing to change the intrinsic character of the produce. The matter of punishment is settled by intentionality. If one has deliberately mixed heave-offering into the produce of someone else, he is culpable; if he did so inadvertently, he is not.

M. Git. 6:1-3 return to the interest in the power of intentionality over the transaction of divorce. The husband's instructions predominate, M. 6:1A-C, since he has set up a condition, which then must be met. When the wife establishes a condition, that condition must be met so long as her husband has not set up a countervailing one. The upshot is that the power of intentionality is worked out, with the husband's taking precedence over the wife's. The issue at M. Git. 6:6, 7:1, involves the assessment of the intention of a person who makes the statement. If we assume that the intention of the man is valid, e.g., he expects to die and does not want his wife to remain linked to a levir, then we carry out the intention. If there is reason not to impute to the man such a valid intention, then we do not. The point at E-F is precisely the same. So here again intentionality plays the decisive role in the transaction of divorce.

The Mishnah's framers again discuss the principle that what has been created through an act of will is dissolved through a valid act of will. Just as the husband's intentionality governs the preparation of the writ, so the wife's governs the receipt thereof. What that means is that the wife must know what she is receiving, M. Git. 8:2A-G, and if she does not know that what she is getting is a writ of divorce, the divorce is invalid. The affect of intentionality on the part of the husband must cease with the writ of divorce. The divorce must totally sever the relationship between the man and the woman, with the result that she is no longer subject to his will or attitude. Accordingly, a stipulation in the writ of divorce that governs the woman's freedom of action after the writ has taken effect is null, so. M. Git. 9:1-2.

13. HAGIGAH

I find nothing pertinent.

14. HALLAH

Leavened bread dough divided into smaller portions to raise other batches of dough is not intended to be baked into bread. The baker of a large volume does not intend to bake the leavening agent into bread. But in assessing liability to dough offering, M. Hal. 1:7, we do not take account of his intention. Dough prepared for this purpose is liable to dough offering, because, as soon as dough is prepared as bread normally is, regardless of the processing that will take place later on, the liability is incurred. We do not take account of the potential change in the status or use of the dough, and we also do not take account of the issue of intentionality in changing the status of something that has reached its fixed and final definition. Finally, when we are not sure of the classification of something, we then appeal to human attitude of will, as at M. Hal. 1:8. Dogs' dough (i.e., dough biscuits) may or may not serve for human use. If human beings regard it as edible, then it falls into the category of ordinary food, and if not, it does not.

15. HORAYOT

M. Hor. 1:1 contributes the principle that one's improper intention is itself subjected to analysis, a complex issue. If one has deliberately performed an action, but has not known that the action itself is improper, and has relied upon a court in forming his improper intention, then he is not liable, for the court is responsible for what he has done. So responsibility enters the assessment of the results of intentionality. If a court gave a ruling to uproot a whole principle of the Torah, it is exempt under the rule of Lev. 4:14; if it was to nullify part and observe part of a rule of the Torah, they are liable under Lev. 4:14; M. Hor. 1:3-5 work out this matter. When the Torah is explicit, there is no excuse for error, and, at that point, we ignore the complication in the assessment of responsibility for incorrect intentionality that is introduced at M. 1:1-2.

16. HULLIN

The issue of M. Hul. 2:7 (inclusive of 2:8-10) is explicit. The intention of a gentile owner of a beast as to the act of slaughter of that beast is effective, because it is the owner that classifies his property. But in the case of an act of slaughter on the part of an Israelite in behalf of the gentile, whose intention is effective? That issue is well stated and worked out explicitly. The point of differentiation at M. Hul. 9:3 is a person's intention in flaying an animal. If the intention is to flay the beast for one purpose, then the rules of connection are defined in an appropriate way for that purpose, and if the intention is for a different purpose, then the rules of connection shift.

17. KELIM

Kelim focuses in the main on an assessment of attitude or intention vis-à-vis the use or purpose of objects, and in that sense, its main point of interest is on the impact of intentionality or attitude upon the classification of objects. It deals specifically with the status, as to cultic cleanness, of useful objects, tools or utensils. The main point is that when an object has a distinctive character, form, use, or purpose, it is susceptible to uncleanness, so that, if it is in contact with a source of uncleanness, it is deemed cultically unclean. If it is formless, purposeless, or useless, it is insusceptible. Three criteria govern the determination of what is useful or purposeful. First come properties deemed common to all utensils, whatever the material. Second are qualities distinctive to different sorts of materials. Third is the consideration of the complex purposes for which an object is made or used, primary and subsidiary. It is here that the intention of the user is determinative. Although intentionality is not the only issue, but it is a primary one. Chapter Four restates essentially the same conceptions about classifying utensils as unclean or clean by appeal to their function or usefulness. The interesting conception is that an object has an intrinsic purpose. If it serves some purpose but not the one for which it was originally made, it is deemed useless and insusceptible, so M. Kel. 4:1-4. Then the attitude of the original owner or maker of the object affects the definition and character of the object, with the stated result. The issue of M. Kel. 5:1-2 is the point at which an oven is deemed useful. The general rule is that when an object is fully manufactured, then it is susceptible to uncleanness. But in the case of a clay oven, the oven may be used even before it has reached its full dimensions. Hence we want to know when it is useful, even prior to the completion of its processing. On the other end, if one is breaking down the oven, at what point is it completely useless? And, along these same lines, what are the appendages of the oven that are essential for using it, hence connected and part of the object, and which ones are not essential and therefore not connected? The criterion of classification throughout is function, not form: use, measured by a common consensus on the matter. So the recurrent taxonomic principle is usefulness, but that is adapted to the consideration of purpose or intentionality. Here is a fine case in which classification is affected—and effected—by issues of attitude and will.

18. KERITOT

The problem of M. Ker. 6:1ff. is the disposition of a suspensive guilt-offering when it is discovered that the person has not in fact committed a sin. If this information comes prior to the slaughter of the beast, then, Meir holds, since the animal was improperly designated, it is set out to pasture; its status has not been changed by the designation, which is null by reason of incorrect intention. Sages say the animal has been properly set aside and sanctified. Eliezer says the animal is offered for some (unknown) sin, if not the one for which it was originally designated. At stake, therefore, is Meir's view that incorrect intentionality is null and has no affect upon the thing that is classified thereby.

19. KETUBOT

I find nothing relevant.

20. KILAYIM[7]

At stake at M. Kil. 2:6-7 (and elsewhere) is not whether we actually are mixing crops, but whether it looks as though we are doing so. This is made explicit at M. Kil. 2:7C, for example: "for it [the point of the angle of the wheat field] looks like the end of his field." So long as each bed can be readily distinguished from another, different kinds may grow in the same field without producing the appearance of violating the law against diverse-kinds. So in this matter the law depends upon attitude and not upon actuality. The same considerations are operative through to M. Kil. 3:7, e.g., M. 3:4: It is permitted to plant two rows each of chate melons or gourds, but not only one, since if it is only one, they do not appear to be planted in autonomous fields (Mandelbaum, p. 8). So too M. Kil. 3:3: "[If] the point of the angle of a field of vegetables entered a field of another [kind of] vegetables, it is permitted [to grow one kind of vegetables in the field of the other kind], for it [i.e., the point of the angle of the vegetable-field] looks like the end of his field," in line with M. 3:5D: "for whatever the sages prohibited, they [so] decreed only on account of appearances." We proceed at M. Kil. 4:1-7:8, to the issue of sowing crops in a vineyard. This is permitted if within or around a vineyard is an open space of the specified dimensions. If there is ample space between the vines, that space may be used. But if the appearance is such that the vines appeared mixed with grain, then the grain must be uprooted. The basic consideration is that grain or vegetables not create the appearance of confusion in the vineyard. Everything in the long sequence of rules derives from that single concern. The prohibition of mingling fibers, with particular attention to wool and linen, occupies M. Kil. 9:1-10. Scripture's basic rule is amplified with special attention to mixtures, e.g., camel's hair and sheep's wool hackled together. Here we assign the traits of the dominant component of the mix to the entire mixture. Items that resemble wool and linen but are not of wool and linen, or that are not intended to serve as garments, are not subject to the prohibition. The issue of intention is explicitly excluded. Even if one does not intend permanently to use a piece of cloth as a garment, it still may not be used at all if it is a mixture of diverse kinds, and so too at M. 9:2F. So here the consideration of intentionality is excluded; all that matters is the fact.

---

[7] The analysis of this tractate is based on the study by Irving J. Mandelbaum, *A History of the Mishnaic Law of Agriculture: Kilayim* (Chico, CA: Scholars Press for Brown Judaic Studies, 1982). Hereinafter referred to as "Mandelbaum."

21. MAASER SHENI

Sanctification is relative and not absolute; it is what the farmer conceives to be holy that is holy, and the attitude is determinative, not the physical object, so M. M.S. 2:5. This is shown also at M. M.S. 2:6. When consecrated and unconsecrated coins are mixed together, the status of the consecrated coins is transferred to a fresh batch of coins.

22. MAASEROT[8]

At M. Ma. 1:1, the rule is that only when the householder by an action claims his harvested produce as personal property must the crop be tithed; in general that is when untithed produce is brought from the field into the home. Hence when the farmer, by an act that expresses his attitude, lays claim on the crop, God responds by demanding his share of that same crop, which is due him as owner of the Land of Israel. In general, therefore, at stake is the interplay of classification and intentionality. God acts and wills in response to human intentions, God's invisible action can be discerned by carefully studying the actions of human beings (Jaffee, p. 5). Jaffee's treatment of this subject shows beyond doubt the variety of ways in which intentionality plays a role in theological thought as well; Eilberg-Schwartz drew upon Jaffee's ideas, but only in his footnotes (see *op. cit.*, pp. 224ff.).

23. MAKHSHIRIN

Lev. 11:34, 37 provide the basic facts of this tractate, but the generative problematic is unknown to Scripture. It is that the attitude or intentionality that a farmer takes when he sees water affect his produce dictates whether or not the produce has been rendered susceptible to uncleanness. Scripture defines the given, that dry food is insusceptible to uncleanness, while wet food is susceptible. But the Mishnah's premise lies beyond Scripture's imagination. The issue of the tractate is the relationship between attitude and actuality. How do we know whether or not the farmer has favored the wetting down of his crop? Do we assess attitude on its own, or do we require an action to confirm our surmise as to attitude? These are the centerpieces of thought. The issue then is, do we decide the character of a person's prior intention upon the basis of what one has done, that is, of what he intended to do? And that issue, as is clear, involves the appeal to

---

[8] The analysis of this tractate is based on the study by Martin S. Jaffee, *Mishnah's Theology of Tithing: A Study of Tractate Maaserot* (Chico, CA: Scholars Press for Brown Judaic Studies, 1981). Hereinafter referred to as "Jaffee."

intentionality to classify whether or not something can become unclean through the application of water.

M. Mak. 3:4-5:8 proceed to classify water vis-à-vis diverse purposes, primary and secondary. If water is used for one purpose, will another purpose be taken into account? M. Mak. 3:4 makes the point that water used for one purpose can impart susceptibility in connection with a second, unrelated purpose. At M. 3:5A-F it is not the man's intention to wet down the wheat. But we ignore that consideration if through his action, not meant to accomplish the wetting down of the wheat, the wheat is nonetheless affected by the moisture. The most important point is at M. 3:5G-I. One's actions define one's (prior) intentions or attitude. Therefore we do not care whether or not a person expressed happiness, but only whether he has done something to take account of the event at hand. At M. 4:2 we take the position that the water is located where it is with the approval of the farmer. The point of M. 4:4-5 is that if the man disposes of the water, in the view of one party, he did not object to its original location. In the other view, the man's ultimate disposition of the water indicates that he never wanted it to begin with. In these and numerous other passages, the same few points are laid out. Intention is confirmed by subsequent action. Intention takes effect, without regard to subsequent action. We take account of intention here; we do not take account of intention there. All of these issues gain power in the setting of classification of substances as unclean or clean.

24. MAKKOT
I find nothing relevant.

25. MEGILLAH
I find nothing relevant.

26. MEILAH
The issue of intention is implicit at M. Meilah 1:1 in the consideration of the inappropriate attitude of the officiating priest, but it is not a principal and generative conception for the composition.

M. Meilah 4:1 reveals that if one's attitude toward a substance is that the substance is null, then if one utilizes that substance for a private purpose though it is holy, he has not violated the laws of sacrilege. So the attitude of the person is principal in determining whether or not to invoke the laws of sacrilege. If something is not valued by the person who uses it, then that thing is not subject to sacrilege, even though it is intrinsically holy. Then holiness depends also upon attitude. This is a firm fact in the present pericope. But it is not a principal proposition here.

M. Meilah 5:1 maintains that sacrilege depends upon the one who does it, not upon the thing to which it is done. That is to say, the category of sacrilege is invoked by the attitude of the person responsible for dealing with a given bit of *materia sacra*. If that person derives benefit from the thing, even without doing injury to it, he has committed sacrilege. That is Aqiba's conception, and it makes attitude the governing consideration. Sages reject this view, and therefore consider null the issue of attitude, regarding sacrilege as intrinsic to the *materia sacra*. M. Meilah 5:4 makes the same point.

The same point is made throughout M. Meilah 6:1-4, 5. Sacrilege is an inadvertent action to begin with; it cannot be done with intention. Misappropriation of *materia sacra* done intentionally is under a different rubric from sacrilege. Now the issue here is whether or not the agent has done what he is told. If he has, then the employer is liable, if not, then he is. The issues then concern doing what one is told.

27. MENAHOT

The issue is the impact of intentionality upon the designation of a meal offering for a given purpose. The offering has to be designated for a specific purpose, such as the meal offering of a sinner, and it must serve for the particular purpose at hand, e.g., the sin that has come to light. If a meal offering is presented under a designation other than the one for which it was set aside—that is, "not for its own name"—it is a valid offering but does not fulfil the obligation of the sinner. The issue, then, is the impact of intention upon the classification of a substance that has been made holy. The substance retains its sanctification, but does not serve the purpose that was meant for it. M. Menahot 1:1-2 present this conception. M. 1:3-4 go on to the issue of the improper intention on the part of the priest to eat the residue of the meal offering or to offer up the handful outside of the correct time or place, respectively. If while effecting one of the four principal actions in connection with preparing the meal offering—which are taking the handful, putting it into a utensil, bringing it to the altar, and offering it up—the priest should form the intention of eating his share or burning the handful outside of the courtyard, the improper intention has classified the meal offering as invalid. This is so even without respect to the actual deeds of the priest. If he has the notion, while doing any one of these four actions, of eating or burning the meal outside the proper time, the offering is rendered refuse. This conception is then qualified. The rule holds only if what renders the offering permissible for priestly use has been offered properly. If it has not, then there is no consideration of refuse at all. In any event we have an otherwise valid offering. But if one has improper intention concerning place, he invalidates the meal offering before he has given play to his other improper intention, which concerns time and which alone brings into play the rules of refuse. Why, he asks, should we declare an already invalid meal offering to be refuse at all? The entire chapter therefore works on the interplay of intentionality and classification of meal offerings.

The next issue explores the impact of improper intention on the parts of the offering, that is, can improper intentionality render unfit not the entire offering but only an element of it? That is indeed the case at M. Men. 2:1. Just as improper intention with respect to either the blood or the sacrificial parts of an animal suffices to impart the status of refuse to the whole, so improper intention either in regard to frankincense or in respect to the handful of meal offering imparts the status of refuse to the whole. The components are inseparable, and what invalidates part invalidates whole. Here is a case in which mixture, classification, and intentionality come together in a single exercise. M. 2:5 goes on to the same problem. One authority takes the view that improper intention affecting the handful but not the frankincense or vice versa will affect the handful, so that it is refuse, and extirpation applies. Another takes the view that the frankincense by itself subjected to improper intention is invalid, but the matter is not refuse and is not subject to extirpation. Sages say that extirpation applies only when the whole of that which renders the offering permitted is made refuse. There are three positions as to the classification of the components of the offering and their interplay. One is that we distinguish the handful of meal offering from the frankincense, but if improper intention regarding the time of offering up the frankincense applies, the sacrifice is merely invalid. The second is that in that case it is made refuse. The third is that extirpation applies only when the whole of that which renders the offering permissible is made refuse. M. Men. 2:2 goes over the ground of M. 2:1. M. 2:3-4 make the point that improper intention concerning what is primary to an offering affects what is secondary, but improper intention concerning what is secondary to an offering does not affect what is primary. If one has an improper intention concerning the thank offering, the bread brought with it is deemed refuse. But if one has an improper intention to eat the bread outside of its proper time, the thank offering is unaffected. M. 3:1 repeats the matter of improper intention with regard to the meal offering.

28. MIDDOT

The category of intention is irrelevant to this tractate.

29. MIQVAOT

At M. Miq. 2:7-9 we ask whether rain water collected in empty wine jars set on a roof is deemed drawn water. If not, then we may simply break the jars and allow the water to flow into a collection-point and form an immersion pool. If one should empty them out, on the other hand, the water falls into the category of drawn water, pure and simple. Joshua takes the position that the rain collected in the jars is rain-water; breaking the jars is permissible, and the water will simply flow into the collection-point. At stake is whether by leaving the wine jars out in the rain I have deliberately collected the water, in which case it should be regarded as drawn water. So the issue is the affect of intention upon the classification of the water. The same matter occupies most of Chapter Four. If one deliberately collects water in a utensil, that falls into the classification of drawn water and thus renders unfit an immersion pool of less than requisite volume, so M. 4:1. Then the issue is, what sort of utensil serves such a purpose? M. 4:2, 3, 4, 5 address this issue, which is subsidiary to the conception that intentionality affects the classification of water.

30. MOED QATAN

I find nothing relevant.

31. NAZIR

M. Naz. 1:5-7 addresses the role of intentionality in the language of a Nazirite-vow. Here there is no issue as to the assessment of the interplay of intentionality and action, however, since the man's own statement governs. But that is as it should be, since it is what he has said that imposes restrictions upon him. The basic issue is how specific the language must be, and, as is common, some authorities want extremely concrete and specific language, which is subject to no ambiguity. Introducing the consideration of intentionality here is misleading, since, as a matter of fact, unstated intention plays no role, and consequent action is not at stake. The issue of M. Naz. 5:1-7 concerns vows taken in error. The issue is again one of intentionality. Does the mere recitation of the formula suffice, or must one mean what one says? The House of Shammai in the opening pericope maintain that a vow made in error is binding; we do not take account of intentionality in assessing the action—here: the speech—of a person. What one says establishes prior intentionality, as is the case in other actions. The

House of Hillel holds that that is not the case. A vow to consecrate something that has been made in error is not binding. But it is binding, M. Naz. 5:4 makes clear, when the prevailing facts assumed by the vower at the time of his vow change after he takes the vow. There is no issue of treating the vow as null on account of things that happen later on. The vow is not binding only if the prevailing facts changed prior to the oath-taking but remained unknown to him at the time of the vow. This issue predominates throughout the chapter.

32. NEDARIM

At M. Ned. 9:1-2 the Mishnah's framers go over the issue of the role of intentionality in the classification of an oath as valid or invalid. One position is that a vow made on an assumption that later proves false is invalid. Hence we take account of intentionality as to an indeterminate future. The other position is that only the facts prevailing at the time of the vow are assumed to be covered by the intentionality of the person who takes the vow. M. 9:3-4 carry the matter further. One cannot use as a pretext something that happens only after the vow has been made; at the moment of the vow, there were no false assumptions that shape the intentionality of the one who takes the vow. But if some things appear to have taken place later on but in fact were already realized by the time of the vow, that is taken into account. M. 9:5-10 pursue the same issues of the interplay of intentionality and actuality in the classification of vows.

33. NEGAIM

M. Negaim 7:3-5 go over how we deal with the removal of tokens of uncleanness. Do we take account of what the priest does not see, that is, what happens prior to actual inspection and certification? The real issue becomes one of intentionality. How do we classify changes effected by the patient, rather than by nature? The regnant opinion is that the entire diagnosis concerns natural phenomena, and the intervention of intentionality is null by reason of the character of the phenomena to be classified. So intentionality is ruled out as a cause, and therefore changes deliberately effected are null.

34. NIDDAH

Intentionality and attitude by definition play no role in this tractate's subject matter. As in Negaim, we deal solely with phenomena produced naturally, not by what a human being does or does not do by an act of will.

35. OHALOT

Chapter Thirteen asks what size of an aperture serves to link two otherwise distinct spaces into one. The issue is expressed in terms of the instrusion of contamination and how an aperture may be diminished from a size capable of allowing the passage of contamination to one too small to do so. The issue then is the same as before: the commingling of space through a whole of sufficient size. The effect of a hole for the transmission of uncleanness is based upon whether it is useful at its present size for the purpose for which it was made. If it was deliberately made only so small as to admit light, then that tiny size will also permit the passage of uncleanness. If not, it will not. We thus take account of the intent of the maker of the whole; if the hole serves the original purpose, it falls into the stated classification as a useful hole, which unites the space between the two rooms joined by the hole.

36. ORLAH

M. Orl. 1:1 takes up the power of intention unaccompanied by deed. The owner's stated intention concerning the use of a newly planted tree determines whether the tree is subject to the law of orlah.

37. PARAH

Water must be drawn with a utensil and mixed by ashes by human intent and action, so M. Par. 6:1. This matter is fresh and important, because it introduces the consideration of intention. The rite must be performed, in every detail, with full intentionality. The ashes must be cast on the water by hand, that is, willingly and knowingly, not by accident. That is the point expressed at M. Par. 6:1A-E, then again at F. M. Par. 9:4 directly addresses the issue of intentionality and the fitness of purification water. If a person forms the intention of drinking the purification water, has the water been made unfit? One party maintains that it has. The other holds that only if someone actually turns up the flask to drink from it is the water made unfit. Intentionality without deed is null; someone may change his mind. Here is the issue of intentionality baldly worked out. M. Par. 12:3 stresses that the sprinkling depends upon the proper intention of the person who does it. If someone has the right intention but the deed does not turn out right, the water that has been sprinkled is validly sprinkled and serves the object on which it has unintentionally come to rest. What water remains on the hyssop may be used for another object, and the hyssop need not be dipped another time.

38. PEAH[9]

At issue in M. Pe. 1:3 is the issue of the relationship of intentionality to action. Following Brooks' reading, the question is whether the farmer must designate produce at the rear corner of his field or whether his designation may apply to any part of the field. Simeon's position is the interesting side. The farmer must designate the proper amount of grain while actually harvesting the rear corner of his field, even if he already has designated produce at the front or middle (p. 46). So the act of designation is null unless accompanied by the correct action that confirms the stated intention. Intentionality by itself has no affect upon the law that specifies precisely where the "corner of the field"-portion is set aside. If that is not a far-fetched reading, then at stake is the interplay of intentionality and action, governed by the objective requirements of the law.

M. 1:4-6 address the classification of crops within the category of peah. How does this come about? The answers derive first from taxonomic definition, then from secondary application of the principle implicit in the definition. M. Pe. 1:4-5 classifies the produce that is liable for peah as that which is agricultural and in the Land of Israel. As at M. Ma. 1:1, when the farmer claims the produce as his own and grows food on it, he must pay for using the earth and leave God's portion for the poor. The evaluation by the farmer of the crop as useful and his act of acquiring the crop mark the point at which peah is to be designated, just as at M. Ma. 1:1 and for the reasons specified there. In general, therefore, at stake is the interplay of classification and intentionality. God acts and wills in response to human intentions, God's invisible action can be discerned by carefully studying the actions of human beings (Jaffee, p. 5). This is made explicit at M. Pe. 1:6: "Produce becomes subject to tithing as soon as the farmer processes it, the critical moment when he takes possession of the food" (Brooks, p. 51). Thus: "At any time [after the harvest, the farmer] may designate [produce] as peah, [with the result that the produce he designates] is exempt from [the separation of] tithes, until [the grain pile] is smoothed over. [At this point, the produce becomes liable to the separation of tithes.]"

When is a field a field, and when is it two or ten fields? That taxonomic problem of how many are one, or how one is deemed many, is

---

[9] The analysis of this tractate is based on the study by Roger Brooks, *Support for the Poor in the Mishnaic Law of Agriculture: Tractate Peah* (Chico, CA: Scholars Press for Brown Judaic Studies, 1983). Hereinafter referred to as "Brooks."

addressed once more at M. Pe. 2:1-8. The principle of division rests upon the farmer's attitude and actions toward a field. If the farmer harvests an area as a single entity, that action indicates his attitude or intentionality with regard to that area and serves to mark it as a field. For each patch of grain the householder reaps separately, however, a peah-share must be designated; the action indicates the intention to treat the area as a single field. But natural barriers intervene; rivers or hills also may mark off a field's boundaries, rendering null the farmer's action and intention. So in classifying an area of ground as a field, there is an interplay between the givens of the physical traits and the attitude, confirmed by action, of the farmer. M. 2:5-8 provide excellent cases for the application of these operative principles. A farmer might harvest a single field delimited by physical barriers, or he may harvest two fields in one lot (Brooks, p. 53). In both cases we ask: do the physical barriers define matters? Or does the attitude of the farmer, confirmed by his action, dictate the field's boundary? And a further issue is whether or not a field produces a single crop. If it does, then a single portion is designated, even if the produce is harvested on a number of different occasions. So Brooks: "Because the householder has ignored the boundaries clearly established by the field's physical characteristics, his actions have no effect" (Brooks, p. 53). A parallel problem has a tract of land planted with different species of a single genus. Here the farmer's actions are decisive, and, consequently, his intentionality enjoys full play. The applied reason involving issues of classification is fully exposed here.

The issue of M. Pe. 5:7ff. is what constitutes forgetting and what defines a sheaf. The point is that if anyone involved in harvesting and binding the grain remembers that a sheaf remains in the field, by definition that sheaf cannot enter the category of the *forgotten* sheaf (Brooks, p. 87). The utter absence of intentionality on the part of the farmer, his workers, and also the poor, who may not practice deception, defines forgetting. So here we are given a fine exercise in the definition of the opposites, forgetting and intentionality. Forgetting on the part of man is deemed the act of intentionality on the part of God. Chapter Six pursues the issue of the role of human intention in determining which sheaves must be left as forgotten produce (Brooks, p. 101). What is the status of a sheaf that the farmer leaves behind with the clear intention of collecting the sheaf later on? What if the farmer binds an unusually large quantity of produce into a single sheaf or places an ordinary sheaf in a special location? The intention is revealed through such an act and the sheaf does not enter the status of forgotten sheaves. Or the fact that the farmer has left the sheaves behind may be decisive. We cannot be certain that the householder will ever retrieve the sheaf, so the intentionality is defined by the action, with the result that this is classified as forgotten sheaves.

M. Pe. 7:7 asks whether the classification of defective clusters depends upon objective facts or subjective attitudes. The taxonomic question is worked out by defining the meaning of "defective," parallel to the sense of the word "forgetting." Is there an objective standard for the shape of a well-formed cluster? In that case, the farmer must give all clusters that do not conform. Then the whole of the vineyard may go to the poor. Eliezer holds that the category of defective cluster applies because of the farmer's evaluation or attitude. If in his view there will be no crop at all, then whatever the condition of the grape clusters, they cannot be rejected. The farmer cannot anticipate leaving the entire crop to the poor; his intentionality will then be taken into account.

39. PESAHIM

The fact that something may be deemed null by reason of inconsequence, M. Pes. 3:2, forms a fundamental principle of dealing with a case of doubt. If people would not pay any attention to such a thing and would deem it as though it were not in existence, then we do not take account of such a thing in assessing whether the law has been violated. One may take the view that that basic principle of nullification by reason of inconsequence appeals to attitude as a consideration in classification. M. Pes. 5:2-3 goes over the issues of M. Zeb. 2:1ff. At stake is slaughtering the animal designated for use as a Passover sacrifice for that particular purpose, that is, for the intention that the farmer has imposed upon the animal, and not for any other purpose: "A Passover sacrifice which one slaughtered under an improper designation ["not for its name," that is, for another purpose than as a Passover sacrifice], or received the blood and tossed the blood of which under an improper designation, or under its proper designation and under an improper designation, or under an improper designation and under its proper designation, is invalid." We have already noted Flesher's treatment of materials in this tractate.

40. QIDDUSHIN

M. Qid. 2:2-3 introduce the notion that intention or attitude bears upon the fulfillment of the stipulations of an agreement. Simeon takes the view that if a deception is intended for the advantage of the deceived party, then it is a valid one, and that means that he tempers the strict requirements of meeting the conditions of a contract with the consideration of attitude or intention as a countervailing force. That interpretation is supported by M. Qid. 2:3, where the opposite viewpoint is introduced. At M. Qid. 2:4D, if the instruction is to betrothe the woman, and is accompanied by information as to her location, then the intent has no bearing on the location of the woman. But, M. Qid. 2:4A, where the instruction bears clear evidence that the location of the women forms a part of the intent, then she is not. So we introduce the consideration of attitude into the interpretation of contracts, this one between the agent and the source of the agency. At M. Qid. 2:6 the intention of the donor plays a role in our interpretation of the result. At M. Qid. 2:7's case, we interpret the attitude of the other parties to the transaction in assessing the outcome. M. Qid. 2:8 pursues the application of attitude and intention (the issue of inadvertent or advertent action) to the use of Holy Things in a betrothal. Everything depends here upon intentionality.

The language of M. Qid. 3:2-3+4 (and see also M. Qid. 3:6) introduces conditions which in fact are deemed to state intentions. If someone says, "On condition that I do such and so," that is deemed a condition that the person intends to meet, and hence, the statement is valid and the intention is fully taken into account. This is in contrast with M. Qid. 3:1, where an intention to take an act at a specified time is deemed null, not a potentiality worth considering. The betrothal takes effect forthwith, and we take for granted the condition will be met. The issue of intention is modified by the matter of responsibility; if there is deceit that has produced an incorrect attitude, then the action that results is null; but if there is no deceit, then the mere fact that a person intended something that was not realized by itself does not nullify the action.

41. QINNIM

I find nothing relevant. Intentionality lies in the background, of course, in the designation of the birds for their several sacrificial procedures.

42. ROSH HASHSHANAH

M. R.H. 3:8-9 raise the question of the relationship between correct intentionality and carrying out one's obligation. In connection with hearing the sound of the shofar, if one heard such a sound adventitiously but upon hearing formed the intention that that sound carry out his obligation to listen to the sound of the shofar, then he has correctly done the action. If not, he has not. The principle is this: "if he paid attention [thereby intending to carry out his obligation], he has fulfilled his obligation. But if not, he has not fulfilled his obligation." So in the cases listed here the correct intentionality is required for fulfilling one's obligation. This explains M. 3:9I: those incapable of forming and expressing correct intention cannot serve the community in fulfilling the shared obligation, hence the deaf-mute, idiot, and minor are excluded.

43. SANHEDRIN

I find nothing pertinent in any direct way, which is an amazing result for this vast and important tractate—and probably a fault of my reading of matters. But I think that we can have had Sanhedrin, nearly whole and complete, without intrusion of the philosophical issues of attitude and intentionality.

44. SHABBAT

M. Shab. 2:5 sets forth, through the contrast of two cases, the stunning conception that the violation of the Sabbath is a matter of not only action but also intention or attitude. If one carries out an action, it may or may not fall into the classification of Sabbath-violation. If one's intent is not for one's own benefit, then the action is not culpable. If it is for a person's benefit, for example, to produce material gain, then the action is culpable. So intentionality forms the indicative point of differentiation. M. Shab. 7:3 goes on to review a taxonomic principle. A person is liable for transporting an object across the boundaries from private to public domain. But there is an intervening principle of taxonomy that tells us if the action is culpable. If someone transports something that is not held to be of worth or value—that is, an object of no consequence—then transporting the object produces no consequences and does not impose liability. Then at M. 7:4 we have a list of the minimum volume or quantity of various sorts of food stuffs for the transportation of which a person is liable. These are minimum amounts of food for which an animal or a human being will find meaningful use, such as a mouthful of food and the like. The upshot is that the attitude or intentionality of a human being is taken into account. But this is not left to subjective considerations, e.g., what an individual person may deem or worth or not of worth. There is a limit as to subjectivity in the objective quantities held to be of value to anyone, if not to a given person. The consideration, then, of what is deemed to be valuable is not left in the hands of the private person. I cannot imagine a more profound statement of that principle of the taxonomic power of intentionality than the one in hand. M. Shab. 10:4 once again introduces the consideration of intentionality. If one intended to violate the law but did not actually do so, he is exempt from punishment. If he intended to transport an object in front of him in the normal way but it slipped around behind him and was carried in an unusual way, he is exempt. If he intended not to violate the law but did so, he is liable. M. 10:5 adds that if one performs a prohibited act of labor for some purpose other than the commission of that act of labor itself, he is exempt from liability. If it is permitted to carry an object and a person happens to carry a container for that object, he is not liable.

The interest of this tractate's framers in defining something's correct purpose and in identifying the intentionality that has affected it, by appeal to that purpose, comes to the fore at M. Shab. 3:6. The principle here is more complex than it appears on the surface. At issue is the classificatory power of oil that has been set aside for use in a lamp on the Sabbath. That act of intentionality has established the character of the oil. It cannot then be carried. When the oil drips into the dish, the dish too cannot be carried. The dish formerly was available for use; it now has been prohibited, and so its status has been changed. If the dish was designated prior to the Sabbath for the particular purpose that it now is made to serve, however, then it is permitted for use in that way. That explains the principle of M. 3:6A. The parallel point concerns an old lamp. It is not used because it is undesirable. It falls into the classification of that which has not been set aside for Sabbath use. The new lamp may be used. So the passage overall works on the principle of the classification of objects— permitted or prohibited for Sabbath use—through the prior act of intentionality. Only in Mishnah-tractate Besah can we locate discussions of the interplay of intentionality and classification of so sustained and penetrating a character. What has been designated or classified in advance for use on the Sabbath may be handled, but what has not been so designated may not be handled. Similarly, at M. Shab. 4:2 the question of an act of intentionality is worked out. A hide is available for use with or without food, since it may be spread out and serve for reclining; it thus falls into the classification of a utensil. Wool shearings are purposed for weaving or spinning, acts not done on the Sabbath. They cannot be used on the Sabbath. If they are used to cover a dish and keep it warm, the dish may be removed but not restored. Here again the conception of a prior act of intentionality that classifies an object and endows it with its purpose and hence its distinctive character vis-à-vis the Sabbath is paramount. The issue of intentionality or inadvertence is introduced in Chapter Eleven in these terms: "This is the general principle: All those who may be liable to sin offerings in fact are not liable unless at the beginning and the end, their [sin] is done inadvertently. [But] if the beginning of their [sin] is inadvertent and the end is deliberate, [or] the beginning deliberate and the end inadvertent, they are exempt—unless at the beginning and at the end their [sin] is inadvertent" (M. 11:6).

The issue of M. Shab. 17:1ff. is handling objects within private domain. The main point is that objects not set apart for use on the Sabbath also may not be handled lest they be used, while those that serve a licit purpose may be handled and used. That principle is not expressed but presumed. The first issue, at M. 17:1, concerns appurtenances of an object that may be handled on the Sabbath. These two may be handled. They are deemed integral to the basic utensil, even when detached. The issue then is one of connection, and connection here is established through function. M. 17:2 catalogues objects that may be handled. These may be destined for purposes that in fact are not licit on the Sabbath, but if the objects are to be used for licit purposes, such as using a plane to cut a piece of cheese, a chisel to open a cask of dates, then they may be handled. So here the principle of classification—permitted or prohibited, with regard to handling— derives from intentionality. Even before one has actually used the object for its intended, licit purpose, he may handle the object, so the attitude or intentionality establishes the classification of the object, without reference to a confirmatory deed. M. Shab. 17:5 reverts to the question of the initial purpose for which an object is made. Has the attitude of the maker or initial user imparted to the object its on-going classification, definition, and character? Or do we allow an object to be reclassified by the intentionality of subsequent users? The anonymous authority holds that if a fragment of a utensil serves any purpose at all, even not for which the utensil has been made, it may be handled; that is to say, it is a perfectly useful object. Judah insists that only if the fragment serves a purpose akin to what it served when it is a whole object may it be handled. Only then, when falling into its initial classification, is the object deemed licit for Sabbath use; otherwise it has not been designated or prepared in advance of the Sabbath for use on the Sabbath and therefore may not be used. M. 17:6 goes on to develop the same point. If a utensil is usable only when joined with an object that normally may not be handled on the Sabbath, the utensil and object may be used when joined, but not when they are separated; this is a refinement. The remainder of the chapter works out analogous problems of thought.

M. Shab. 23:1-5 go over actions of speech. The first point is that one may not conduct a business transaction, e.g., a loan, on the Sabbath. One may request a gift and pay the gift back, but one may not establish those conditions that indicate the presence of a formal business exchange. One may not hire workers on the Sabbath for work to be done afterward or ask someone else to do so or wait at the Sabbath limit to do so. Abba Saul distinguishes between speaking of something one may do on the Sabbath, on which account one may wait at the Sabbath limit, and not speaking of something one may not do on the Sabbath, on which account one may not wait at the Sabbath limit. And that distinction carries in its wake a further one, between something one may not do on the Sabbath but may plan on the Sabbath to do afterward, and something one may not plan or prepare on the Sabbath to do afterward. The example has to do with care of a corpse. The upshot is that expressions of intentionality are governed by the requirements of the Sabbath, and actions that convey a prior intentionality likewise are governed by those requirements. Here is a primary instance of the appeal to intentionality in classifying actions, and also speech, as to permissibility or impermissibility.

45. SHABUOT

I find nothing pertinent to this problem.

46. SHEBIIT[10]

M. Sheb. 3:1-4:1 turns to the problem of cultivating the land during the Seventh Year, with special attention to the difference between actually doing so and appearing to do so. There are acts of labor that will not necessarily benefit the field in the Seventh Year, but which may appear to others to do so. For example, one may store manure in the field. But what if this actually enriches the soil during the Seventh Year? Then doing so is prohibited. So how are we to do the work in such a way that we do not appear to be manuring the field? One brings out three dung heaps per seah of land, each of considerable size; then people will not think that it is to manure the field, the heaps being too few and too scattered, so M. Sheb. 3:2. Along these same lines, one may not appear to clear the field for planting (M. Sheb. 3:5-4:1). One can open a stone quarry, so long as it does not appear that the farmer is clearing the land of stones and so preparing it for cultivation. One who tears down a stone fence in his field may remove only the large stones, to indicate that he is not clearing the land, so M. 3:6-7. Newman states, "The sanctity of the Seventh Year depends in the last analysis upon the actions and will of the people of Israel." From a philosophical perspective, what is important is the power of intentionality (in this case: will) in solving taxonomic problems, assigning to the class of forbidden or prohibited actions things that the

---

[10] The analysis of this tractate is based on the study by Louis E. Newman, *The Sanctity of the Seventh Year: A Study of Mishnah Tractate Shebiit* (Chico, CA: Scholars Press for Brown Judaic Studies, 1983). Hereinafter referred to as "Newman."

attitude of the community at large deems to be work associated with the Seventh Year or not.

What grows in the Sabbatical Year is classified as holy. God owns the crop. Everyone has a right to an equal share. Individuals may not dispose of crops of the Seventh Year as they do of their own produce. That is the fact that generates the interesting problems of M. Sheb. 8:1-6, 7-11. The problem of M. 8:1-2 addresses interstitial classes of produce, which may serve either animals or human beings. How do we know its classification? The matter depends upon human intentionality. If someone gathered it with the intention of using the produce for both human beings and cattle, for instance, it is classified by that intention; or, if someone gathered it only for burning, it is so classified. Here is a classic example of the ambiguous case, in which human attitude or intentionality that defines matters. These same considerations are expressed in the notion of "ordinary mode of utilization," M. Sheb. 8:2. We assume that the prevailing attitude applies in any individual case. We do not take account of an individual's asymptomatic attitude or intentionality, therefore, we classify by the prevailing attitude. M. 8:3ff. then set forth rules for the disposition of crops within the stated rules. The main point concerns the treatment of crops in a manner different from that characteristic of other years of the Sabbatical cycle.

The law that crops must be removed from one's house when crops of the same classification cease to grow in the fields presents its set of taxonomic problems in M. 9:1-6. Specifically, the Mishnah's authorities address the interstitial issues involved in cases in which it is unclear when the law of removal takes effect. These cases derive from a situation in which the entire species of produce may or may not be subject to removal at a single time—just the sort of problem of sorting matters out that the philosophy of classification is meant to solve. Here the solution derives from a variety of taxonomic indicators. First, farmers in various regions harvest the same crop, for example wheat, at different times. So one thing becomes many things and is so classified. Sometimes part of the crop has been removed from the field, while part of the same species is growing in a private courtyard or is not yet ripe. Since part of the crop is not yet harvested, the rule of removal should not take effect. But since the species is not now available to everybody all at once, perhaps the law does apply. The taxonomic indicator is whether the inability of certain classes of persons to gather and eat produce can affect the point at which the law of removal applies (Newman, p. 179). A second possibility is that the law is not invoked until the last of that species disappears, without regard to whether particular classes of persons can or cannot gather it. As Newman says:

The first theory is that man through his actions and capacities determines when the law of removal takes effect. If Israelite farmers harvest a single species of produce in two or more separate lots, each crop is deemed a separate entity. Similarly, the ability of Israelites to harvest and use crops of the Sabbatical Year is decisive. As soon as produce of a given species is no longer available...the householder must remove that same species from the home. Finally, the way in which man stores produce after he has harvested it likewise is probative. If a householder stores several distinct species of produce in a single jar, the whole is treated as a single entity. The principle underlying these rules is that man is the center of his world. Through their actions...farmers and householders order the world in accordance with their wishes.... The opposing theory is that the law applies separately to each species of produce, no matter how Israelite farmers may handle them... These rules express the notion that it is God's action, not man's [attitude], which determines the point at which the law takes effect. (Newman, p. 180)

47. SHEQALIM

I find nothing relevant to this matter, although the tractate does present some interesting exercises of classification based on the designation or attitude of a donor. But the facts of intentionality here are systemically inert.

48. SOTAH

I find nothing pertinent here.

49. SUKKAH

I find nothing pertinent here.

50. TAANIT

I find nothing pertinent here.

51. TAMID

I find nothing pertinent here.

52. TEBUL YOM

The question is whether the Tebul Yom imparts uncleanness through certain substances to objects connected to those substances are connected. The tractate joins together three issues: intention, connection, and the distinction between firm connection and dubious connection. Intention is at issue at M. 1:1A-C; since the beggar plans to separate the pieces of dough, do we deem them connected for the nonce? The House of Shammai ignores the intentionality and classifies the dough as connected by reason of the deed that has been done. One's intent is fully exposed in one's deed, and, since one can change his mind, the deed is all that matters. The contrast between uncleanness of the Tebul Yom and that of all other classifications of uncleanness is drawn at M. 1:1M as against 1:2I-J. The types of connections are the usual: substances that are thoroughly mixed together and entirely connected, substances that remain distinct from one another and not wholly connected, substances that are in no way to be deemed related.

53. TEMURAH

Though the issue of intentionality makes its appearance, it is not a generative principle of the tractate and scarcely stands behind the formation of any analytical problems, so far as I can discern.

54. TERUMOT[11]

At stake at M. Ter. 1:1-2, 3 is how produce is classified so that part of it falls into the category of heave-offering, that is to say, is sanctified. The Israelite is central to the process of classification, that is, sanctification. So Avery-Peck (p. 3): "The holy heave offering comes into being only if man properly formulates the intention to sanctify part of his produce and indicates that intention through corresponding words and actions. The centrality of human intention in this process is illustrated by the fact that individuals deemed to have no understanding, e.g., imbeciles and minors, and therefore no power of intention, may not validly designate heave-offering." No produce is intrinsically holy. All depends upon the intentionality, as to classification, of the householder. That accounts for the interest at M. 1:1-2 in an act of classification accomplished through full intentionality of someone with the power of intentionality. The indicative traits of those excluded from the process then bear the generalization. We come to the interplay of action and intentionality, with intentionality ruled out of bounds. M. Ter. 1:8 explains how the act of separation takes place. What is required is negative: there must not be a predetermined and measured quantity of produce. The produce that falls into the classification of holy must be so classified by fortune, that is, by accident and not by intention. So the act of classification must be intentional, but carrying out the act must be left in the hands of God. That forms an important limitation upon the role of intentionality, a distinction between the arena in which human intentionality operates, and the boundaries beyond which it does not

---

[11] The analysis of this tractate is based on the study by Alan J. [Avery-] Peck, *The Priestly Gift in Mishnah: A Study of Tractate Terumot* (Chico, CA: Scholars Press for Brown Judaic Studies, 1981). Hereinafter referred to as "Avery-Peck."

extend. The basic principles of the separation of heave offering having been set forth—intentionality as a distinction, speciation as a consideration—we come at M. Ter. 2:1-2 to the systematic composition of a grid in which the two sets of principles are joined in a common, complex expression. The established rules are [1] heave offering may not be separated from one genus of produce on behalf of produce of a different genus; [2] if the householder owns different species within the same genus of produce, heave offering should be separated from the species which is of the higher quality (Avery-Peck, p. 81). M. 2:1-3 begin the work by specifying that heave offering may not be separated from produce of one genus on behalf of another now with reference to cultic cleanness. The unclean must be treated in distinction from the clean. If one has done so, the act is valid. But what about deliberately doing so, since the unclean is useless and of less value? M. Ter. 2:2 then invokes the consideration of intentionality. If one intentionally separated unclean for clean, his act is null; if unintentionally, his act is valid. Here, therefore, intentionality joins as a principal criterion for classification. The role of intentionality in the classification of part of the crop as heave offering is spelled out at M. Ter. 3:5. The farmer must express his will distinctly and clearly, meaning he must say where, in his intentionality, the portion of the crop that is distinguished as heave offering is located within the larger batch. So the oral declaration is required, not merely a decision reached within one's heart, and that oral designation must be detailed and concrete. Only after the offering has been so designated is part of the batch separated and given to the priest. M. Ter. 4:1-6 complete the presentation of rules on the classification of produce. M. Ter. 4:1 allows for the possibility that an owner may wish to give more than the minimum portion of his crop for heave offering. The established principles are worked out within this context. The issue of intentionality is introduced, now with reference to the volume of the crop that a farmer wishes to set aside for this purpose. The taxonomic power of intentionality comes into play when it comes to violating the sanctity of heave-offering. If a non-priest has eaten heave-offering, how do we classify the act? If he has done so intentionally, he is subjected to one set of sanctions, and if unintentionally, a different set of sanctions. As specified at M. Ter. 6:1D, the principal and added fifth are restored to the priesthood for intentially misappropriating the sanctified produce. The added fifth is a fine through which the non-priest makes atonement for his improper intention (Avery-Peck, p. 193). The task is to indicate who is liable to pay the principal and added fifth, and what produce may be used for that purpose. While the whole of Chapter Six works on these questions of detail, what generates the questions to begin with is the power of classification deriving from intentionality.

Produce in the status of heave offering may not be permitted to go to waste. It must be used for the purpose for which it has been designated, that is to say, for the benefit of the priest. The taxonomic principle that governs the utilization of produce in the status of heave offering is this initially intended purpose. The intentionality of the farmer in designating this portion of the crop for the priest governs the disposition of the crop, yet in another important way intentionality forms a primary taxonomic indicator in the formation of the rules of this tractate. Chapter Eleven spells the matter out. M. 11:1-3 presents the governing theory: produce in the status of heave offering must be prepared in the manner customary for unconsecrated produce of the same type. What this means is that the intentionality of the farmer-donor is limited by the prevailing practice or rule, though I do not think that that is a principal consideration here. All portions of the produce that normally are eaten must be available for eating (Avery-Peck, p. 295). If produce is processed in an abnormal way, for example, so that what is usually eaten is pressed for juice, the skin would go to waste; that must not happen. M. 11:4-7 proceeds to produce that normally is not eaten but may be consumed. Such an interstitial category demands attention. How do we resolve the matter? If the priest deems that produce worthy as food, then it is in the consecrated status of heave offering. What the priest does not deem food is treated as inedible and therefore not in the status of heave offering. Here intentionality has paramount power of classification. M. 11:8-10 deal with produce of an ambiguous classification. It is unclean and may not be eaten by the priest; or he may not want it as food. But it may be used for some other purpose, e.g., fodder or lamp oil. Since it cannot be used as food, it does not have to be eaten; but it may not be permitted to go to waste.

55. TOHOROT

The issue of intentionality is introduced at M. Tohorot 1:1-8. At stake is whether or not vegetable matter falls into the category of food. Is intention to eat the food required for the food to fall into the category of that which can impart food-uncleanness? The answer is that intentionality serves as a taxonomic indicator in cases of choice, but not in cases in which, in general, something is deemed edible. The basic point introduced at M. Toh. 9:1-10:8 concerns the taxonomic power of intentionality: liquid that is not wanted does not have the power to make something susceptible to uncleanness (cf. Mishnah-tractate Makhshirin), while liquid that is wanted makes something susceptible to uncleanness. That taxonomic principle is fully exposed in the treatment of the special liquids at hand, olive oil and wine.

56. UQSIN

At M. Uqs. 2:1, the Mishnah's framers focus on the question of whether things connected to a foodstuff are part of it. The issue is resolved through the user's intention. If a merchant wants the hair of a cucumber, for instance, it is deemed connected, and if not, it is deemed null. Similarly, if the one who pickled the cucumber deemed the leaves merely for the sake of ornament, then the leaves are not regarded as part of the plant. Hence the attitude or intentionality of the owner of the produce is taken into account when we assess whether or not an extrinsic part of the produce is regarded as joined with the main part or is deemed not a component of it at all.

A similar issue is addressed at M. Uqs. 2:5. If a man began to pull the produce apart, we have no reason to suppose that the process of disconnection will inevitably continue; therefore only the food actually taken apart is deemed disconnected. Hence we dismiss the potentiality of what one may do, even though one's intention is to do exactly that; we take account only of what one actually has done.

According to M. Uqs. 3:1, some things become susceptible to uncleanness only after the application of liquid, even though a person's intention has no effect on whether they are deemed edible. Other items require a person's intention to be considered edible, but are susceptible to uncleanness without application of water. Still other items require both intention and application of water, while others require neither. This issue is discussed further at M. Uqs. 3:2, 3, 9.

M. Uqs. 3:4 reveals that once dill has imparted its flavor, it has carried out its intended purpose and is no longer susceptible to uncleanness as food. The issue of intentionality remains decisive, for it governs the herb's function and therefore its classification.

57. YADAYIM

I find nothing pertinent.

58. YEBAMOT

The issue of intentionality does not arise. But that judgment must be qualified. In those pericopae, such as Chapters Nine and following, in which the capacity to express intentionality is a taxonomic indicator or criterion, there we have to admit that intentionality is an issue. But it forms an inert fact and does not generate problems; it is systemically neutral in this tractate.

59. YOMA
The topic does not occur in any way I can discern.

60. ZABIM
The issue of intentionality is explicitly excluded in Chapter Two. A study of intentionality in the philosophical system of the Mishnah will focus not only upon points at which intentionality plays a taxonomic role but also upon those at which it is explicitly omitted, as in the present case. M. 2:2, 3 make the important point that the condition must be natural and not self-induced; that is, there must be clear evidence that we deal with not semen, which is sexually generated, but flux, which is an abnormal emission from a person's sexual organs. This forms part of the issue of analogical thinking; since flux is not semen, nothing that causes semen can be admitted in evidence of the Zab's condition. We see that the omission of intentionality forms part of a taxonomic exercise in distinguishing flux from semen.

61. ZEBAHIM
The basic consideration that is operative in Chapters One (1:1) through Four (4:6) and Chapter Six (6:7) is that the priest must carry out his duties with the correct intentionality. That involves several considerations. First, he must conduct the rite in accord with the owner's intentionality. If the owner has designated ("sanctified") the beast for a given offering—such as a sin-offering or a guilt offering or peace offering—then the rules for that sacrifice must govern. Second and more important, the priest must not form the intention of eating his share of the meat outside of the correct location in which the meat must be eaten, and he must not form the intention of tossing the blood outside the specified time period during which the beast's blood must be tossed on the altar. If he should do so, then he has classified the beast as unacceptable. This is accomplished not through deed but solely through the improper intention that he has formed for himself. M. 1:1-3 deal with the first of the two considerations of intentionality, that is, preserving the animal within the classification for which the owner has designated it. If the priest slaughters a beast other than for its proper designation, it ordinarily remains valid (with the specified exceptions), even though, as to the owner's personal obligation for this offering (incurred by inadvertent sin, for instance), that must be met with a different beast; the stress here is that the beast must be designated for the particular sin that the owner of the beast has inadvertently carried out. Intentionality then plays a role in classification here in that the priest has done the deed with an

improper attitude and that has classified the beast in a manner other than the donor has intended; the priest's intentionality is paramount.

M. Zeb. 2:1 lists ten categories of persons or actions that invalidate a rite. What is important is the contrast drawn to what follows, namely, that attitudes that have the same taxonomic power. M. 2:2-5 set forth the issue of intentionality. If a priest slaughters the animal sacrifice, while intending at the moment of the action to toss the blood outside its proper location or to burn the entrails or to eat the flesh outside the correct location, the sacrifice is invalid. That is the rule of M. 2:2. If the priest performs the sacrifice with one of these improper intentions, then the offering is deemed refuse, and anyone who eats of that meat incurs the penalty of extirpation. M. 2:3 generalizes: if the false intention has to do with the place in which the action is done, then the sacrifice is invalid, and extirpation to begin with does not pertain to it. If it has to do with time, the sacrifice is refuse, and extirpation does pertain. M. 2:3 furthermore qualifies this position by positing that these considerations apply only if what permits the sacrifice to be eaten by the priests or donor has been properly offered up. It is then, but only then, that the sacrifice comes within the category of being subject to the rule of refuse—that is to say, the consideration of intentionality—and therefore also of extirpation. But if what permits the offering to be eaten is not properly offered, which is to say, if the blood is not properly tossed, at which point sacrificial portions of the sacrifice are burned on the altar and the priest's share of the meat may be eaten by him, then the sacrifice is not subject at all to the rule of refuse; the consideration of attitude or intentionality does not pertain. M. 2:4 gives examples of both cases, first, the proper offering of that which permits the offering to be eaten, then the improper offering of that which permits the offering to be eaten. In the former case we have slaughtering without proper intention, then receiving, conveying, and tossing the blood with improper intention as to time; or improper slaughtering, then proper disposition of the blood; or improper intention in regard to time as regards slaughtering, then receiving, conveying, and tossing the blood. Intentionality plays it role here, since it is a factor in consideration whether or not that which permits the offering to be eaten has been properly offered. That which permits the offering to be eaten is not properly offered if the act of slaughter took place with the disqualifying intention of eating the meat outside the proper place, and the blood was received, conveyed, and tossed with the intention of eating the meat at the improper time; or if the slaughter was accompanied by improper intention as regards the time of eating, and the blood was received, conveyed, and tossed with improper intention as regards the place of eating the meat, and so forth. M. 2:5 adds that the act of intentionality must pertain to a sizable portion of the meat, namely, an olive's bulk or more. If the intentionality pertains to less than that bulk, it is null. M. 3:1 then proceeds to assess the power of intentionality imputed to people who are not supposed to have a role in the rite at all, or who can carry out one part of the rite but not some other. M. 3:2 completes that matter. M. 3:3-5 deal with improper intention concerning matters that are improperly conceived to begin with, such as an improper intention to eat at the wrong time things that are not normally eaten at all, or to burn in the wrong place things not usually burned at all. M. 3:6 goes on to the limitations of intentionality. Improper intention concerning something that is not normally done is null. Chapter Four draws to a close the discussion of the role of intentionality in the sacrificial act and process. The discussion both pursues secondary issues and then closes with a powerful generalization. M. 4:1-2 ask, with the sprinkling of which particular drop of blood is the false intention to eat part of the sacrifice outside of its proper time going to invoke the status of refuse for that sacrifice? This is surely a secondary consideration. M. 4:3 lists things that are not subject to the law of refuse at all; to these intentionality does not apply. Whatever is subject to the proper offering of that which renders the offering permissible, for example, for eating by the priest or for burning on the altar, also is subject to the law of refuse, and whatever is not subject to such a condition is exempt, a familiar consideration. M. 4:4 carries forward the same definition. M. 4:5 introduces the matter of the relationships between liability to refuse and liability to the prohibition of remnant, which is to say, leaving meat beyond its proper time. That is the action to which invalidating intention involved in refuse is relevant. The consideration of carrying on the rite in a state of uncleanness is here introduced as well. Things which are not liable to refuse are liable to the prohibitions as to remnant and uncleanness, except for the blood. That a variety of taxonomic considerations are in play then is self-evident. M. 4:6, given above, tells us that the intentionality of the officiating priest, not of the donor-owner of the beast, is determinative.

What is now clear, and hardly requires extensive reiteration, is that lexical studies provide only limited data, therefore unreliable conclusions, in the study of the philosophical and theological conceptions of a document such as the Mishnah. The reason is that the character of the Mishnah is violated by the identification of pertinent data solely through word-choices. The Mishnah's authorship expresses ideas through its account of relationships, that is to say, within the idiom of hierarchical classification, and it is entirely feasible, on that account, to make the same point through a variety of cases, and, it follows, of word-choices. The correct medium for Mishnaic speech is abstract symbol, but, having no such symbolic vocabulary at its disposal, the Mishnah's authorship chose the next best thing: picayune cases of such monumental specificity as to require, for intelligible discourse, a process of generalization and abstraction. God lives in the details—therefore not only in the word.

Chapter Four

Reading Tradition, Writing System: Structural Separation and the Role of the Reader in the Talmud of Babylonia

Roy Kreitner
Brown University

> A text is made of multiple writings, drawn from
> many cultures and entering into mutual relations of
> dialogue, parody, contestation, but there is one
> place where this multiplicity is focused and that
> place is the reader...[1]

If the reader is actually the most important person in literature, then criticism has often neglected its topic. But indeed the reader is not always a central consideration of even the literary process itself. Literary cultures define different roles for readers at different times, in response to (and resulting in) shifting conditions. The reader's responsibility changes over time, from genre to genre, from document to document, even from style to style. Given the changing position of the reader vis-à-vis the documents he or she reads, raising questions about the reader's place will provide important insights into a text and its interpretation.

Once the initial questions are raised, the task of applying them to an existing document remains. The choice of any document is somewhat arbitrary, but some documents prove more useful than others. The most

---

[1] Roland Barthes, "The Death of the Author," in *Image, Music, Text*, trans. Stephen Heath (New York: Hill and Wang 1977) p. 148.

useful thing a document could offer us is a framework within which to pursue our questions. But from where does this framework spring? The answer is, from a body of critical opinion—that is, a history of *reading*, of engagement of readers with the text—which addresses (explicitly or implicitly) or neglects our specific questions. One such document with a particularly rich history of reading is the Talmud of Babylonia (a.k.a. Bavli). Jewish readers have defined the Bavli as the "central pillar" of Judaism and claimed it as the authoritative statement of rabbinic tradition. Jews have read the Talmud and encouraged its continued reading from one generation to the next as a traditional document. So the framework which we may borrow from that history of reading is the question of tradition.

Before bringing this question to the Bavli, it is important to set out some definitions of traditional and non-traditional—that is, systemic —literatures, so as to understand the methodological framework before applying it to a specific text.[2] For our specific purposes, it will be most useful to divide the definition into two parts, which are connected but clearly distinguishable. The first involves the (internal) workings and justification of the literatures; in other words, we must identify how the literatures function. The second part of the definition regards the role of the reader.

In the composition of traditional literature, the key element is the transmission of unquestioned fundamental truth, basically intact. New information is unimportant except as it fits into an already present (re-presented) truth. This necessitates a traditional document's placement within a body of existing works, all reliant on the same origin for their authoritative statement. In a different context (that of a transition to modern poetics), John Freccero describes this double characteristic (transmission of truth, placement within body of work) of traditional literature:

> ...the "truth value" of Augustine's narrative depends...upon the privilege granted to God's word as the ultimate significance of all discourse. The fig tree, under the shade of which all this takes place, stands for *a tradition of textual anteriority that extends backward in time to the Logos and forward to the same Logos at time's ending*... (italics added)[3]

---

[2] When discussing these terms, I will concentrate on "literary process," disregarding another perfectly valid side of "tradition." The other meaning regards structure and content (as opposed to literary process) and does not directly touch our larger question, which is literary, not theological. This distinction is informed by *The Bavli and Its Sources* by Jacob Neusner, (Atlanta: Scholars Press, 1987) p. 2.

[3] John Freccero, "The Fig Tree and the Laurel: Petrarch's Poetics" in *Literary Theory/Renaissance Texts*, Patricia Parker and David Quint, eds. (Baltimore: Johns Hopkins University Press, 1986) p. 25.

But the significance of a document's reliance on "textual anteriority" is not (and is never intended as) merely an archeological point of interest about the text. The traditional makeup of a document has specific impact on its consumer, the reader. By pinning its validity on prior texts and on their authoritative origin, the traditional text locks the reader out of the process of its own construction. This is a necessary conclusion of a literary process which attempts to portray its authority as unchallengeable. It considers itself as having been "always already" complete, and is thus not receptive to input from the reader. Speaking of the reader of this kind of "classic text," Roland Barthes writes:

> This reader is thereby plunged into a kind of idleness – he is intransitive; he is, in short, serious: instead of functioning himself, instead of gaining access to the magic of the signifier, to the pleasure of writing, he is left with no more than the poor freedom either to accept or reject the text: reading is nothing more than a *referendum*.[4]

With these features of tradition in mind, it becomes easier to define systemic literature in opposition to the traditional. First, in contrast to the traditional document's reliance on textual anteriority, the system relies on some internal logic for its cogency. That is, instead of implicit or explicit reference to a prior agent of authority, the systemic document will refer to itself, and will build an interior network of connections which hold it together and take on the task of "verifying" the document. It is not going too far to suggest that this mode of internal interaction of the parts of a systemic document then becomes its focus, outweighing its "message," which would certainly be the focus of the traditional document. In this context Barthes writes: "In operational terms, the meanings I find are established...by their *systematic* mark."[5] This point is crucial in that it attributes the production of meaning to the play of elements within the text rather than to reference points outside it. The locus of production of meaning is the basis for the distinction between the systemic and the traditional.

The internal production of meaning points to another element which separates the systemic from the traditional text; namely, its

---

[4] Roland Barthes, *S/Z*, trans. Richard Miller (New York: Hill and Wang 1974, original published 1970) p. 4.

[5] He continues: "There is no other proof of a reading than the quality and endurance of its systematics; in other words: than its functioning. To read, in fact, is a labor of language. To read is to find meanings, and to find meanings is to name them; but named meanings are swept toward other names; names call to each other, reassemble, and their grouping calls for further naming." *S/Z*, p.11.

independence. While the traditional text is meaningless (even non-existent) without its precedent texts, the systemic document can stand on its own, pursuing its own program. The truly traditional text has no choice about its program (it is always pre-programmed) while the systemic text('s author) has very wide choices (limited by social conditions, power of language etc. rather than other textual programs). Again, this independence of program is not trivial. The reliance on internal connections to produce meaning puts the burden and responsibility of construction on the reader. Here, the "text's unity lies not in its origin but in its destination."[6] The reader, then, is forced to assume an active position with regard to the text, since drawing out the meaning requires making connections within the text.

At this point we can take the question of tradition and its implications for the reader and apply them to our specific text, the Babylonian Talmud. When trying to distinguish between tradition and system in Bavli, the definitional question becomes more pointed and somewhat clearer. The question—is the Bavli a traditional or systemic document?—can be addressed in two parts: the first is the form and content of Bavli's internal workings, and the second is Bavli's connection to and possible reliance on other parts of the Judaic canon.

As far as Bavli's internal workings are concerned, the structure and content of the document force *reader intervention* in the text, cancelling the possibility of a passive reader, and making a strong case for Bavli as a systemic text. The justifications for such a claim are varied. A truly traditional document will try to maintain seamlessness, pushing attention away from its own writing, but the Bavli, on the contrary, calls attention to this process. To begin with, it is written in Hebrew and Aramaic, two distinct languages, immediately disrupting any notion of a smooth cognitive process in reading (even if a sonic smoothness, through melody, can be achieved). This same process of disrupting the cognitive flow of the text is carried out by the half-articulated and often unattributed citations of passages from other texts. These often inject a different style of Hebrew into the discourse (usually Mishnaic), which Bavli makes no attempt to imitate. But this particular technique serves a double function. It is not only a call to reader intervention in recognizing language difference and the references, but in fact, it brings to light incongruities (the unharmonious) in the sources and the heterogeneity of the evidence (ranging from Amos to Mishnah to Leviticus etc.), which would be unthinkable for a traditional text. A simple example of disagreeing sources reads: "One Tanna [authority says], 'They may bless the light of a furnace,' and another Tanna [says], 'They may not bless it.'"[7]

---

[6] Barthes, "The Death of the Author," p. 148.

[7] All translations of the Bavli are from Jacob Neusner, *Invitation to the Talmud* (San Francisco: Harper & Row 1984) pp. 247-270.

More important than these surface disruptions however, are the Bavli's mode of address and logic of cogent discourse. The mode of address constantly points to the seams or the contradictions within the document. Following are two examples of direct pointing to contradiction which closely follow each other:

> 1. But [we must conclude] that the prohibited [flame] is present, but when he blesses, it is over the additional [flame], which is permitted, that he blesses.
>
> *If so, lo a gentile['s flame kindled] from a gentile['s flame] also [should be permitted].*

> 2. ...If the majority are Israelites, he blesses it.
>
> *Lo, the statement is self-contradictory.*

In fact, the mode of address assumes a constant critic (the reader), paying very close attention. Evidence of the assumption of a critical presence outside (but involved with) the text may be seen in the repeated phrasing, "If *you* like, I can argue that..." It is abundantly clear that there is a constant internal argument going on in the Talmud (between houses, sages, etc.), but what is equally important is the role of someone outside the Talmud (again, the reader) inside the argument. The reader is hailed, commanded to engage the text.[8]

This leads us, finally, to the Bavli's most important systemic characteristic, which is its internal logic. This takes precedence over the mode of address because while a personalized mode of address may disguise any document, a systemic logic is not reproducible in a traditional text. Bavli's logic of cogent discourse is based on a process of building syllogisms, or philosophical propositions.[9] The key factor in these syllogisms is that the reader is responsible for piecing them together, and often for fleshing out the conclusions.[10] A series of propositions which may serve as an example begins:

---

[8] An extended digression on the mode of study of talmud could be in place here. The role of the yeshiva, and of study by argumentation is clearly essential to the writing and preservation of the talmud.

[9] One example that comes to mind is the tradition which calls on each individual to imagine her/himself as being present at revelation (or the exodus). Each person is called on personally, but revelation remains unchanging.

[10] That the reader is responsible for drawing conclusions through rationality also comes out in the Bavli's rejection of unchallengeable evidence, for instance, "They do not pay attention to an echo from heaven." When that kind of evidence is accepted, as in, "That is true, but it is prohibited by decree..." it is an unusual exception, which is noted distinctly and so highlights the rule.

Our rabbis have taught: [If] one was walking outside of a village and saw a light, if it was as thick as the opening of a furnace, he may bless it, and if not, he may not bless it.

The series then continues, pitting one tannaitic teaching against another in regard to related problems of when to bless. It is left to the reader to connect this series to the propositions which have preceded it, and by longer extension to the opening of the larger section, the Mishnah reference, "They do not bless..." This is a simple pericope, but the more difficult ones require more sustained effort to connect propositions. This work of connection, which must be carried out by the reader, is the key in making Bavli systemic.

As far as its relationship to other parts of the Judaic canon, the Bavli never threatens to sink into a traditional literary style. The first place one would look for this would be in Bavli's connection to the Mishnah, whose exegesis it performs. But, rather than conforming to the Mishnah's own program and transmitting its truth with some glosses, Bavli takes the ultimate systemic liberty with the Mishnah by dividing it into small units and not reading it as a whole, unified work. It reads the Mishnah in what Barthes would call the "step-by-step method" through "a systematic use of digression."[11] No respect for the "sanctity" of a transmitted *truth* is present. Bavli views the Mishnah as a systemic document in itself, and then deals with it systemically, never as tradition, never parroting its conclusions. Bavli's connection to Yerushalmi and the rest of the Judaic canon prior to it is exhaustively analyzed in *The Bavli And Its Sources*, yielding almost no trace of reliance on those texts for Bavli's own program. Even with Yerushalmi, which shares the Bavli's program of Mishnah exegesis, points which are pursued in common are few. In Chapter Eight of tractate Berachot, an example representative of many talmud passages, the two Talmuds go their separate ways from the very first questions addressed to a Mishnaic passage.[12] The Bavli makes no attempt to unify its predecessors, and offers no summary of them.

This analysis has made the case that the Bavli is a systemic document. The Bavli satisfies the conditions set out here—for being systemic and for not being traditional—by requiring an active reader through its internal logic, reliant on reason. It pursues a program independent of its predecessors and places little or no weight on the

---

[11] Barthes, *S/Z*, pp. 12-13: "the step-by-step commentary is of necessity a renewal of the entrances to the text, it avoids structuring the text excessively, avoids giving it that additional structure which would close it."

[12] Yerushalmi, after citing Tosefta, pursues an extrapolation of the rule from Shabbat onto Havdalah; Bavli begins by questioning a particular phrase, "What is 'another matter'", reaching havdalah later and even then asking different questions in regard to it.

transmission of an original truth. Everything in the Bavli is subject to change. But this assertion is not a dead end. Since Bavli is Judaism's authoritative statement, holding that it does not in fact continue the program of its predecessors in the canon disrupts the unity of that canon. The idea of Bavli as system then activates us as readers of all of Judaism, letting us divide the canon into, not a unified tradition, but a set of texts independent of one another. We are called on to take the first step, that of division, in reading the entire canon of Judaism, systemically.

Part Two

SOCIETYAND LITERATURE

Chapter Five

The Magician as Outsider: The Evidence of the Hebrew Bible

Stephen D. Ricks
Brigham Young University

Several recent studies on magic in antiquity have stressed its continuity, rather than cleavage, with religion. According to these studies, magic in antiquity was not regarded as a separate institution with a structure distinct from that of religion, but was rather a set of beliefs and practices that deviated sharply from the norms of the dominant social group, and was thus considered antisocial, illegal, or unacceptable.[1] The evidence of the Hebrew Bible corresponds to this

---

[1] David E. Aune, "Magic; Magician," in Geoffrey W. Bromiley, ed., *The International Standard Bible Encyclopedia* (Grand Rapids, MI: W. B. Eerdmans, 1986), 3:213. Cf. Aune, "Magic in Early Christianity," in Wolfgang Haase, ed., *Aufstieg und Niedergang der Römischen Welt* (Berlin: Walter de Gruyter, 1980), 2:23:2, p. 1515. In a similar vein, see Haralds Biezais, *Von der Wesensidentität der Magie und Religion*, in *Acta Academiae Aboensis, Series A: Humaniora* 55:3(1978); note the comment of Jorunn Jacobsen Buckley in the *Abstracts: American Academy of Religion/Society of Biblical Literature Annual Meeting 1986* (Decatur, GA: Scholars Press, 1986), 53, concerning a Mandaean document that "lends itself well to defend the thesis that there is no difference between 'religion' and 'magic'—this distinction is a scholarly evaluative fiction." Among the more recent literature that maintains a solely or primarily structural distinction between "religion" and "magic," see Stephen Benko, "Magic," in Paul J. Achtemeier, ed., *Harper's Bible Dictionary* (San Francisco: Harper and Row, 1985), 594-96; Piera Arata Mantovani, "La magia nei testi preesilici dell'Antico Testamento," *Henoch* 3(1981): 1-21; J. B. Segal, "Popular Religion in Ancient Israel," *Journal of Jewish Studies* 27(1976): 6-7. Among the older works, see, e.g., Arvid Kapelrud, "The Interrelationship between Religion and Magic in Hittite Religion," *Numen* 6(1959): 32-50; A. Lods, "Le rôle des idées magiques dans la mentalité israélite," in *Old*

view of magic. There, it is not the nature of the action itself, but the conformity of the action (or actor) to, or deviation from, the values of Israelite society—as these values are reflected in the canonical text of the Bible—that determines whether it is characterized as magical. Further, magic (as this and related words have been understood in the Hebrew and rendered in versions from the Septuagint to the new Jewish Publication Society translation) is quintessentially the activity of the "outsider" in the Bible.[2] As I am using the term, "outsider" includes both the non-Israelite as well as the native Israelite whose practices deviated sharply from the Israelite norm, particularly because these acts were perceived as being performed through a power other than Israel's God. In this paper I discuss the traditional distinction between magic and religion that has prevailed in Western scholarship since the Reformation, and contrast it with the view of magic and religion in antiquity. Further, I consider accounts from the Hebrew Bible as examples of the magician as "outsider," and show that the characterization of activities in ancient Israel as magical is based upon the norms of Israelite society.

The traditional view of the structural cleavage between magic and religion that has prevailed in Western scholarship in recent centuries is the result, in part at least, of the sharp Protestant reaction to certain Roman Catholic sacraments and other practices. This position was represented at least as early as 1395 by the Lollards in their "Twelve Conclusions":

> That exorcisms and hallowings, made in the Church, of wine, bread, and wax, water, salt and oil and incense, the stone of the altar, upon vestments, mitre, cross, and pilgrims' staves, be the very practice of necromancy, rather than of the holy theology. This conclusion is proved thus. For by such exorcisms creatures be charged to be of higher virtue than their own kind, and we see nothing of change in no

---

Testament Essays: Papers Read Before the Society for Old Testament Study (London: Charles Griffin and Company, 1927), 55-76; A. Lods, "Magie hébraïque et magie cananéenne," *Revue d'Histoire et de Philosophie Religieuses* 7(1927): 1-16.

[2] The matter of the translation and subsequent interpretation of words traditionally rendered as magic is an important one that should not be overlooked in investigations of magic, since the choice of words used in a translation reflects a whole host of *a priori* assumptions made by the writer or translator. For a convenient list of biblical Hebrew terms related to sorcery and their Septuagint equivalents, see G. André, "$ka\bar{s}\bar{a}p$," in G. Johannes Botterweck, Helmer Ringgren, and Heinz-Joseph Fabry, eds., *Theologisches Wörterbuch zum Alten Testament* (Stuttgart: W. Kohlhammer Verlag, 1984), 4:376-77.

such creature that is so charmed, but by false belief, the which is the devil's craft.[3]

According to the Lollard Walter Brute, the very procedures of the priests were modeled on those of the magician. Both thought their spells were more effective when pronounced in one place and at one time rather than another; both turned to the east to say them; and both thought that mere words could possess a magic virtue.[4] But if the Protestants criticized holy water and the consecration of church bells, they launched a frontal assault against the central Catholic doctrine of the Mass. In the view of one Reformer, transubstantiation differed in no significant way from conjurations, "the pretense of a power, plainly magical, of changing the elements in such a sort as all the magicians of Pharaoh could never do, nor had the face to attempt the like, it being so beyond all credibility." John Calvin wrote that the Roman Catholics "pretend there is a magical force in the sacraments, independent of efficacious faith." According to Bishop Hooper, the rite of the Roman Mass was "nothing better to be esteemed than the verses of the sorcerer or enchanter...holy words murmured and spoken in secret."[5] The essential features of magic thus came to be understood as consisting of the automatic efficacy of ritual words (incantations) and procedures (magical operations). Based on this view of the automatic and immediate efficacy of ritual words, a different relationship to Deity (or deities) was posited: magic was said to be manipulative and coercive, while religion (based on the Reformers' views of efficacious faith) was perceived as supplicative.

In contrast to this view of magic that developed during the period of the Reformation, magic in antiquity was viewed as "that form of religious deviance whereby individual or social goals are sought by means alternate to those normally sanctioned by the dominant religious institution."[6] As Jonathan Z. Smith and Morton Smith have shown in the case of the Greco-Roman world, magic and magical practices are *par excellence* the activities of the outsider.[7] According to Jonathan

---

[3] Cited by H. S. Cronin in "The Twelve Conclusions of the Lollards," *English Historical Review* 22(1907): 298.

[4] John Foxe, *The Acts and Monuments of Matters Most Special and Memorable* (London: Adam Islip, Foelix Kingston and Robert Young, 1632), 3:179-80, cited in Keith Thomas, *Religion and the Decline of Magic* (New York: Charles Scribner's Sons, 1971), 52.

[5] Thomas, *Religion and the Decline of Magic*, 53.

[6] Aune, "Magic in Early Christianity," p. 1515.

[7] Jonathan Z. Smith, "Good News Is No News: Aretalogy and Gospel," in *Map Is Not Territory* (Leiden: Brill, 1978), 163, and Morton Smith, *Clement of*

Smith, in the Greco-Roman world "Magic was not different in essence from religion, but rather different with regard to social position.... The one universal characteristic of magic" is that "it is illegal,... and it carried the penalty of death or deportation."[8] In the same vein, Morton Smith notes, "In the Roman Empire, the practice of magic was a criminal offense (Paulus *Sententiae* 5:23.14-18), and the 'magician' was therefore a term of abuse. It still is, but the connotation has changed: now it is primarily fraud; then it was social subversion."[9] As in the Greco-Roman world, magic in the Bible was a practice of the outsider. It was also perceived as a form of subversion, and was consequently severely punished, since it was viewed as undermining Israel's religious foundations.

The biblical accounts that most lucidly show magicians as outsiders and refute a simple definition of magic as the employment of words and actions that function *ex opere operato* (i.e., have their desired effect merely by being performed or spoken) are the stories of Moses and Aaron and Pharaoh's wise men and magicians, Joseph and the wise men and magicians of Pharaoh, and Daniel and the Babylonian astrologers and wizards. According to the account in Exodus 7-9, the Lord said to Moses and Aaron, "When Pharaoh speaks to you and says, 'Produce your marvel' (Heb. מוֹפֵת), you shall say to Aaron, 'Take your rod and cast it down before Pharaoh.' It shall turn into a serpent" (Ex. 7:8-9). They went before the Pharaoh and did precisely that: Aaron cast down his rod in the presence of Pharaoh, and it turned into a serpent. The Pharaoh then summoned his own wise men (חֲכָמִים) and sorcerers (מְכַשְּׁפִים), and the Egyptian magicians did the same thing with their spells (כְּ וַיַּעֲשׂוּ גַם־הֵם חַרְטֻמֵּי מִצְרַיִם בְּלַהֲטֵיהֶם) (Ex. 7:11). Though the rods of the Egyptian magicians were able to become serpents, Aaron's rod swallowed all of their rods. The Egyptian wise men and sorcerers were further able to imitate Moses and Aaron in the turning of the bodies of water of Egypt into blood and in bringing frogs upon the land by their spells (בְּלָטֵיהֶם), but they failed in their efforts to produce lice (כִּנִּים); they were fully discomfited when the boils affected them as they did

---

Alexandria and a Secret Gospel of Mark (Cambridge, MA: Harvard University Press, 1973), 221.

[8] J. Z. Smith, "Good News Is No News," 163; cf. Jules Maurice, "La terreur de la magie au IV. siècle," *Comptes rendus de l'Academie des Inscriptions et Belles-Lettres* (1926): 188.

[9] M. Smith, *Clement of Alexandria*, 221. In the light of this statement, it is significant—and telling—that one of Smith's subsequent books is entitled *Jesus the Magician*.

the other Egyptians, so that they were not even able to stand before Pharaoh.

In Genesis 41, Pharaoh had dreams that left him troubled. He sent for his magicians (חַרְטֻמֵּי מִצְרַיִם) and for his wise men (חֲכָמֶיהָ) to interpret his dreams for him. After Pharaoh had told them his dreams, the magicians and wise men said that they were not able to interpret them for him. At this point the chief cupbearer remembered Joseph, who was then called before Pharaoh and was able, through the gift of God (Gen. 41:16) to interpret Pharaoh's dreams to his satisfaction.

In Daniel 2, Nebuchadnezzar, like Pharaoh, had dreams that left his spirit agitated, whereupon he called his magicians (חַרְטֻמִּים), exorcists (אַשָּׁפִים), sorcerers (מְכַשְּׁפִים), and Chaldaeans (כַּשְׂדִּים) to tell him what he had dreamed. They were threatened with death if they failed to produce for him both his dream and its interpretation, but they claimed that such a demand as the king was making of them had never been made of a magician, exorcist, or Chaldaean before: "The thing asked by the king is difficult; there is no one who can tell it to the king except the gods whose abodes are not among mortals" (Dan. 2:11). Thereupon the king flew into a violent rage, and gave an order to kill all of the wise men of Babylon. However, Daniel, who would also have fallen under this death order, was able to interpret the dream through the power of the "God of heaven," thereby saving himself and the others from death.

Several significant features in these stories that are relevant to our subject are worth noting: In each of these three instances, Israelites are pitted against practitioners of the religion of non-Israelite "outsiders," and in each instance the superior power of God is shown. When the magicians and wise men of Pharaoh are not able to produce lice by their own spells, they exclaim to Pharaoh, "This is the finger of God" (הוא אֶצְבַּע אֱלֹהִים) (Ex. 8:15). Daniel similarly emphasizes Israel's God as the source of his power and its superiority to the power of the wise men and magicians: "The mystery about which the king has inquired—wise men, exorcists, magicians, and diviners cannot tell to the king. But there is a God in heaven who reveals mysteries, and He has made known to King Nebuchadnezzar what is to be at the end of days" (Dan. 2:27-28). Further, in the instances of Joseph and Daniel, there is no clear indication given of the specific manner in which they show themselves superior to the Egyptian and Babylonian magicians, except through prayer and the power of God. However, in the case of Moses and Aaron in Pharaoh's court, the action by which the effect was achieved was the same (וַיַּעֲשׂוּ גַם־הֵם חַרְטֻמֵּי מִצְרַיִם בְּלָהֲטֵיהֶם כֵּן). In addition, the very word used here in the text for the Egyptian magicians—חַרְטֹם (in the phrase חַרְטֻמֵּי מִצְרַיִם)—is borrowed from the Egyptian ḥr tp, "lector priest," one who, in Egyptian materials at least, is not generally associated with magic (for which the regular Egyptian word is ḥkʾ).[10] This suggests to me an implicit polemic in the text against all practitioners of Egyptian religion; they are all magicians because they are non-Yahwists.

In contrast to my analysis, Jacob Milgrom has interpreted the Moses passage with a principle that reflects Reformation assumptions about magic. Milgrom has pointed out that before the performance of each miracle, Moses is silent; Pharaoh's magicians, on the other hand, are only able to copy Aaron's actions "by their spells" (בְּלָטֵיהֶם—if we follow the rendering of the new Jewish Publication Society translation, rather than the more traditional translation, "by their secret arts").[11] By acting alone, and not speaking, Moses behaves in a manner that is distinct from that of the Egyptians (which is, by implication, "magical"). I find this position somewhat unsatisfying. As Milgrom himself notes, later Israelite prophets do not refrain from speaking while performing their wonders. Thus, Elijah said to King Ahab, "As the Lord, the God of Israel lives, whom I serve, there will be no dew nor rain in the next few years except at my word" (1 Kings 17:1). During his contest with the priests of Baal on Mount Carmel, Elijah both speaks and acts (1 Kings 18:16-46). Similarly, Elisha speaks and acts when miraculously providing oil for the widow (2 Kings 4:2-7). If the essence of magic is acting and speaking together when performing wonders, why are these prophets never referred to as "magicians" or "sorcerers" in the text of the Bible, despite its rich vocabulary for describing practitioners of such arts? Furthermore, practitioners of numerous normative religious traditions, both ancient and modern, include both words and actions in their rites. By the definition of magic that Milgrom uses, these actions would also become "magical." His definition is based upon notions that only gained wide currency during the Reformation (described above). That is, they are the direct result of the protestant polemic against Catholicism. Milgrom's interpretation thus stems from theological assumptions extrinsic to the Hebrew Bible.[12] Instead, the decisive element in all of these accounts—of Elijah and Elisha, as well as Moses—is the Israelite, Yahwist context.[13] Since the prophets represent Israel's God, they are

[10] Adolf Erman and Hermann Grapow, *Ägyptisch-Deutsches Wörterbuch*, 6 vols. (Leipzig: J. Hinrichs, 1929), 3:177.

[11] Jacob Milgrom, "Magic, Monotheism, and the Sin of Moses," in H. B. Huffmon, F. A. Spina, A. R. W. Green, eds., *The Quest for the Kingdom of God: Studies in Honor of George E. Mendenhall* (Winona Lake, IN: Eisenbrauns, 1983), 251-65.

[12] Aune, "Magic," 213.

[13] I readily concede that Moses may be shown as refraining from speaking in order to distinguish him from the "magicians" and "sorcerers" in Pharaoh's court, but I question whether these Egyptians are thus described because they

not magicians. Their opponents, who have no link to Yahweh or to normative Israelite society, are by definition magicians.

Probably the best-known list of prohibited practices in the Pentateuch is found in Deut. 18:10-11: "Let no one be found among you who consigns his son or daughter to the fire, or who is an augur (קֹסֵם קְסָמִים), a soothsayer (מְעוֹנֵן), a diviner (מְנַחֵשׁ), a sorcerer (מְכַשֵּׁף), one who casts spells (חֹבֵר חָבֶר), one who consults ghosts or familiar spirits (שֹׁאֵל אוֹב וְיִדְּעֹנִי), or one who makes inquiries of the dead (וְדֹרֵשׁ אֶל הַמֵּתִים)." These activities are typically the practices of the outsider, as the context of the list makes clear: not merely are they considered abhorrent practices (תּוֹעֵבֹת) when performed by Israelites, but their abhorrent nature is at least in part the result of their being observed by Israel's neighbors, as the wider context of the pericope shows. The verse immediately preceding the list of prohibited practices begins: "When you enter the land that the Lord your God is giving you, you shall not learn to imitate the abhorrent practices of those nations." Further, these practices of the people of the land form one of the grounds for their being dispossessed, as the passage following the list indicates: "For anyone who does such things is abhorrent to the Lord , and it is because of these abhorrent things that the Lord your God is dispossessing them before you. You must be wholehearted with the Lord your God. Those nations that you are about to dispossess do indeed resort to soothsayers and augurs; to you, however, the Lord your God has not assigned the like" (Deut. 18:12-14).

There are a score or so of words in the Hebrew Bible that refer to practices or practitioners of magic (as it is generally understood), falling roughly into the categories of magic in general or sorcery, divination, and astrology (these categories, it should be pointed out, are not explicit in the Bible itself: in none of these lists are these types of magical practices expressly divided).[14] The terms and roots from which words generally understood as magic and sorcery are derived include: אַשָּׁף,[15] חַרְטֹם,[16] כֶּשֶׁר,[17] כשׁף,[18] לחשׁ,[19] שׁחר.[20] To the groups of words

---

speak when performing their acts, rather than because they are non-Israelites and non-Yahwists.

[14] These categorical distinctions are to be found in G. André, "ka͏̄ṣ̌ap," 379.

[15] Dan. 1:20, 2:2, 10, 27, 4:4, 5:7, 11, 15.

[16] Gen. 41:8, 24; Ex. 7:11, 22, 8:3, 14, 15, 9:11; Dan. 1:20, 2:2, 10, 27, 4:4, 6, 5:11.

[17] Dan. 2:2, 4, 5, 10 (2x), 4:4, 5:7, 11.

[18] Ex. 7:11, 22:17; Deut. 18:10; 2 Kings 9:22; Is. 47:9, 12; Jer. 27:9; Micah 5:11; Nahum 3:4; Mal. 3:5; Dan. 2:21.

[19] 2 Sam. 12:19; Is. 3:3, 20, 26:16; Ps. 41:8, 58:6; Eccles. 10:11.

[20] Is. 47:11, 15.

denoting divination belong אוֹב,[21] חבר,[22] יִדְּעֹנִי,[23] נחש,[24] ענן,[25] and קסם.[26] The groups of words denoting astrology include גזר (probably),[27] שָׁמַיִם חֹבְרֵי,[28] and הַחֹזִים בַּכּוֹכָבִים.[29] Roughly three-quarters of the occurrences of these words refer, explicitly or implicitly, to non-Israelite practitioners or activities. Indeed, some of these words (אַשָּׁף "exorcist," גזר "astrologer," חַרְטֹם "magician") are used exclusively of non-Israelites. At least three (אוֹב "familiar spirit, sorcerer," אַשָּׁף, חַרְטֹם) are most likely of foreign origin. As I have noted above, חַרְטֹם is Egyptian in origin, אַשָּׁף derives from Akkadian, while אוֹב appears to be a non-Semitic migratory word that is found in Sumerian, Akkadian, Hurrian, Hittite, and Ugaritic.[30]

The remaining quarter of the occurrences of the terms for magicians and magical practices refers to prohibited Israelite practices or to Israelites engaged in these forbidden practices. In no case have I found any of these terms used favorably of an Israelite practice. For example, in Isaiah 3:2, the "augur" (קֹסֵם) is mentioned together with warrior, priest, and king; in Micah 3:6, 7, 11, the "augur" (קֹסֵם) is mentioned together with the prophet. If there is no explicit disapproval of the diviner in either of these passages, neither is there anything like approval: both passages occur in oracles of doom prophesied against all of these persons.

Even in those instances where there is no strongly negative tinge to the words for magic and magician, they refer either to non-Israelites or to Israelites in a non-Israelite setting.[31] Thus, Laban says to Jacob at one point, "If you will indulge me, I have learned by divination that the Lord has blessed me on your account" (Gen. 34:27). Similarly,

---

[21] Lev. 19:31, 20:6, 27; Deut. 18:11; 1 Sam. 28:3, 7, 8, 9; 2 Kings 21:6, 23:24; Is. 8:19, 19:3, 29:4; 1 Chron. 10:13; 2 Chron. 33:6.

[22] Deut. 18:11; Is. 47:9, 12; Ps. 58:6

[23] Lev. 19:31, 20:6, 27; Deut. 18:11; 1 Sam. 28:3, 9; 2 Kings 21:6, 23:24; Is. 8:19, 19:3; 2 Chron. 33:6.

[24] Gen. 30:27, 44:5, 15; Lev. 19:26; Num. 23:23; Deut. 18:10; 1 Kings 20:33; 2 Kings 17:17, 21:6; 2 Chron. 33:6.

[25] Lev. 19:26; Deut. 18:10, 14; 2 Kings 21:6; Is. 2:6, 57:3; Jer. 27:9; Micah 5:11; 2 Chron. 33:6.

[26] Num. 22:7, 23:23; Deut. 18:10; Jos. 13:22; 1 Sam. 6:2, 15:23, 28:8; 2 Kings 17:17; Is. 3:2, 44:25; Jer. 14:14, 27:9, 29:8; Ezek. 12:24, 13:6, 7, 9, 23, 21:26, 27, 28, 34, 22:28; Micah 3:6, 7, 11.

[27] Dan. 2:27, 34, 45, 4:4, 5:7, 5:11.

[28] Is. 47:13.

[29] Is. 47:13.

[30] Harry A. Hoffner, "ôbh," in G. Johannes Botterweck and Helmer Ringgren, *Theological Dictionary of the Old Testament*, tr. John T. Willis (Grand Rapids: Eerdmans, 1974), 1:131.

[31] E.g., Gen. 30:27, 44:5, 15; 1 Kings 20:33.

Joseph tells his servant to follow after Joseph's brothers and to accuse them of having willfully taken his cup: "Up, go after the men! And when you overtake them, say to them, 'Why did you repay good with evil? It is the very one from which my master drinks and which he uses for divination" (Gen. 44:5).

The three divinatory instruments regularly associated with the Israelite cultus—lots (גּוֹרָל),[32] Urim and Thummim,[33] and ephod[34]— have a distinct vocabulary associated with them. Unlike any of the words mentioned above, these terms are used primarily in connection with Israelites, only occasionally with non-Israelites,[35] and invariably in a favorable, or neutral, context. Nowhere in the Hebrew Bible is there a detailed description of the method by which these divinatory instruments are used. Because of this, there is no way to compare the divinatory methods used in connection with the lot, ephod, and Urim and Thummim with the techniques used by the אוֹב, מְעוֹנֵן, מְנַחֵשׁ, יִדְּעֹנִי, חֹבֵר, and קֹסֵם, all of whom were viewed as magicians by the writers of the Hebrew Bible viewed as magicians. The decisive difference between the two groups is their association with, or estrangement from, Israel's religion and cultus: the ephod, Urim and Thummim, and lots are acceptable because they are Israelite, while the others are rejected because they are not.

Haralds Biezais, in his study on the relationship between religion and magic, denies any formal distinction between the two, claiming that all such presumed differences are ideologically motivated.[36] Although starkly formulated, I think that Biezais' observation contains a fundamentally important insight: where on the religion-magic continuum religion ends and magic begins depends upon the stance of the person speaking or writing since it is not possible to divide religion and magic on the basis of any objective set of criteria.[37] In the

---

[32] Lev. 16:8; Num. 26:55; Josh. 7:14, 14:2; 1 Sam. 10:16-26, 14:42; Dan. 12:13; Joel 1:3; Ps. 22:18; Prov. 18:18; 1 Chron. 24:5, 25:8, 26:13. The פּוּר explicitly identified with the גּוֹרָל in Esther 3:7, was used by Haman to determine the month and day on which to carry out the pogrom against the Jews.

[33] Ex. 28:30; Lev. 8:8; Num. 27:21; Deut. 33:8; 1 Sam. 14:41, 28:6; Ez. 2:63, Neh. 7:65.

[34] 1 Sam. 23:9-12, 30:7-8.

[35] E.g., Jonah 1:7; Obad. 11; Nahum 3:10.

[36] Biezais, Wesensidentität, 30.

[37] Based on empirical differences reported by field workers among modern nonliterate peoples, the anthropologist William J. Goode, in three studies, "Magic and Religion: A Continuum," Ethnos 14(1949): 172-82; Religion among the Primitives (Glencoe, IL: Free Press, 1951), 50-55; and, most recently, in "Comment on: 'Malinowski's Magic: The Riddle of the Empty Cell,'" Current Anthropology 17:4 (December 1976): 677, has suggested a more reticulated model of "nondichotomous empirical differences" between magic and religion than that proposed by Biezais. However, in Goode's model, too, the element of

case of the Hebrew Bible, the major factor dividing acts that might be termed "magical" from those that might be termed "religious" is the perceived power by which the action is performed. Acts performed by the power of Israel's God are, in the view of the writers of the Hebrew Bible, by that very fact nonmagical, even where they may be formally indistinguishable from those that are depicted as magical. "Magic," "magician," and related terms describing practices mentioned in the Hebrew Bible thus remain useful designations in discussions of the life of ancient Israel only as long as one takes into consideration the internal categories of the writers of the Bible itself and retains a sensitivity to the subjective nature and potentially pejorative connotations of these terms.

---

group and individual perspective remains a dominant feature, and his view of the continuity between magic and religion underscores the subjective nature of the distinction between the two.

Chapter Six

PASSOVER LEGISLATION AND THE IDENTITY OF THE CHRONICLER'S LAW BOOK

Judson R. Shaver
Seattle University

The books of Chronicles, Ezra, and Nehemiah create a literary world in which divine retribution is a given. The characters in this world must obey the law of Yahweh in order to prosper; if they disobey they will surely perish. Fortunately for them, it is not difficult to determine exactly what God requires. This is because a Book of Law exists in this literary world, a book which Yahweh gave to Israel through Moses at the time Israel became his people.

But what exactly did this book contain? We find no clear answer in the books of Chronicles, Ezra, and Nehemiah. We do find, however, many explicit references to this book of law,[1] most of which disclose something of the history, nature, or contents that the Chronicler attributes to it.[2] Thus we learn that Yahweh gave the Torah *book*, not just Torah, to Moses (2 Chr. 34:14), that it was available during the time of David (1 Chr. 16:39f.), and that it was taught throughout Judah

---

[1] It is variously described as "the book of Moses" (2 Chr. 25:4; 35:12; Ezra 6:18; Neh. 13:1), "the law of Moses" (2 Chr. 23:18; 30:16; Ezra 3:2), "the book of the law of Moses" (Neh. 8:1), "the law of God" (Neh. 8:8), "the law of YHWH" (1 Chr. 16:40; 2 Chr. 31:3; 35:26), "the book of the law of YHWH" (2 Chr. 17:9; 34:14; Neh. 9:3), "the book of the law of God" (Neh. 8:18), "the book of the law" (2 Chr. 34:15; Neh. 8:3), or simply "the book" (2 Chr. 34:15, 16, 21, 24; Neh. 8:5, 8).

[2] I use the term for convenience. I take the Chronicler's History Work to be the books of Chronicles, Ezra, and Nehemiah, but assume that they have had a long and largely unrecoverable editorial history.

135

during the reign of Jehoshaphat (2 Chr. 17:7-9). On its authority Jehoiada initiated a religious reform (2 Chr. 23:18), it was obeyed by Amaziah (2 Chr. 25:4), and it authorized Hezekiah's reform (2 Chr. 29-32). Having apparently been lost during the reigns of Manasseh and Amon, it was discovered in the reign of Josiah (2 Chr. 34). According to Ezra and Nehemiah, it provided the basis on which the returned exiles rebuilt the altar (Ezra 3:1-3) and reestablished the sacrificial cult in Jerusalem (Ezra 6:4, 18). Ezra read it to the assembled people (Ezra 7, Neh. 8-9), and both Ezra and Nehemiah enforced it (Ezra 9-10, Neh. 13).

In short, according to the Chronicler the book of Torah originated in Mosaic times, and had provided the authoritative blueprint for Israelite life and worship ever since. The Chronicler cites this divine, written authority when on thirteen occasions he uses the formula "as it is written in the book of Moses" (ככתוב בספר משה), or its equivalent, to describe the manner in which some (usually ritual) act was (or should have been) carried out.[3]

These citations, with their emphasis on the divine authority of the law book, heighten the reader's interest in the book's identity. To what exactly did the Chronicler refer when he wrote "as it is written in the book of Moses" (ככתוב בספר משה)?

Since ancient times the Chronicler's law book has been identified as the Torah or Pentateuch.[4] In the modern period Wellhausen held this position, and it continues to find support.[5] An analysis of the Chronicler's accounts of Passover and Unleavened Bread, however, will show that it is untenable. Although the formulaic expressions "as it is written" (ככתוב), "according to the Torah of Moses" (כתורת משה), "according to the word of Yahweh by Moses" (כדבר-יהוה ביד משה), "according to the ordinance" (כמשפט), and "as it is written in the book of Moses" (ככתוב בספר משה) usually refer to legislation now in the Pentateuch (in collections of legal material generally identified as

---

[3] 2 Chr. 35:12. See also 2 Chr. 23:18; 25:4; 30:5, 18; 31:3; 35:26; Ezra 3:2, 4; 6:18 (Aramaic); Neh. 8:15; 10:35, 37. Cf. 1 Chr. 16:40 (לכל-הכתוב) and 2 Chr. 34:21 (ככל-הכתוב).

[4] b. Baba Bathra 14b-15a; cf. 2 Esdras 14:37-48.

[5] Julius Wellhausen, *Prolegomena to the History of Ancient Israel* (Gloucester, 1957), pp. 405-410. See Otto Eissfeldt, *The Old Testament: An Introduction* (New York, 1965), p. 557; Ernst Sellin and George Fohrer, *Introduction to the Old Testament* (Nashville, 1968), p. 192; Jacob M. Myers, *Ezra. Nehemiah* (Garden City, 1965), pp. 62, 153; H. H. Schaeder, *Esra der Schreiber* (Tübingen, 1930), p. 63f.; H. Cazelles, "La Mission d' Esdras," *VT*, IV (1954), 113-140; R. J. Coggins, *The Books of Ezra and Nehemiah* (Cambridge, 1976), p. 108; Peter Ackroyd, *1 and 2 Chronicles, Ezra, Nehemiah* (London, 1973), p. 298, apparently; F. Charles Fensham, *The Books of Ezra and Nehemiah* (Grand Rapids, 1982), p. 105; H. G. M. Williamson, *1 and 2 Chronicles* (Grand Rapids, 1982), pp. 402, 406.

either JE, D, H, P, or late supplements either to P or to the Pentateuch as a whole), the cited book cannot be identified with the Pentateuch or any of its posited sources or major redactional stages.[6]

Passover and Unleavened Bread

The present books of Chronicles, Ezra, and Nehemiah describe three celebrations of the feast of Passover and Unleavened Bread. The people kept the feast as a part of Hezekiah's reform following the repair and rededication of the temple (2 Chr. 30:1-27), as a part of the reforms of Josiah, following the repair of the temple (2 Chr. 35:1-19), and finally as a part of the post-exilic restoration of the cult in Jerusalem immediately following the dedication of the second temple (Ezra 6:19-22).

The descriptions of the feasts of Hezekiah and Josiah include a number of details on the exact manner in which the feast was kept. Moreover, at several points in these narratives the Chronicler notes explicitly that some of these details conformed to the written law.[7] Clearly the Chronicler believed that the correct ritual for Passover and Unleavened Bread was based on authoritative texts. But which ones? Many scholars, following Wellhausen, have found the influence of P pervasive in the Chronicler's History. Roland de Vaux, a representative of this view, argued that the Chronicler's descriptions of the feast are in accord with P and not Deuteronomy.[8] Gerhard von Rad, by contrast, argued at length that the Chronicler was influenced at least as much by Deuteronomy as by P,[9] and specifically that the Chronicler's descriptions of Passover and Unleavened Bread depend almost entirely on Deuteronomy.[10] My analysis of the texts in question yields more complex results.

I begin by describing the canonical stipulations for Passover and the feast of Unleavened Bread as they are found in the various pentateuchal law codes and Ezekiel. I then examine the Chronicler's three accounts of the feast. By comparing these accounts with the legislation surveyed in the first part of the article, I am able to show that some of the details of the Chronicler's accounts of Passover and Unleavened Bread conform to the requirements of P, some to D, and others to one of the other pentateuchal legal collections. Some of the details, however, appear to reflect the program of Ezekiel, and others,

---

[6] 2 Chr. 30:5, 16, 18; 35:6, 12, 13.

[7] "As it is written" (כַּכָּתוּב) occurs at 2 Chr. 30:5, 18; 35:12. Cf. 2 Chr. 30:16; 35:6, 13.

[8] Roland de Vaux, *Ancient Israel* (London, 1961), p. 487.

[9] Gerhard von Rad, *Das Geschichtsbild des Chronistischen Werkes* (Stuttgart, 1930), pp. 38-63.

[10] von Rad, *Geschichtsbild*, pp. 52-53.

although attributed to the book or law of Moses, have no antecedent basis in the Hebrew Bible.

Israel's Early Traditions

Israel's earliest religious calendars, Ex. 23:14-17 and Ex. 34:18-23, both describe the feast of Unleavened Bread (חג המצות), but neither refers to Passover.[11] The Yahwist's instructions for Passover (Ex. 12:21-23, 27b, 39) are likewise ancient, but make no mention of the feast of Unleavened Bread.[12]

According to Ex. 23:15, the feast of Unleavened Bread was one of the three annual pilgrimage feasts kept to Yahweh. The verse has probably been expanded at the end, but in its original form it stipulated a seven-day feast in the month of Abib during which unleavened bread was to be eaten.[13] Exodus 34:18, likewise expanded, provides the same instruction, but nothing further.[14]

Passover is not included in these early calendars for two reasons. In the first place, the three annual feasts were Canaanite agricultural feasts which Israel adopted and then kept to Yahweh,[15] while Passover had a different origin.[16] Secondly, as the J account of the Passover ritual (Ex. 12:21-23, 27b) makes clear, Passover—at least after the settlement in Canaan—was not a pilgrimage feast but a family celebration; it was only later joined to the feast of Unleavened Bread.[17]

The Yahwist (Ex. 12:21-23, 27b, 39), by contrast, does not mention the feast of Unleavened Bread, but does provide detailed instructions for keeping the Passover. The elders of the community must select a lamb or kid (צאן) for their respective families. Each elder then kills the Passover victim (שחט הפסח) for his family and dabs its blood around the doorway of the house in which the family observes the Passover. If the Yahwist originally included a date for this meal, it was lost in

---

[11] de Vaux, *Ancient Israel*, pp. 471, 486. Ex. 34:25 refers to Passover and terms it a "pilgrimage feast" (חג), probably influenced by the reference to a חג in the parallel Lev. 23:18 (which, however, does not refer to Passover). Since Passover is not identified as a חג until Deuteronomy, the editing of these texts must be later than D. Cf. Martin Noth, *Exodus* (Philadelphia, 1962), pp. 190-192, 264f.

[12] But cf. v. 39 which mentions the quickly made "unleavened cakes" (מצות).

[13] Noth, *Exodus*, p. 190. The date is not specified because the feast was originally tied to the harvest which would vary from year to year. de Vaux, *Ancient Israel*, pp. 471.

[14] Noth, *Exodus*, p. 265.

[15] Noth, *Exodus*, p. 190f.; de Vaux, *Ancient Israel*, p. 471.

[16] Cf. de Vaux, *Ancient Israel*, pp. 488-490; J. B. Segal, *The Hebrew Passover: From the Earliest Times to A.D. 70*, (London, 1963), pp. 78-113.

[17] de Vaux, *Ancient Israel*, p. 488; Noth, *Exodus*, p. 191.

the editorial process of incorporating J's instructions for the Passover into the P narrative of Ex. 12.

Deuteronomy

The religious calendar of Deuteronomy (16:1-17) in its section on Passover and the feast of Unleavened Bread (vv. 1-8) introduces a number of important changes and additions to the required ritual. The most important of these is the transformation of the formerly familial Passover celebration into a pilgrimage feast. Passover is no longer to be celebrated "within any of your towns...but at the place which the Lord your God will choose" (Deut. 16:5f.). The people must assemble in Jerusalem for Passover and return to their homes *the next morning* (v.7). The requirements for the seven-day feast of Unleavened Bread, which assume that the people have already returned home from the pilgrimage, are clearly secondary.[18]

As a consequence of this centralization of the celebration, Passover becomes a part of the temple's sacrificial ritual. The people no longer simply kill (שחט, cf. Ex. 12:21, J) the Passover victim; they now sacrifice (זבח, Deut. 16:2, 5) it.[19] The people may now sacrifice an ox as well as a lamb or kid (v. 2, צאן ובקר), but in any case they must boil (בשל, v.7) it. Finally, as in former times, Passover occurs on the evening of an unspecified day in the month of Abib (vv. 1, 6).

The Holiness Code

The religious calendar of the Holiness Code (Lev. 23) reflects two major developments in the manner of keeping Passover and the feast of Unleavened Bread. In the first place, the two are now clearly associated; and secondly, both are precisely fixed in the liturgical calendar (Lev. 23:5-8). Passover takes place on the fourteenth day of the seventh month and is followed by the seven day feast of Unleavened Bread. The text says nothing more about Passover, but emphasizes instead the ritual of the feast of Unleavened Bread. For seven days the people must eat unleavened bread (v. 6). On the first and seventh day they may do no work; it is a holy convocation (מקרא־קדש vv. 7f.). Finally, fire offerings (אשה) are to be presented (קרב) on each of the seven days of the feast (v. 8).

Ezekiel

Passover and the feast of Unleavened Bread are first associated in the Holiness Code; in Ezek. 45:21-24 they are for the first time viewed

---

[18] As are 3a$^\beta$, 4. von Rad, *Deuteronomy*, p. 112f.; de Vaux, *Ancient Israel*, p. 485f. Note also that the Deuteronomistic account of the Passover of Josiah (2 Kgs. 23:21-23) indicates that it was a pilgrimage feast kept in Jerusalem, and that it too lacks any reference to the feast of Unleavened Bread.

[19] זבח is used in Ex. 34:25, but is an addition to J based on D. Cf. n. 11.

as one feast (חג, v. 21). As in Lev. 23 the feast begins on the fourteenth day of the first month; the people must eat unleavened bread for seven days during which time the prince must also arrange for required daily animal sacrifices. Ezekiel does not mention a holy convocation (מקרא־קדש) on the first and last day of the feast, but—unlike the Holiness Code—specifies the required sacrifices. On the fourteenth of the month, the people offer a bull (פר) as a sin offering (חטאת) and on each of the following seven days they sacrifice seven bulls and seven lambs (אילים) as a burnt offering (עולה) as well as one goat (עז) as a sin offering. In addition, they must make cereal and oil offerings in specific measure. Finally, although unparalleled in Israel's codes of law, Ezekiel requires the prince (נשיא) to provide all the animals, cereal and oil for these sacrifices.[20]

The Priestly Code

Our survey of biblical texts which describe the requirements for observing Passover and the feast of Unleavened Bread has to this point revealed a progressive development. The two celebrations have been brought together, dated precisely, and made a part of the central sacrificial cult. In addition a number of details specifying the source, kind, number, and manner of the sacrifices have been added. The Priestly Code's treatment of Passover and Unleavened Bread (Ex. 12:1-20) does not, however, continue on this trajectory. Instead, on major issues P rejects Deuteronomic and subsequent stipulations in favor of earlier practices.

The most obvious and important of these changes is that P completely removes Passover and Unleavened Bread from the temple cult. Gone are all references to burnt offerings and sacrifices, including even the fire offerings (אשים) of H (Lev. 23:8). The lamb or kid, no longer sacrificed as in Deuteronomy (16:2, 5, 6), is now simply killed (שחט, v. 6) as in J (Ex. 12:21). This takes place not in Jerusalem (cf. Deut. 16:5ff.) but in each private home (v. 5f.). As in J (Ex. 12:22) blood is smeared on the doorway (v. 7). In a direct correction of Deut. 16:7, P (Ex. 12:8f.) stipulates that the lamb or kid be roasted with fire (צלי־אש) and not boiled in water (ובשל מבשל במים).[21] Finally, the animal is to be eaten in haste with unleavened bread and bitter herbs in memory of the exodus; what is uneaten must be burned (vv. 8, 10f., 14).

---

[20] The people contribute to the prince who then apportions the material as the ritual requires (Ezek. 45:13-16).

[21] von Rad, *Deuteronomy*, p. 112, suggests that the Deuteronomic requirement of boiling the meat "probably corresponds to the custom at the sanctuaries where the meat to be eaten by the worshipping congregation was boiled in large cauldrons (1 Sam. 2:12ff.)." If this is correct the requirement that it be roasted and not boiled may be a part of P's decentralization of the Passover.

P has not, however, changed every detail. Passover is still closely joined to the feast of Unleavened Bread.[22] The dates remain the same (Ex. 12:18), and like the Holiness Code (Lev. 23:7), but unlike Ezekiel, P stipulates that Unleavened Bread begin and end with a holy convocation (מקרא־קדש, Ex. 12:16).

There are also certain refinements. According to P the selection of the passover animal must take place on the tenth day of the first month (v. 3), and the animal itself must be an unblemished one year old male from the flock (שה, vv. 3, 4, 5), either a lamb or a kid (כבש, עז, v. 5).

Numbers 28:16-25

No trace of P's revision remains in Num. 28:16-25, the latest stratum of pentateuchal legislation for Passover and the feast of Unleavened Bread. In fact, nothing is said of Passover itself except that it is on the fourteenth day of the first month. While this is also the date in P (Ex. 12:6, 18), it is clear from the virtual identity of Num. 28:16-19a, 25 and Lev. 23:5-8 (H) that this late text depends on H rather than the priestly Ex. 12:1-20. Thus, like Lev. 23:5-8, our text stipulates that Passover is on the fourteenth day of the seventh month and is followed by the seven-day feast of Unleavened Bread, the first and seventh day of which are marked by their mandatory holy convocation (מקרא־קדש, vv. 16, 17, 25). Moreover, following H (Lev. 23:8) instead of P, daily offerings by fire (אשה) are to be made for the duration of the feast. Numbers 28:16-25 goes beyond H at this point, however, and in doing so is reminiscent of Ezek. 45:21-24. In particular, the required daily offering by fire (אשה, Lev. 23:8, Num. 28:19) is further identified as a burnt offering (עולה) and its contents are specified: two young bulls, one ram and seven male lambs a year old together with specified amounts of flour and oil for a cereal offering, and finally one male goat for a sin offering (vv. 19-24). As we have seen, Ezek. 45:23f requires a very similar burnt offering (עולה) on each of the feast's seven days.

Passover and Unleavened Bread
in the Chronicler's History

Having reviewed all of ancient Israel's canonical legislation for Passover and the feast of Unleavened Bread, I turn now to the Chronicler's three narrative accounts of the feast. As I have indicated above, the Chronicler claims in a number of texts that various details of the ritual were performed "as it is written" (ככתוב), "according to the Torah of Moses" (כתורת משה), "according to the word of Yahweh by Moses" (כדבר־יהוה ביד משה), "according to the ordinance" (כמשפט), or "as it

---

[22] It is difficult, however, to imagine Israel having a peaceful seven day feast of Unleavened Bread following the night of the Passover in Egypt. Cf. Noth, *Exodus*, p. 97.

is written in the book of Moses" (כתוב בספר משה).[23] A comparison of these details with the requirements of the legislation surveyed above will demonstrate the Chronicler's complex and eclectic use of Israelite legal tradition. Although he regards legislation from each of the Pentateuch's legal collections as authoritative, his book of law is neither the Pentateuch nor any of its sources.

The Passover of Hezekiah: 2 Chronicles 30:1-27

The Chronicler's first and longest narrative of a feast of Passover and Unleavened Bread is not derived from 2 Kings. It is widely regarded to be the Chronicler's own composition, although it may have been based on a description of Unleavened Bread which can no longer be recovered.[24] In what follows, I will examine the specific details of how the feast was celebrated and attempt to describe their relationships to antecedent Israelite law.

1) <u>The place where Passover and Unleavened Bread was kept.</u>
2 Chronicles 30:1, 3, 5, and 13 stress the requirement that all Israel should assemble in Jerusalem for the feast of Passover and Unleaveı ed Bread. Verse 5 even notes that the people "had not kept it in great numbers as prescribed" (כתוב).[25] The Chronicler, it appears, knows a text which he takes to be the authority for holding Passover in Jerusalem. One thinks immediately of Deut. 16:1-8, the first text to state such a requirement, but Ezek. 45:21-24, Num. 28:16-25, and the Holiness Code (Lev. 23:5-8) all presuppose Jerusalem as the site of the daily burnt offerings of Unleavened Bread.[26] What can be said with

---

[23] 2 Chr. 30:5, 16, 18; 35:6, 12, 13.

[24] Scholars differ on the question of the event's historicity. E. L. Curtis and A. L. Madsen, *A Critical and Exegetical Commentary on the Books of Chronicles* (Edinburgh, 1910), p. 471, and de Vaux, *Ancient Israel*, p. 487, view it as a product of the Chronicler's imagination, while J. Myers, *II Chronicles* (Garden City, 1965), p. 178, thinks the Chronicler's story is not wholly invented. Williamson, *1 and 2 Chronicles*, pp. 360-365, reviews the issues and argues that Hezekiah did in fact celebrate Unleavened Bread in the second month (but not Passover as it was not joined to Unleavened Bread until the time of Josiah), and that the Chronicler had an account of the event which he completely rewrote. Cf. Segal, *The Hebrew Passover*, p. 228ff.

[25] Adam C. Welch, *The Work of the Chronicler: Its Purpose and Date* (London, 1939), p. 133ff., assumes the "they" in this clause to refer exclusively to people from the north, who had not been able to keep Passover as prescribed (by Deut.) because their sanctuaries had been destroyed by Assyria. The verse itself, however, identifies the subject as the people of all Israel "from Beersheba to Dan," that is Judeans and Israelites.

[26] von Rad, *Geschichtsbild*, p. 52, argues that the location of Passover in Jerusalem is the Chronicler's main point, that it derives from Deut. 16:1-8 and 2

certainty is that the Chronicler is not following the stipulations of J (Ex. 12:21ff.), nor is it the Priestly Code (Ex. 12:1-20) with its decentralized family celebration to which the Chronicler refers and on which his description depends.

2) The date of Passover and Unleavened Bread.
According to 2 Chr. 30:15, Hezekiah's Passover was kept on the fourteenth day of the second month. But v. 2f makes clear that the normal practice was to keep the Passover on the fourteenth day of the first month, the month long delay having been necessitated by a lack of sanctified priests and the peoples' need for additional time to make their way to Jerusalem. As we have seen, from the Holiness Code (Lev. 23:5) on, all of Israel's traditions set the fourteenth day of the first month as the date for Passover. The authorization to delay the Feast, however, is found in Num. 9:6-11, a P text. There the question is put: What if a person is unclean or away on a journey at the appointed time for Passover? The answer provided by Yahweh is that such a person should celebrate the feast one month later, on the fourteenth day of the second month.

Arguing that the grounds for postponing the celebration in 2 Chr. 30:3 and Num. 9:10 are quite different, von Rad held that the Chronicler was not following this P text.[27] There is some merit to this objection. For P, Passover is celebrated at one's home so the reference to a journey (Num. 9:10) can not refer to a pilgrimage to Jerusalem as 2 Chr. 30:3 would require. In addition the uncleanness in Num. 9:6ff. is corpse contamination while 2 Chr. 30:3 refers simply to "unsanctified priests." An alternative explanation is offered by Talmon, who argued that the delay was to accommodate people from the North whose calendar was a month behind that of the South.[28] While this is an attractive suggestion, the fact is that according to the Chronicler Passover could not have been kept in Jerusalem at the normal time because the temple was not sanctified until the sixteenth day of the first month (2 Chr. 29:17). Despite von Rad's arguments it seems more likely that the text reflects the extent to which the Chronicler found room to interpret for his own day the spirit of Num. 9:6-11.[29]

3) The animal sacrifices of Passover and Unleavened Bread.
At Hezekiah's Passover, the victim is termed הפסח (RSV: "the passover lamb"), and it is killed (שחט) not sacrificed (2 Chr. 30:15, 17).

Kgs. 23, and that therefore the Chronicler is following D and rejecting P's *häusliches Fest*.

[27] von Rad, *Geschichtsbild*, p. 53.

[28] Shemaryahu Talmon, "Divergencies in Calendar Reckoning in Ephraim and Judah," *VT*, VIII (1958), 48-74. Cf. 1 Kgs. 12:32f.

[29] Ackroyd, *1 and 2 Chronicles, Ezra, Nehemiah*, p.184.

144   Judson R. Shaver

This phrase (שחט הפסח), which occurs in each of the Chronicler's
Passover narratives, occurs elsewhere only in Ex. 12:21 (J).[30] According
to P (Ex. 12:6), the victim is killed (שחט), but it is never referred to as
הפסח; in Deut. 16:2, 5 the animal (never הפסח) is sacrificed (זבח).[31]

During the seven days of Unleavened Bread the people sacrificed
peace offerings (זבחי שלמים) consisting of bulls (פרים) and sheep and goats
(צאן vv. 22-24). According to Deut. 16:2, the Passover sacrifice could
come from the flock (צאן) or the herd (בקר), but Deuteronomy makes no
mention of sacrifices during Unleavened Bread. The Holiness Code
(Lev. 23:8) mentions a daily offering by fire (אשה), but only Ezek. 45:21-
24 and Num. 28:19-22 specify the sacrificial animals, namely: bulls,
rams, and goats (פרים, עזים and אילים) in Ezekiel; and bulls, rams, lambs
(כבשים) and goats in Numbers. P does not even refer to sacrifices during
Unleavened Bread, and yet the phrase used by the Chronicler for these
sacrifices (זבחי שלמים)—which is associated with Unleavened Bread
nowhere else in the Hebrew Bible—is a favorite of the priestly
writers.[32] The term "peace offering" is also used to describe a part of
the covenant ratification ritual (Ex. 24:5, JE) and the covenant renewal
ceremonies at Shechem (Deut. 27:7) and Mt. Ebal (Josh. 8:31). Most
significantly, however, according to 1 Kgs. 8:63 peace offerings (זבחי
שלמים) were offered at Solomon's dedication of the temple. Although
neither mentions this fact, both Myers and Williamson point out that
the Chronicler's model for Hezekiah's Passover was Solomon's
dedication of the temple.[33] Both were kept for fourteen days rather
than the required seven (2 Chr. 7:8f., 30:23), but it was Sukkoth that
followed the dedication of the temple and Passover which follows
Hezekiah's rededication. The זבחי שלמים (peace offerings) of Solomon's
feast (1 Kgs. 8:63), simply השלמים in the Chronicler's account of that
event (2 Chr. 7:7), appear to have been transferred to his account of
Hezekiah's Passover (2 Chr. 30:22) for which he had no *Vorlage* in
Kings. Thus it is likely that this phrase, although a characteristic of
P, is present in our text due to the influence of 1 Kgs. 8:63 rather than
the Priestly Code.

The source of the animals sacrificed as peace offerings is not as
explicit as one could desire, but it seems likely that the meaning of v. 24
is that they were all provided by Hezekiah and the princes (השרים),
presumably from their own possessions (cf. 2 Chr. 31:3). According to 1

---

[30] 2 Chr. 30:15, 17; 35:1, 6, 11; Ezra 6:20. The Passover victim is termed פסח
elsewhere only in 2 Chr. 35:7, 8, 9, 13.

[31] von Rad, *Geschichtsbild*, p. 53, argues that the Chronicler basically follows
the Deuteronomic Passover legislation, but allows that this is an exception.

[32] F. Brown, S. R. Driver and C. A. Briggs, *A Hebrew and English Lexicon of the
Old Testament* (Oxford, 1907), p. 257b.

[33] Myers, *II Chronicles*, p. 179; H. G. M. Williamson, *Israel in the Books of
Chronicles* (Cambridge, 1977), pp. 119-125.

Kgs. 8:63 (and 2 Chr. 7:5) at the dedication of the temple Solomon sacrificed peace offerings from the herd (בקר) and flock (צאן). The implication is that they belonged to him. Strangely, however, none of the Pentateuchal texts which require sacrifices during the feast of Unleavened Bread indicate who is responsible for providing the animals. Only Ezekiel addresses this question. The people contribute them to the prince (הנשׂיא), who then provides them as they are required for the sacrificial ritual (Ezek. 45:15, 17, 21). While these instructions may have influenced the Chronicler, it seems likely that here again he is following the Solomonic precedent described in 1 Kings, which, unlike Ezekiel, says nothing about the people's contribution. For the Chronicler, Hezekiah's wealth, like Solomon's, is sufficient for him to provide "from his own possessions" (2 Chr. 31:3).[34]

4)   Official functions of priests and Levites.

According to 2 Chr. 30:13-15a, a large congregation (including a few people from the Northern Kingdom, v. 11) assembled in Jerusalem, removed unacceptable altars, and "killed the passover lamb" (*RSV*; MT: וישׁחטו הפסח). The zeal of these laymen put the priests and Levites to shame (v. 15b). They therefore sanctified themselves, brought burnt offerings into the temple and took their posts "according to the law of Moses" (כתורת משׁה v. 15bf.). The Levites then slew the paschal offering (שׁחט הפסח) for those not ritually prepared, and the priests manipulated the blood (v. 16f.).

Myers, following Rudolph, suggests that having the Levites slay the Passover sacrifice was probably a misunderstanding since the law (he cites Ex. 12:6 and Deut. 16:6) assigned that task to the heads of families.[35] I think it more likely that the Chronicler has not so much misunderstood the law as supplemented it. The Hebrew Bible has no instructions at all for Levitical or priestly participation in the Passover ritual.[36] The Chronicler's formulaic "according to the law of

---

[34] Williamson, *Israel*, p. 122; Williamson, *1 and 2 Chronicles*, p. 373.

[35] Myers, *II Chronicles* , p. 178f.; Wilhelm Rudolph, *Chronikbücher* (Tübingen, 1955), p. 301. It is understandable that P, with its familial Passover ritual, would not assign a role to priests or Levites, but with the centralized observance of Deut. one would expect the clergy to take over functions previously assigned to the heads of families. Deut. 16:6, in fact, contrary to Myers' assertion, is ambiguous in regard to who exactly makes the sacrifice. It does not mention the heads of families or the clergy, but stresses instead the place at which the Passover sacrifice is to be made.

[36] Ezek. 44:10-16 may be connected with this, however. It does not deal specifically with Passover, but does say that the Levites are to slay (שׁחט) the burnt offering (עולה) and sacrifice (זבה) of the people.

Moses" (כתורת משה) in v. 16 claims legal authority, but refers to no canonical text.[37]

The Passover of Josiah: 2 Chronicles 35:1-19

For his account of the Passover held in the eighteenth year of Josiah, the Chronicler had at his disposal the deuteronomistic account of the same event (2 Kgs. 23:21-23). That account stresses that in accordance with the newly discovered book, Passover was kept in Jerusalem in a way unparalleled since the rise of the monarchy. But how exactly was this Passover different? The text is brief and provides little information about how the Feast was kept. It gives no specific date, says nothing about the role of priests or Levites, and provides no information about the kind or number of animal sacrifices. We are told only that the Passover was kept in Jerusalem in accordance with the book. But as I have noted above, the great innovation of the book, that is of Deuteronomy, is that it changed the nature of Passover from a familial meal to a pilgrimage feast. Thus it appears that the one detail provided by 2 Kgs. 23:21-23, namely that it was kept in Jerusalem, is precisely the detail which made Josiah's Passover so extraordinary.[38]

The Chronicler reproduced in his own account all the information provided him by his *Vorlage*. Even the problematic statement that no such Passover had been previously kept during the entire period of the monarchy is included.[39] Moreover, the command by Josiah in 2 Kgs. 23:21 to "keep the Passover as it is written in this book of the covenant," while not quoted, is essentially reproduced in 2 Chr. 35:1-19—not just once but three times. We find in v. 6 the command to the Levites to discharge their cultic obligations "according to the word of the Lord by Moses" (כדבר־יהוה ביד־משה); in v. 12 it is said that the burnt offerings were set apart to be offered "as it is written in the book of Moses" (ככתוב בספר משה), and in the following verse the Passover sacrifice is claimed to have been roasted "according to the ordinance" (כמשפט).

---

[37] "As it is written" (ככתוב) in v. 18 is similar. The context deals with people who are not ritually prepared (clean) for Passover. The Hebrew Bible does not include specific instruction on how to prepare oneself for Passover, but does recognize that uncleanness disqualifies one from participation (cf. Num. 9:6-13). A striking feature of the passage is that the written requirements of the law are suspended to allow the sincere, although unclean, to participate.

[38] de Vaux, *Ancient Israel*, p. 486ff.

[39] Rudolph, *Chronikbücher*, p. 329, identifies the role of the Levites in Josiah's Passover as the new thing. But while it is true that 2 Chr. 35 describes their activities in more detail than we find in 2 Chr. 30, the Levites had the principal role in Hezekiah's Passover. Cf. Welch, *The Work of the Chronicler*, p. 113.

In his expanded version of the Kings account of Josiah's Passover, therefore, the Chronicler describes an event which, like Hezekiah's Passover, was kept in Jerusalem in accordance with the Deuteronomic prescription. Unlike that of Hezekiah, however, it was kept on the fourteenth day of the first month, that is, on the date first specified at Lev. 23:5 (H) and unchanged in subsequent cultic calendars. There is, however, no real discrepancy between the dates observed by Hezekiah and Josiah. As we have observed, the Passover of Hezekiah was postponed due to extraordinary circumstances and on the authority of a P text (Num. 9:9-12). Thus it appears that the Chronicler requires that in normal circumstances Passover be a pilgrimage feast (חג) observed in Jerusalem on the fourteenth day of the first month. As we have seen, the place of the celebration and its character as a חג derive from D (Deut. 16:5f., cf. 2 Kgs. 23:23), while the date—never specified in D— reflects later priestly texts.

With regard to the sacrificial victims and the official cultic roles of priests and Levites, the Passover of Josiah again closely parallels that of Hezekiah. The same kinds of animals are provided by the king and his princes, the Levites "killed the passover lamb" (וישחטו הפסח), and the priests sprinkled the blood "as it is written in the book of Moses" (ככתוב בספר משה v. 11f.). We noted above in connection with Hezekiah's Passover that the Pentateuch—indeed, the Hebrew Bible—nowhere assigns these or any other functions in the Passover ritual to priests or Levites. In the case of Josiah's Passover it is further stated that "they set aside the burnt offerings" (v. 12), presumably parts of the paschal victims, for the laity to offer to Yahweh. As Rudolph pointed out, the Hebrew Bible says nothing about this ritual which the Chronicler attributes to the book of Moses.[40] The practice may, however, reflect a development from Ezek. 45:21-24 and Num. 28:16-25, which, like the Chronicler, view Passover and Unleavened Bread as a single feast (חג), and require a daily burnt offering (עולה) for the seven days of the feast.

A second point not mentioned in connection with Hezekiah's Passover but noted in our present text (v. 13) is that the Passover victim was roasted (ויבשל הפסח באש) according to the ordinance (כמשפט). Myers translates the phrase as "boil in the fire" and finds here "a conflation of Ex. 12:8f. (P), which requires roasting, and Deut. 16:7, which requires boiling."[41] If this is true it provides important further evidence that the Chronicler regarded both D and P as authoritative and thus attempted to reconcile their differences. The text, however, may not be such a conflation. The Deuteronomic stipulation is that the victim be boiled (בשל, Deut. 16:7), while P (Ex. 12:8f.) requires that it be roasted

---

[40] Rudolph, Chronikbücher, p. 327. The Chronicler, he believes, has been influenced by Lev. 3:6-16.

[41] Myers, II Chronicles, p. 211. So also Williamson, 1 and 2 Chronicles, p. 407.

(צְלִי־אֵשׁ) and not boiled (בָּשֵׁל בַּמַּיִם). The contrast is between cooking[42] in water and cooking in fire, and in this instance the Chronicler follows P.[43]

The Passover of the Restoration Community:
Ezra 6:19-22

This brief account describes a feast of Passover and Unleavened Bread very similar to those of Hezekiah (2 Chr. 30:1-27) and Josiah (2 Chr. 35:1-19). Even the context is the same: After the dedication of the (second) temple, Passover and Unleavened Bread was celebrated, as in the former instances, in Jerusalem on the fourteenth day of the first month.[44] Once again the Levites killed the Passover victim (וַיִּשְׁחֲטוּ הַפֶּסַח) and the feast of Unleavened Bread was celebrated for seven days.[45]

Conclusion

"As it is written in the book of the law of Moses," or its abbreviated equivalent, is a recurring formula in the books of Chronicles, Ezra and Nehemiah. Analysis of this claim to written authority in these books' accounts of Passover and Unleavened Bread suggests that the Chronicler had a single coherent notion of how to observe the Feast in accordance with the law book. Although various scholars have identified this law book as D, P, or the Pentateuch, I have shown that the Chronicler's portrayal of the feast reflects the authority of a variety of sometimes conflicting legal traditions. It does not depend exclusively on D or P, nor does it simply combine them. Instead, it draws in varying degrees from the various legal collections of the Pentateuch. But the practice of Passover and Unleavened Bread, as recorded by the Chronicler and attributed by him to the written Torah, is not based exclusively on pentateuchal legislation either. Ezekiel appears to have been influential, and although they were claimed to have been derived from the law of Moses (2 Chr. 30:16) and from the book of Moses (2 Chr. 35:12), the much emphasized ritual functions of the priests and Levites have no antecedent legislative basis elsewhere in the Hebrew Bible.

---

[42] בשל many times simply means "cook" (cf. Brown, Driver, Briggs, Lexicon, p. 143a.

[43] Even von Rad, whose thesis is that the Chronicler has essentially based his descriptions on D, recognized that in this instance we have a deviation from D which conforms to P (cf. Geschichtsbild, p. 53).

[44] Hezekiah's Passover was an exception, but the context makes clear that the normal date was the fourteenth day of the first month. See above, p. 14f.

[45] Note, however, that the text lacks any reference to the authority which warranted these activities.

Although the Chronicler's History is usually dated to the late Persian period, about the middle of the fourth century, it is difficult to draw conclusions about the historical setting from which this eclectic conception of Passover derives.[46] We have little certain knowledge of the editorial history of the books of Chronicles, Ezra, and Nehemiah, or of the degree to which the views of the text reflected the thinking and practice of the larger community. The text gives little support, however, to the hypothesis that its authors had a pentateuchal canon at their disposal. Yet it does emphasize the importance of *written* authority. And it is precisely this conviction that *texts* are authoritative that generates the question a canon answers, namely: *Which* texts?

---

[46] This is a widely shared view. Cf. Ackroyd, *1 and 2 Chronicles, Ezra, Nehemiah*, p. 25f.; Eissfeldt, *Introduction*, p. 540; Williamson, *1 and 2 Chronicles*, p. 15f. A number of scholars, however, date the work slightly earlier in the first half of the fourth century. Cf. W. F. Albright, "The Date and Personality of the Chronicler," *JBL*, XL (1921), 104-124; W. Rudolph, *Esra und Nehemia mit 3. Esra*, (Tübingen, 1949), p. XXIVf.; J. Myers, *I Chronicles* (Garden City, 1965), p. LXXXVII; F. M. Cross, "A Reconstruction of the Judean Restoration," *JBL*, XCIV (1975), p. 12.

Chapter Seven

The Maccabean Revolution

Joseph P. Healey
Hobart College

"It is an old maxim of history that those who rule the present command our vision of the past...."[1] History is written by the victors. The past is interpreted to the present. Thus all history is mediated and each intermediary views history from a peculiar perspective.

This problem of hermeneutics is particularly evident in the research done on biblical texts. An entire era of scholarly research has passed in the pursuit of sources, forms, and models by which to interpret the scriptures of the Judeo-Christian Testaments.[2] What is clear from this research is that we have come to understand the complex nature of the data we have been given and the even more complex nature of the process of making *history* out of mere *facts*. Hayden White has observed:

> Critics of historiography as a discipline, however, have taken more
> radical views on the matter of interpretation in history, going so far as

---

[1] Richard Marius, *Thomas More: A Biography* (New York: Knopf, 1984) 177. The problem here is the nature of historical truth and the hermeneutics of objectivity. See on this Hans Georg Gadamer, *Wahrheit und Methode Grundzüge einer philosophischen Hermeneutik* (Tübingen: Mohr, 1960); also Bernard Lonergan, *Method in Theology* (New York: Herder and Herder, 1972); Karl Löwith, *Meaning in History: The Theological Implications of the Philosophy of History* (Chicago: University of Chicago, 1959).

[2] For an excellent summary of the current state of the discussion see Brevard Childs, *Introduction to the Old Testament as Scripture* (Philadelphia: Fortress, 1981); John H. Hayes and J. Maxwell Miller eds., *Israelite and Judean History* (Philadelphia: Westminster, 1977); John H. Hayes, *Introduction to Old Testament Study* (Nashville: Abingdon, 1979); John Barton, *Reading the Old Testament: Method in Biblical Study* (Philadelphia: Westminster, 1984).

to argue that historical accounts are nothing but interpretations, in the establishment of the events that make up the chronicle of the narrative no less than in assessments of the meaning or significance of those events for the understanding of the historical process in general. Thus, Levi-Strauss concludes, historical facts are in no sense "given" to the historian but are, rather, "constituted" by the historian himself "by abstraction and as though under the threat of an infinite regress."[3]

In approaching the causes of the Maccabean Revolution we are faced with all these problems on a grand scale. To begin with, our sources of information on the period are extremely limited. We know that among the canonical books of the Hebrew Bible our only contemporary source is Daniel, a book notable for its enigmatic character, apocalyptic language, and intense use of symbols and symbolic language. The historical interpretation of Daniel is always open to suspicion. In the Greek Bible we have the two books of the Maccabees. These both contain information that can be shown to be contemporary with the events in the books, but both of them are written after the fact and must be viewed as "interpreted" history. The third source available is Josephus, who writes of the period both in the *Jewish War* and in the *Antiquities*.[4] Josephus, however, is not a reliable, first hand source for the period since he is here dependent on his own sources, which for this period are limited.[5]

The rabbinic materials for this period are very skimpy and of no independent value as sources. They are all dependent on one another or the sources already cited. One could note also that the rabbinical attitude toward the Hasmoneans is mixed in the early materials.[6] The

---

[3] Hayden White, *Tropics of Discourse: Essays in Cultural Criticism* (Baltimore: Johns Hopkins University Press, 1978) 55. See also Shimon Applebaum, "Josephus and the Economic Causes of the Jewish War," Unpublished paper courtesy of Professor Louis Feldman.

[4] *The Jewish War* I, 37; *Antiquities of the Jews* XII.

[5] See H. St. John Thackerey, *Josephus: The Man and the Historian* (New York: Jewish Institute of Religion 1929, rpt KTAV 1967); also Victor Tcherikover, "Wars I, II as an Historical Source," in *The Jews in the Greco-Roman World*, M. Amit ed. (Tel Aviv: 1961) 135-145; also *Hellenistic Civilization and the Jews* (Philadelphia: Jewish Publication Society, 1959) 392-297 (after, HCJ); Elias Bickermann, *Der Gott der Makkabäer* (Berlin: Schocken Verlag, 1937). Bickermann sees Josephus as a fairly reliable source for the period in contrast to Tcherikover who regards him as of little value.

[6] There are three works of considerable value and interest in reviewing the rabbinic evidence: Phillip Kieval, *The Talmudic View of the Hasmonean and the Early Herodian Periods in Jewish History.* (Unpublished Diss., Brandeis University, 1970); Samuel Schafler, *The Hasmoneans in Jewish Historiography* (Unpublished Diss., Jewish Theological Seminary, 1973); Joseph Sievers, *The*

general interest of this literature relates more to the purification of the Temple and the Hannukah festival than to any real appreciation of the causes and progress of the Maccabean Revolution. Certainly no discussion of the idea of "hellenism" or the process of "hellenization" can be found. Some allusions to the period may be present in Ben Sira.[7] From a historical point of view the hard evidence for the Maccabean period and the causes of the revolt is very limited. And each writer who approaches this material must carefully consider what questions can be fruitfully addressed and what answers may be reasonably expected.

The standard interpretation of these texts produces a scenario in which a small group of "hellenizers" attempted to overthrow the ancient and established Law of Moses, under the inspiration and with the direct complicity of Antiochus IV Epiphanes. He instigated the events through the application of a vast program of "hellenization" which was an attempt to find a basis of unity for his vast empire. This paper will attempt to show that this perspective does not represent any scientifically verifiable account of the events. It is not historical, but catechetical. It interprets the events of the early Maccabean period from the perspective of a small group within the larger nation— mistaking this smaller group's specific religious and political *agenda* for the structure of actual historical events. In fact, the causes of the Revolution lie in intrinsic and long-standing anomalies in the constitution of Israel and Judaism itself.

Hellenism-Hellenization-Hellenizers

It is common for scholars to speak of the period of the Maccabean Revolution as a time of intense "hellenization." A serious problem arises. What exactly is meant by Hellenism or Hellenization? Saul Lieberman, in his two books on the subject, is at pains to show a very significant Greek influence in the period of the Maccabees.[8] But a

---

Hasmoneans and Their Supporters from Mattathias to John Hyrcanus (Unpublished Diss., Columbia University, 1981).

[7] Shimon Applebaum, "Josephus and the Economic Causes of the Jewish War," 21-25, notes allusions to economic factors in Sir. 13:15-20.

[8] Saul Lieberman, *Greek in Jewish Palestine: Studies in the Life and Manners of Jewish Palestine in the II-IV Centuries C.E.* (New York: Jewish Theological Seminary, 1942); S. Lieberman, *Hellenism in Jewish Palestine* (New York: Jewish Theological Seminary, 1950; rpt. KTAV, 1962); also S.K. Eddy, *The King is Dead: Studies in Near Eastern Resistance to Hellenism* (Lincoln: University of Nebraska, 1961); Martin Hengel, *Judaism and Hellenism.* Translated by John Bowden, Volume One: Text; Volume Two: Notes and Bibliography (Philadelphia: Fortress, 1981).

careful examination of his work shows that Greek influence, if measured by use of language and terms, is found precisely in the areas one would expect: technical words, commercial words, and common words. The famous passage in the Talmud in which Rabbi Gamaliel is said to have had a thousand young men studying, five hundred studying Torah and five hundred studying *hokmah yovanit*,[9] ties in with the further observation that this was permitted because Rabbi Gamaliel had to have dealings with the government.[10] It is not surprising, then, to find among the upper class and governing groups in Palestinian Judaism a familiarity with the language of the ruling power. Indeed, given the later antipathy of the Rabbis to Greek learning (or their supposed antipathy), the example of Rabbi Gamaliel shows that even in circles not generally favorable to Greek ideas, the practical need for Greek was understood.[11]

Hellenism and hellenization were certainly more than knowledge of the Greek language. Hengel argues for an extensive process of Hellenization which began as early as the third century B.C.E. and spread all across the Levant. This process involved not only the acquisition of Greek for purposes of conducting business and political affairs, but the exposure to Greek literature, Greek ideas, Greek politics and life, and Greek styles of art and dress, at levels varying from very profound to quite superficial.[12]

The features of Hellenistic culture that distinguished it from the old Semitic civilizations that had dominated the area were: a) a political system based on the idea of a *polis* governed by a monarch but also by a series of constitutional instruments and customs; b) an emphasis on the "secularization of religion" (that is the lack of a distinct, priestly caste); c) the use of schools and gymnasia as instruments not simply for strengthening the military capacity of the state, but also as places for the dissemination of ideas and for the pursuit of pleasure as an end in itself; d) a growth of the idea of the individual as opposed to older "tribal" notions of identity.[13]

---

[9] TB, *Baba Kama*, 82b-83a.

[10] TB, *Baba Kama*, 82b-83a.

[11] It should be noted that the rabbinic evidence is late and that there is serious dispute about the meaning of the rabbinical statements concerning Greek learning. See Liebermann, *Greek in Jewish Palestine.*

[12] See Hengel, *Judaism and Hellenism*, 56-57.

[13] These features parallel remarks made by Professor Morton Smith (7/10/85, NEH Seminar, Yeshiva University) where he noted that each of the features of "hellenistic" civilization was a development or even a corruption of the "classical" Greek way of life.

The culture of Hellenism rapidly became the dominant culture of the whole region. And at every major center of the old culture a new symbiosis emerged. This symbiosis was most evident among the groups with the strongest interest in the development of the new culture. By and large the groups that would be most readily receptive to these influences were the upper classes and the educated elites of the old cultures (although Greek culture was also pervasive among some segments of the lower classes who were directly involved with Greek manners: soldiers, sailors, etc.).[14] The growth of a Jewish-Greek symbiosis outside ancient Palestine is beyond dispute. The Alexandrian community provides well-documented examples of this mix and of the fruitful outcome that it could produce.[15]

The question posed most sharply, then, is whether the Jewish community of Judea can be seen as substantially different from the Judaism of the Diaspora on the issue of hellenistic influence. This is the thrust of Hengel's thesis. There is, in his view, no *substantial* difference between the two areas. And in this assertion a growing number of scholars support his view.[16] These views are not entirely new. Both Tcherikover and Bickermann, as well as Lieberman argued the same point in the last generation. The evidence for hellenistic influence in Palestinian Judaism is not as immediate and self-evident as

---

[14] See Solomon Zeitlin, *The Rise and Fall of the Judean State: A Political, Social and Religious History of the Second Commonwealth.* Vol. I 332-37 B.C.E. (Philadelphia: The Jewish Publication Society, 1962) 53; Liebermann, *Greek in Jewish Palestine,* 21; Wayne Meeks, "Moses as God and King," *Religions in Antiquity,* ed. Jacob Neusner (Leiden: E.J. Brill, 1970) 354; Klaus Bringmann, *Hellenistische Reform und Religionsverfolgung in Judäa: Eine Untersuchung zur judisch-hellenistichen Geschichte (175-163 c. Chr.)* Abhandlugnen der Akademie der Wissenschaften: Philologisch-Historische Klasse, Dritte Folge, Nr. 12 (Göttingen; Vandenhoeck und Ruprecht, 1983) 67.

[15] See the excellent discussion of this diaspora Judaism in V. Tcherikover, *HCJ,* 269-380; one might also give thought to the continuing discussion of the relation of Wisdom literature to Greek ideas. For more on this see John Collins, *Between Athens and Jerusalem: Jewish Identity in the Hellenistic Diaspora* (New York: Crossroads, 1983); A. Dilella, "Conservative and Progressive Theology: Sirach and Wisdom," *Studies in Ancient Israelite Wisdom,* ed. James Crenshaw (New York: KTAV, 1976) 401-416; Hengel, *Judaism and Hellenism,* 110-175.

[16] See Hengel, *Judaism and Hellenism,* 105 and notes; also Collins, *Between Athens and Jerusalem,* 10-12; Henry A. Fischel, "Story and History: Observations on Greco-Roman Rhetoric and Pharisaism," *Essays in Greco-Roman and Related Talmudic Literature,* ed. H. Fischel. Library of Biblical Studies, ed. Harry M. Orlinsky (New York: KTAV, 1977) 443-472.

that for the Diaspora but the cumulative effect of literary and other evidence is compelling, though not universally acknowledged.[17]

Despite these challenges I would argue that the weight of past evidence, and the continuing growth of more evidence of a similar nature, indicates that we have only scratched the surface of hellenistic influence in Palestine. The evidence may be divided into five areas:

        a) Greek words
        b) Greek literary forms
        c) Greek philosophical ideas
        d) Greek social forms
        e) Greek art

In all these areas the evidence from our sources is substantial enough to make clear that a more than superficial contact with hellenism has taken place. Morton Smith states the case:

> Jewish material has come down to us heavily censored. This censorship has been double—an external censorship by Christian authorities and a domestic censorship by Jews.... Yet even this preserved material, as we have seen, testifies *consistently* to the hellenization of ancient Judaism.[18]

In point of fact, the Judaism we receive as normative is probably simply a variety of a rather complex set of Judaisms.[19] And, more significantly, hellenism itself is a broad-ranging term that can signify the presence of any or all of the qualities noted above. If we try to define a specific set of criteria for what is or is not hellenistic, we find ourselves very quickly in the realm of impressions or feelings rather than in a world of reasonably objective data. The terms hellenism and hellenization relate to a complex of ideas and practices that are loosely associated with the classical Greek republics and their self-understanding as articulated by philosophers and writers. It is clear that where the Greek language is spoken and known we have hellenization of one kind, and where Greek religion or Greek philosophical schools are present we have a different kind of hellenization. But in both cases it is hellenization.

It would also seem reasonably clear that hellenization was also a process of absorbing the older traditions of the pre-Greek civilizations.

---

[17] See Louis H. Feldman, "Hengel's *Judaism and Hellenism* in Retrospect," *JBL* 96 (1977) 371-382.

[18] Morton Smith, "The Image of God: Notes on the Hellenization of Judaism with special reference to Goodenough's Work on Jewish Symbols," *BJRL* 40 (1957/58) 473-512.

[19] Morton Smith, "Goodenough's *Jewish Symbols* in Retrospect," *JBL* 86 (1967) 53-68, esp. 62-63.

There can be little doubt that the differences between classical Greece and Ptolemaic Egypt were as much the product of the interaction of Greek and Semitic or Egyptian culture as they were the result of inner-Greek development.[20] One should be careful to note that in every case the mix of cultures would or could produce a different result.[21]

If, as the literature suggests, the causes of the Maccabean revolution were related directly to hellenization and its impact on Judaism, we have little or no idea what we are dealing with under the title hellenization. But can we even identify with clarity the other party to the clash: Judaism? There is substantial evidence to suggest that we cannot.

Judaism

What we know of the origins of Judaism is passed on to us in three sources: The Torah and Canonical Writings; the Rabbinic literature; and in Jewish writers of the early period, particularly Josephus.[22] In addition, if the Rabbinic traditions for the earliest period are to be believed, there was a body of received tradition, an oral Torah, which is equal in weight to the written Torah.[23] Thus the body of received tradition from which Judaism draws its inspiration was open to a variety of influences (particularly the oral forms) and of interpretations. And variety was certainly the mark of early Judaism.[24]

Josephus noted that the Jewish community in the time of the revolt against Rome was divided into four philosophies. This classic division names Pharisees, Sadducees, Essenes, and "Zealots" as the principal

---

[20] See S.K. Eddy's *The King is Dead;* Saul Liebermann, *Hellenism,* 110-115; Cyrus Gordon, *Before the Bible: The Common Background of Greek and Hebrew Civilization* (Collins: London, 1962) 226.

[21] Gordon, *Before the Bible,* 286.

[22] See Jacob Neusner, *Early Rabbinic Judaism* (Leiden: E.J. Brill, 1976) 209-215; Shaye Cohen, *Josephus in Galilee and Rome* (Leiden: E.J. Brill, 1979); John Collins, *Between Athens and Jerusalem,* 60-101; Hengel, *Judaism and Hellenism,* 107-174.

[23] Geza Vermes, *Scripture and Tradition in Judaism.* Studia Post-Biblica IV (Leiden: E.J. Brill, 1961) 1-10 and passim; Neusner, *Early Rabbinic Judaism,* 3-33.

[24] Morton Smith, *Palestinian Parties and Politics that Shaped the Old Testament* (New York: Columbia University, 1971); R.H. Pfeifer, *The History of New Testament Times with an Introduction to the Apocrypha* (New York: Harper and Brothers, 1949) 46-59.

groups in the first century C.E.[25] It is interesting to note that G. F. Moore could say Judaism "is the monument of the Pharisees" (*Judaism* II, 193) without challenge. The statement of course is a contradiction. It raises the ethos of one group to the height of a definition, though that group vied with many others to determine what would finally define Judaism. We know that there was an inner-Jewish struggle to define the meaning of Judaism. And we know that if a normative Judaism ever existed, it existed only as an uneasy compromise among distinct groups.

If we further consider that it is indisputable that the Judaism of Palestine and the Judaism of the Diaspora were equally Judaism, yet quite distinct, then we are secure in deducing that a definition of normative Judaism is not possible in the first century C.E. and *a fortiori* in the earliest period.[26] In the period of the richest cross-fertilization between hellenism and the Jewish culture, hellenism was a broadly-based literary, cultural, and philosophical movement centered on a process of "*polis*-ification"[27] while Judaism was a diverse ethnic, religious and philosophical (in the broadest sense) movement centered on the process of keeping faith with the traditions of the "fathers."

But neither hellenism nor Judaism in this early period could be defined so clearly and distinctly as to make of them antithetical views of life.[28]   Having said all this, we are now prepared to ask the question as to why the Maccabean revolution took place at all? It seems reasonably clear that the mere encounter, even on a profound level, with hellenism was not a problem for the vast majority in the ancient world. What peculiar conditions, then, could cause this encounter to lead to such dramatic events as those described in the books of the Maccabees and in Daniel?

---

[25] Josephus, *Antiquities* 18:1, 2-6; 13:5, 9; 10:5-20; *Jewish War* 2:8, 2-14. Note that the identity of the fourth philosophy in Josephus is disputed. See Pfeifer, *History*, 59.

[26] The great works of G. F. Moore and to a large extent of E. R. Goodenough are based on (indeed Moore established) the idea of a "normative Judaism" which was present in a developed form at this time. But normative Judaism simply does not exist until well past the destruction of the second Temple and the revolts against Rome, if it exists at all! See M. Smith, "Palestinian Judaism in the First Century," in Fischel, *Essays*, 183-197; E. Bickermann, *From Ezra to the Last of the Maccabees*. Foundations of Biblical Judaism (New York: Schocken, 1962).

[27] E. Rivkin, "Pharisaism and the Crisis of the Individual in the Greco-Roman World," in Fischel, *Essays*, 508-509.

[28] Hengel, *Judaism and Hellenism*, 153-175; Pfeifer, *History*, 53.

Palestine in the Period of the Revolution

The destruction of Jerusalem in 589 B.C.E. and the exile or flight of the upper classes and leadership groups to Babylon or Egypt brought to an end the history of Israel. After the exile we cannot really appropriately speak of the history of Israel but we must talk about the history of Judaism or the Jewish people. The reasons for this change are many but not the least significant of them is the fact that the state and the ethos of Israel were intimately united not simply through politics but, more profoundly, through the religious traditions embodied in the Torah.[29]

The end of the exile is not, however, the restoration of the old state. That had long disappeared. Through wars and population shifts the character of the Davidic empire was radically altered. When Cyrus frees the Jews of Babylon he does not restore the kingdom of David and Solomon. He simply restores the rights of the upper classes and priests to return and re-establish Jewish law and custom in the city of Jerusalem.[30]

Ezra and Nehemiah reestablished Jerusalem as a city state. The state they reestablished was hardly the restored Zion of Is. 40-66. The dreams of the visionaries and prophets of the early exile, of a glorious new Israel, were soon to fade in the face of the reality of the restored state. Now the great conflict between kings and prophets would cease, not because the messianic ruler had arrived to bring them together, but because the restored state would have no kings or prophets but a priestly bureaucracy dedicated to the service of the Temple.[31]

There is considerable dispute about the ways in which the returnees and the resident Judeans managed to restore the religion and customs of Israel. For the purposes of our discussion I have adopted the views elaborated by Paul Hanson in *The Dawn of Apocalyptic* building

---

[29] On the question of the formation of Israel and the role of the monarchy in defining the national ethos see B. Halpern, *The Constitution of the Monarchy in Israel*, Harvard Semitic Monographs 25 (Chico: Scholars Press, 1981).

[30] Ezra 1:1-4, notes that Cyrus is given the mission "to build a Temple at Jerusalem in Judah," in thanksgiving because "Yahweh, the God of Heaven (*ba'al shamim!*) has given me the kingdoms of the earth." No Kingdom of Israel is restored, however, only the Temple.

[31] Zeitlin, *The Rise and Fall*, 23-33; F.M. Cross, "A Reconstruction of the Judean Restoration," *JBL* 94:1, 4-18; Paul D. Hanson, *The Dawn of Apocalyptic: the Historical and Sociological Roots of Jewish Apocalyptic* (Philadelphia: Fortress, 1975).

on the programmatic article of Frank M. Cross.[32] The crux of Hanson's
position is that Israel in the post-exilic period was divided into two
major "parties." On the one hand was the Palestinian Jewry left behind
in the exilic period bereft of priestly leadership and largely
impoverished. On the other hand were the old leadership cadres now
"Babylonized" through forty years of contact with that culture, but
still retaining (indeed glorying in) the Torah traditions of the old
kingdom. This hierocratic party viewed the restoration of the Temple
as a pragmatic reassertion of the basic values of the old Temple.[33] In
their view the loss of kingship was not critical but the loss of the
Temple was. The resident group was much less concerned with the
Temple and more concerned with the individual's ability to be in touch
with the visionary future in order to define the meaning of history as
God's history.[34] This division, if Hanson is correct, is paradigmatic for
understanding the emergence of apocalyptic and for the later division
into specific parties which aligned themselves to the right and left on
the issue of the "future."[35]

The situation in Palestine, then, at the dawn of the Maccabean era
is one in which Jewish and Greek/Hellenistic cultures are interacting in
a matrix in which the struggle between the visionaries and the
hierocrats remains unresolved. For, though the hierocratic party is
ascendant and politically dominant, the visionary party has not lost
its force. If the divisions originally were between the powerful,
priestly castes and the lay parties associated largely with rural
groups, then the same division may have continued to exist into
hellenistic times when the process of hellenization affected most

---

[32] Hanson, The Dawn of Apocalyptic; (and) F.M. Cross, "New Directions in the
Study of Apocalyptic," Journal for Theology and The Church (1969) 157-165.

[33] Hanson, The Dawn of Apocalyptic, 211-220.

[34] Hanson, The Dawn of Apocalyptic, 234.

[35] In a personal note E. Sanders wrote to me, he cautions on Hanson's view:
"There may be visionary and hierocratic emphasis in surviving literature, but
giving a literary emphasis a sociological Sitz-im-Leben is very dubious. No one
today who works on apoc., [sic] except maybe Hanson, would agree with
Vielhauer that apocalyptic material came from apocalyptic conventicles.

"Further, hierocrats had visions and visionaries lusted for power. For the
latter, the proof is Qumran. Visionary, maybe; hoping to take over and run the
Temple, certainly. For the former, the visionary and charismatic Rabbis and
Pharisees are the proof."

These caveats received I would still hold that Hanson's model is closer to the
reality than any other. The continuing debate about the use of sociological
method in biblical study is now at fever pitch but the field, it seems to me,
belongs to those who can judiciously apply the models of sociology to the
materials we have.

immediately and most profoundly the same urban, priestly, politically potent groups which had earlier defined the Jewish ethos through the restoration of the Temple and its cultic apparatus.

The persecution of Antiochus IV Epiphanes is seen in the books of Maccabees as the tyrannical and arbitrary actions of a king who resolved to revoke the ancient privileges of the Temple-state, in favor of a new, alien religion. The events are outlined for us in the Books of I-II Maccabees and very schematically in the book of Daniel. The opening of the crisis period is the deposition of the legitimate high priest Onias by his brother Jason. This action is the result of a bribe offered to Antiochus on his accession (II Macc. 4:7 ff.). Jason, according to Macc., introduced the way of the Greeks. A gymnasium is built; Athletic contests are celebrated. Some among the community seek to have their circumcision removed. The ephebate is established. And, as the book of II Macc. wryly notes:

> As a result, the priests no longer had any enthusiasm for their duties at the altar but despised the Temple and neglected the sacrifices.... They placed no value on their hereditary dignities, but cared above everything for Hellenic honours (II Macc. 4:14-16).

Here, of course, the blame seems to fall on the shoulders of the priests. In I Macc. greater responsibility is laid on the king:

> The king [Antiochus IV] then issued a decree throughout his empire: his subjects were all to become one people and abandon their own laws and religion (I Macc. 1:41-42).

The process of hellenization or persecution moved slowly. The Temple rituals were originally untouched. And the priests under Jason continued the observance of the Mosaic Law regarding the Temple. However, a second *coup d'état* took place. This time one Menelaus, who had been sent by Jason on a mission to Antiochus IV, took the occasion to outbid his master Jason for the office of the High Priesthood. Further, Menelaus is said to have purchased the murder of the deposed Onias who had arrived in Antioch to argue the case of the Jews against the usurpers (II Macc. 4:34). Menelaus and his brother Lysimmachus proceeded to plunder and ravage the Temple and the City and to wholly neglect their religious duties. In these circumstances the various groups opposed to the different candidates or occupants of the High Priesthood began agitating for one or another of them. Antiochus IV himself was preoccupied at the same time with a campaign against the Ptolemies of Egypt. In 169 B.C.E. and again in 167 B.C.E. he successfully engaged the Egyptians. On his return from the first campaign he plundered the Temple.[36]   This was an act apparently in keeping with family traditions![37]

The exact sequence of events in the opening of the Revolution is widely disputed. For our purposes I have adopted the outline of Klaus Bringmann.[38] The sequence follows:

a)   The overthrow of Onias by Jason-175 B.C.E. (II Macc. 4:7-8).

b)   Jason's petition to create Antioch of Judea, a Greek *polis* in Jerusalem and the royal permission to "enroll" those who would be citizens-175 B.C.E. II Macc. 4:8-10).

c)   Menelaus overthrows Jason as high priest-172 B.C.E. (II Macc. 4:23-38).

d)   Antiochus' victory over the Egyptians and the plunder of the Temple-169 B.C.E..

e)   Antiochus' pyrrhic victory over the Egyptians prompting Roman intervention to halt his campaign-168-67 B.C.E. (II Macc. 5:2).

f)   Jason seizes power from Menelaus but cannot hold the City for want of popular support-168 B.C.E. II Macc. 5:11-26).

g)   The second plundering of the Temple by Appolonius the Mysarch-168 B.C.E.

Jerusalem is reduced from a *polis* to a *katoikia* (I Macc. 1:29-40; II Macc. 5:24).

h)   The "decree" of Antiochus forbidding the Mosaic Law-167 B.C.E. (I Macc. 1:41-50).

i)   The incident at Modein and the opening of the revolution - 167 B.C.E.[39]

---

[36] This is in contrast to his earlier visit on the way to Egypt when: "The Judeans of the City marched through the streets carrying blazing torches in honor of the king." S. Zeitlin, *The Rise and Fall*, 82.

[37] His father had plundered the temples at Ecbatana and Elam. See F.E. Peters, *The Harvest of Hellenism: A History of the Near East from Alexander the Great to the Triumph of Christianity* (New York: Simon and Schuster, 1970) 244, 256.

[38] The dating of the events is disputed. In my reconstruction I follow Klaus Bringmann, *Hellenistic Reform*, 29-40. Bringmann argues for the priority of Daniel for the reconstruction of the events which are reported confusedly in the books of the Maccabees.

[39] One should note also the episode of Heliodorus which II Macc. 3:7-40 records as an early attempt at a persecution. E. Bickermann argues a) for the historicity of the event, and b) for its character as a normal bureaucratic procedure. See E. Bickermann, "Héliodore au Temple de Jerusalem," *Annuaire de l'Institut de Philologie et d'Histoire Orientales et Slaves* VII (1939-44), 161-191.

Even a cursory glance at the table of events should make it clear that the persecution has strong elements of a political character. The actual "edict" forbidding the practice of the Mosaic Law comes directly on the heels of a civil disorder involving at least three groups: Jason's followers, Menelaus' party, and the people who apparently supported neither of them (II Macc. 5:5-10).

One ought to note the sequence of events. Jason is made high priest and the Greek *polis* is established in 175 BCE. The edict of persecution is "issued" in 167 BCE, fully eight years later. In the intervening eight years what significant events have taken place? Three: a) the two campaigns of Antiochus to Egypt, one totally successful, the other militarily successful but politically suicidal because of the Roman intervention; b) the change of high priests a second time and the subsequent increase in the tribute price that was exacted to seal the bargain made by Menelaus; c) a civil rebellion in which both Jason and Menelaus are involved but out of which neither seems to gain anything in the nature of popular support. The decrees on religion follow the dismantling of the city walls and the reprisals by Appolonius on the citizenry, which includes the reduction of the city (with the subsequent economic dislocation and loss of revenue for the privileged classes at least), and the erection of the Akra as the new polis. Into this Akra would go Menelaus and his party and an assortment of Jewish and non-Jewish military personnel. In all, it is hard to escape the impression that the religious persecution was at best an afterthought rather than the core of some program of hellenization foisted on Jerusalem by Antiochus IV.

If the persecution is religious in nature, what are the elements of this religious persecution? There are several listed in the sources:
1.   The introduction of a foreign God;
2.   The injunctions against the Law of Moses;
3.   The erection of the "Abomination of Desolation" in the Temple and the sacrifice of swine and unclean animals to/on it.[40]

The problem of the decree is that there is no other evidence of such persecution in antiquity. It is utterly contradictory to the policies of both the Ptolemies and the Seleucids.

> It is best to confess, however, that there seems to be no way of reaching an understanding of how Antiochus came to take a step so

---

[40] I Macc. 1:51.

profoundly at variance with the normal assumptions of governance in his time.[41]

Of all these changes certainly the most drastic would seem to be the change of deities. But this is very difficult to establish. Since we know of many instances of the successful blending of hellenistic religious ideas and local religion, one must exercise great caution in assuming that the change of name was, in fact, a change of deities.[42] Bickermann notes that the change of names to Zeus Olympius was simply a way of "registering" the Temple God of Jerusalem in the official Greek language of the *polis*.[43]

> The tradition concerning the designation of the Temple, the fact that it was taken over for a new cult, and the probability that this cult was not anthropomorphic all these data prove that the God of Zion remained the same even after the "destruction of the temple." The God but not the temple service.[44]

Still more significant is the fact that there is considerable doubt that the decree itself was authentic.[45]

It is therefore, highly questionable that Antiochus IV personally took such interest in the religious affairs of Jerusalem that he would specifically forbid the practice of the Mosaic Law there or anywhere.[46] But the dissatisfactions of certain inner-Jewish groups would certainly coalesce around changes which might be perceived as dramatic innovations.

From all that has preceded we can perhaps make some attempt to wrest an understanding of what actually happened in the Maccabean Revolution. I would take it for a given that the simplistic idea of Greeks versus Jews can be dismissed. And I would hold that the idea of a religious persecution *ab extra* is on very thin ground historically. What appears most evident is that the struggle is basically an inner-Jewish struggle.[47] This, of course, coincides perfectly with the work of

---

[41] Fergus Millar, "The Background to the Maccabean Revolution: Reflections on Martin Hengel's *Judaism and Hellenism*," *JJS* 29 (1978) 17.

[42] This subject is treated definitively by Bickermann. *Der Gott der Makkabäer*, 90-96.

[43] E. Bickermann, *The God of the Maccabees: Studies on the Meaning and Origin of the Maccabean Revolt*. Trans. Horst R. Moehring (Leiden: E.J. Brill) 65.

[44] Bickermann, *The God of the Maccabees*, 68.

[45] See the discussion in M. Hengel, *Judaism and Hellenism*, 284.

[46] F.E. Peters, *The Harvest of Hellenism*, 250-252.

[47] An excellent discussion of the issue is found in Joseph Sievers, *The Hasmoneans and Their Supporters*, 22-30.

M. Hengel and his programmatic statement: "From about the middle of the third century BC *all Judaism* must really be designated 'Hellenistic Judaism'."[48] The inner-Jewish struggle is not a simple struggle between opposing religious factions. It is a complex struggle which harkens back to the divisions of the proto-Apocalyptic period and which involves as much economics as it does religion.

The exact conflict from which the Revolution arises goes back to the struggle between aristocratic families in the 3rd century BCE. It is most clearly reflected in the struggle between the Tobiads and the Zadokite priests in charge of the Temple. The Tobiads are known to us from the *Antiquities* and other sources. The Tobiads generally favored the Ptolemies in the contest between them and the Seleucids. A critical point in the development of this struggle was the assumption of the office of *prostates,* or tax collector, by Joseph, the son of Tobiah the founder, in 230 BCE. This office he snatched from the high priest Onias (Ant. XII, 162). As Tcherikover then notes: "Thus occurred the first breach in the edifice of the theocracy of Jerusalem."[49]

The rivalry between these families would determine the play for the next century until the emergence of the Hasmoneans and the re-unification of the priestly and civil offices. The economic factors that are at work during this period are, of course, difficult to discover. But any attempt to understand the Maccabean Revolution must reckon with the fact that the struggle was, at first, among the Jewish upper classes for control of the Temple which was not only the religious but the economic center of the Jerusalem city state.

The effects of hellenization were largely economic. The culture of the Greek cities provided a basis for the expansion of economic markets. In addition to the creation of a variety of new needs which were to be met, the cities which were chartered were given a wide berth in the development of their commercial contacts. Some of them were allowed to mint their own coinage, thus allowing a more universally acceptable means for purchasing foreign goods and selling their own goods. Of course these benefits were largely divided among the wealthy, though perhaps some early form of "trickle-down" economics might have been possible.[50]

---

[48] Hengel, *Judaism and Hellenism,* 104.

[49] V. Tcherikover, *HCJ,* 132, and 149.

[50] See Hans G. Kippenberg, *Religion und Klassenbildung im antiken Judäa* (Göttingen: Vandenhoeck und Ruprecht, 1978) 82-94; Bickermann, *Der Gott der Makkabäer,* 128; Heinz Kreissig, "A Marxist View of Josephus' Account of the Judean War," Unpublished, courtesy of Professor Louis H. Feldman.

The general picture we have of the Temple state at this time suggests a tripartite society: a) the priestly ruling class subdivided into a variety of families; b) the landed "gentry"[51] and upper class merchants or professional groups; c) the group largely encompassed by the term 'ammê ha'aretz.[52] This latter group was to bear the burden of the economic growth of the hellenistic period. Since both the system of taxation and the sources of wealth were changing to favor the urban elite or their country cousins of the aristocracy.[53] Thus, the same groups where the earlier apocalyptic, visionary elements largely resided were again the victims of the vagaries of the ruling hierocratic (now also bureaucratic) party.

The entry of hellenism into the scene seems hardly the problem at all. The problems must be seen in the light of the economic and social benefits that were being shared or not being shared at this critical point. The creation of the Greek-style polis of Jerusalem was not a matter of religion, it was a matter of economics.

> Zahlreichen Judean, insbesondere Angehörigen der priestlichen Obersicht, war die übernahme der Gesellschaftlischen und politischen Instituionen der griechischen Städte erwünscht und willkommen.[54]

In a rather blunt and not wholly objective remark Heinz Kreissig noted:

> Allein religiöse Widersprüche haben noch nie und nirgends zu grossen Volksbewegungen geführt.[55]

One ought to take such statements with great caution but the truth of the matter is that revolutions are seldom if ever the product of *one* overriding idea or concern, but tend always to emerge from complex problems and ideas that are often contradictory. In a perceptive remark on this complex process E. Rivkin wrote:

> The shift from relatively primitive agricultural-priestly society to a far more complex agricultural urbanized one began in the Persian period with the steady growth of an agricultural surplus which enriched the

---

[51] The landed "gentry" must be reckoned with also as a group of particular significance to the growth of both the religious and cultural life of Jerusalem. See R.N. Whybray, *The Intellectual Tradition of the Old Testament* (Berlin: DeGruyter, 1974) 61-65.

[52] S. Zeitlin, *The Rise and Fall*, 65-73; Tcherikover. *HCJ*, 150-151.

[53] A. Mittwock, "Tribute and Land Tax in Seleucid Judah," *Biblica* 36 (1955) 352-61; H. Kreissig, "Der Makkabäeraufstand zur seiner sozialökonomischen Zusammenhange und Wirkungen," *Studi Classice* 4 (1962) 143-175.

[54] Bringmann, *Hellenistische Reform*, 67.

[55] Kreissig, "A Marxist View," 14.

culture, and proceeded at a heightened tempo under the pressure of the polisification process that transformed the economic, social and political structures of the Ancient Near East.[56]

And Tcherikover noted that:

It was not the revolt which came as a response to the persecution but the persecution came as a response to the revolt.[57]

I would propose, then, that the Maccabean Revolution was a classic model of revolution. The scenario of the revolution is laid out as follows:

a) the returned exiles bring back the Temple and establish a hierocratic state largely based on the Jewish legal traditions and increasingly wedded to a priestly, hierocratic view of the community;

b) the people left behind in Palestine, having established a visionary program for the new Jerusalem based largely on the prophetic critique of the kingdom and the cult, are forced to compromise or go "underground." Though defeated in the public forum they remain powerful;

c) the process of hellenizing the civilized world was a vast movement across nations, cultures, and religions involving every aspect of human life but particularly emphasizing the *polis* and the urban life (hence also the individual) as the center in which the hellenistic view of life could be articulated;

d) the struggle to define Judaism was also international in scope and was waged both in Palestine and in the rest of the Diaspora. The process of hellenization affected *all* the parties who were involved in the struggle at certain points more obviously and directly than at others (e.g. Alexandria or Samaria);

e) the economic factors that were present may be anachronistically, but perceptively defined as class conflicts. The *'ammê ha'aretz*, initially descendants of an honored class (indeed the heart of the old Yahwistic religion), now became "peasants." This class was largely left outside the process of economic growth experienced by the urban elites, and as the bearers of the "visionary" strains in Judaism, they bore within them the seeds of a religious revolution;

f) the struggle over the Temple priesthood, the control of the bank of the Temple, the marketplace, in short, the economic

---

[56] E. Rivkin, "Pharisaism," 508-509.

[57] Tcherikover, *HCJ*, 191.

center of Judea, namely Jerusalem, set the major families of the aristocracy against one another and for or against the Zadokite priests.

Taken together these factors all indicate that Palestinian Judaism was ripe for revolution.[58] One significant factor present, besides the growing divisions in the upper classes, was what Gurr referred to as "relative deprivation." That is the fact that the urban poor, the small craftspeople, and others whose livelihood was drawn from the Temple as it was customarily constituted, and the rural poor, all saw the growing luxury of city living and, at the same time, found themselves overburdened with taxation and victimized by the growth of large estates. Thus they were classic economic victims and likely saw themselves as experiencing "relative deprivation," that is, a sense of a gap between expectations and perceived capacity to achieve them economically, politically, or socially. Among the upper classes it is clear that the clash was not between hellenizers and Jews but between various groups vying for economic and political power. So the rise and fall of the "hellenizers" has less to do with opposition between religious values and more to do with the control of power in the state.[59]

There is an ancient opposition which, I believe, lies beneath the surface of the conflict. That opposition is partly revealed in the conflict between visionaries and hierocrats, but its roots are more remote in Israel's history. The process of defining Israel and the process of defining Judaism are parallel processes. They both involve the revolutionary upheaval of an existing but debilitated social system under the impetus of a religious and nationalist movement. From this follows the redefinition of ethnos and ethos.

This opposition has been admirably outlined and skillfully argued by Norman K. Gottwald in his *The Tribes of Yahweh*. There Gottwald decisively, I believe (though not without some cautions[60]), argues that Israel emerged from the destruction of the old Canaanite/Phoenician city state system by disaffected groups which came together under the

---

[58] In his classic work *The Causes of the English Revolution 1529-1642* (New York: Harper Torchbooks, 1972) Lawrence Stone discusses succinctly a variety of theories of revolution. Note especially the discussion on pp. 12-15. "It is in societies experiencing rapid economic growth that trouble usually occurs" (p. 14).

[59] K. Bringmann, *Hellenistische Reform*, 92-93. Even the Pharisaic party which emerges out of this matrix, and is most popularly associated with anti-hellenism, is, in fact, just as likely to have been, in the words of Fischel, "The most Hellenized group in Judah." ("Story and History," 466).

[60] See the discussion in B. Halpern, *The Emergence of Israel in Canaan*. SBL Monograph Series 29 (Chico: Scholars Press, 1983) 47-63.

impetus of the religion of Yahweh. The thrust of the movement was the creation of an egalitarian and idealist society.[61] The city, in general, has not served as the model for that society.[62] Applebaum notes:

> The city governments of Judea consisted largely of landowners from city-territories.... The tendency, therefore would have been to see the city-councilors as the enemies of the rural laborers, the small holder, and the tenant. The social gulf and the resulting hostility between city and country in the classical period have been emphasized more than once.[63]

As we have seen, the emergence of the polis as the center of activity in both economic and social-political matters was a mark of hellenistic culture. Thus the ancient dispute over cities could be easily re-invoked in such circumstances.[64] The opposition between the goals of liberated Israel and the city state models are particularly evident in the Yahwist source in the Pentateuch.[65]

It is particularly important to realize, however, that the paradigm and the reality of what constituted early Israel are not necessarily the same. A paradigm is a model against which experience can be weighed and measured until such a time as experience shows the paradigm not to work and a new paradigm is required.[66] Thus, the classic opposition between the "Way of the Canaanites" and the "Way of Israel" is paradigmatic for early Israel's self understanding. But the reality of the relation between the Canaanite city culture and Israelite "country" culture is much more complex. The values of the revolutionary party necessarily needed to be articulated in opposition to the status quo, to the old order, to the repressive system. But, in fact, the old system was not destroyed but absorbed. Indeed the old system eventually became the new system as the model for Israel's self-

---

[61] Norman K. Gottwald, *The Tribes of Yahweh: A Sociology of the Religion of Liberated Israel 1250-1050 BCE* (Maryknoll: Orbis, 1979) 584-587 and passim.

[62] On the various ideas about the city see the excellent study by Frank S. Frick, *The City in Ancient Israel.* SBL Dissertation Series 32 (Chico: Scholars Press, 1977), 201-227.

[63] Applebaum, "Josephus and the Economic Causes," 28.

[64] See the interesting reflections of Jacques Ellul, *The Meaning of the City* (Grand Rapids: Eerdmanns, 1970) for a contemporary discussion of the theology of the city; also John M. Halligan, *A Critique of the City in the Yahwist Corpus* (Ph.D. Diss. Notre Dame University, 1975).

[65] Halligan, *A Critique,* 218.

[66] Thomas S. Kuhn, *The Structure of Scientific Revolutions.* 2d Edition, Int'l Encyclopedia of the Unified Sciences, Vol. 2, No. 2 (Chicago: University of Chicago, 1970) 43-51.

governance through leagues and tribes, sheiks and judges, ceded to the idea of kingship, kingdom, and temple priesthood.[67]

The same paradigm, in my view, applies to the conflict of the Maccabean era. From the opening of I Macc. where the story of Mattathias is consciously built on the model of Phinehas in Numbers 25, to the setting of the struggle initially outside the city, in the hill country, from whence liberated Israel first emerged, through the model of the sons of Mattathias built on the model of the judges (where leadership passes not by right of primogeniture but through charisma) every aspect of the books of the Maccabees seems to present a picture approximating the great struggle to free the land from the Canaanites. One could argue that the denouement of the story is the restoration of kingship and priesthood in the Hasmoneans, the new Davidides.[68] History comes full cycle. The coalescence of the factors present in the social and economic sphere, through the zeal of certain religious factions (we know of one at least, the *assidaioi*[69]), led to the emergence of a perceived dichotomy in the minds of the revolutionaries. The rallying cry was against "hellenism" and the "hellenizers" and thus for Judaism. But neither term, as we have seen, had any carefully defined content. But the political maneuvering which centered on the sale and desecration of the priesthood—particularly with Menelaus and his followers—and the subsequent change of the *rites* in the Temple (not the religion however!) provided the religious motivation. In a sense the religious groups provided the cement that held the political and social factions together initially.[70]

Thus, the hellenizers are to be rightly identified with the Canaanites if the paradigm is correct. And as Gottwald shows and the biblical accounts themselves indicate, the opposition between the Canaanites and the Israelites had only a limited historical basis. But it was essential to the propaganda of the liberating Yahwists. In this sense the model of the conquest of "Canaan" by Israel is now transmogrified into the conquest of the Hellenizers by the Jews.

If this is so, then the evidence which continues to mount of the hellenization of Palestinian Judaism finds no contradiction in the biblical story of the Maccabean Revolution. It is paradigmatic, and modeled on the classical locus of cultural contact in Israel's formative

---

[67] Gottwald discusses this process of opposing and at the same time absorbing and being absorbed by the dominant culture in *The Tribes of Yahweh*, 498-583.

[68] See the discussion of this dual role in Peters, *The Harvest of Hellenism*, 281-296.

[69] See Sievers, *The Hasmoneans*, 56-60.

[70] Gottwald, *The Tribes of Yahweh*, 498-503; 571-583.

period. But they (the biblical books) do not adequately deal with or display the reality of the historical situation. To resume our opening thought, history is written by the victors. The story that is told in Maccabees is mythical. It is a tale told to prove a point. The central point is the legitimacy of the Hasmonean dynasty as the authentic heirs to David's throne. The paradigm the writer(s) chose is the story of kingship in Israel, itself a construction intended to legitimate David's kingship. The setting, plot, characters, and language of the story are all artfully constructed on the foundation of a series of "factual" events. Like a good historical novel, the book instructs in a point of view through careful attention to creating the appearance of objectivity.[71] But this is not a simple retelling of events. This is the story of Israel's rebirth. The story of the Hasmonean victory can even be called the story of a new Exodus. In this case the Hasmoneans and their followers define the struggle between the Jewish "parties" in terms which evoke the liberation of Israel from Egypt and Canaan.

---

[71] Hayden White, *Tropics*, 121-134.

Chapter Eight

Patterns of Mystical Prayer in Ancient Judaism: Progression of Themes in *Ma'aseh Merkavah*

Michael D. Swartz
University of Virginia

Ma'aseh Merkavah is an important text in the literature of Merkavah Mysticism, the visionary Jewish mysticism which flourished in Palestine and Babylonia in the second through eighth centuries C.E. These texts, known as Hekhalot literature, contain some of the earliest evidence for Jewish mysticism and theurgy. Unlike other contemporary texts of Rabbinic religion, these texts center not on law, theology, or biblical exegesis, but on journeys purportedly undertaken by their authors through the *Hekhalot*, the heavenly "palaces" or chambers, to the Divine Chariot-Throne, the *Merkavah*.[1]

Ma'aseh Merkavah is primarily an anthology of mystical prayers ranging in form and content from prayers similar to the standard Babylonian Jewish liturgy to practical magic. In *Ma'aseh Merkavah* prayer plays an active role, more so than in any other Hekhalot text. Prayers are seen in the text as the instruments by which the protagonists ascend, experience the vision of the upper realm, and protect themselves from the dangers of that vision.

---

[1] G. Scholem, *Major Trends in Jewish Mysticism* (second ed., New York, 1954); *Jewish Gnosticism, Merkavah Mysticism, and Talmudic Tradition* (second ed., New York), 1965. An overview of the phenomenon is presented in J. Dan, "The Religious Experience of the *Merkavah*," in A. Green (ed.), *Jewish Spirituality From the Bible to The Middle Ages* (New York, 1986), 289-307.

At the same time, *Ma'aseh Merkavah* also provides evidence for the changing function of prayer within the Hekhalot tradition. Form-critical analysis demonstrates that the text underwent a process of evolution from a collection of prayers to be recited in community with the heavenly hosts, to a prescription for the active cultivation of the individual's ascent to and vision of the upper realm—that is, an evolution from liturgy to theurgy.

This process of evolution becomes evident in striking contrasts between the form and content of the prayers in the text, on the one hand, and the function attributed to them in their redactional framework, on the other. This relationship has been demonstrated in this writer's larger study of *Ma'aseh Merkavah*.[2] This article will focus on the initial stage in this process of development, through an analysis of the major themes in the prayers themselves. When these prayers are seen apart from their narrative context, striking thematic patterns emerge. These patterns illustrate the purpose of the prayers which formed the basis for the text.

Ma'aseh Merkavah

Ma'aseh Merkavah was first published in excerpts by Alexander Altmann,[3] then in full by Gershom Scholem.[4] The text is included in Peter Schäfer's definitive synoptic edition of Hekhalot literature, which forms the basis for this study.[5] Schäfer has shown that for many of the Hekhalot texts, an *Urtext* cannot be established.[6] His conclusions demonstrate that it is necessary to treat the literature not as a unitary corpus representing a single phenomenon, but as a highly

---

[2] This article began as a paper presented to the History and Literature of Early Rabbinic Judaism Section of the Society of Biblical Literature at the SBL 1987 annual meeting. It is based on my forthcoming study of *Ma'aseh Merkavah*, which originated as my doctoral dissertation, "Liturgical Elements in Early Jewish Mysticism: A Literary Analysis of *Ma'aseh Merkavah*," (New York University, 1986). I wish to thank Professor Lawrence Schiffman, my principal thesis adviser, and Professor Gary Anderson, who read a version of this paper. On prayer in *Ma'aseh Merkavah* see also M. Swartz, "'Alay le-shabbeah: A Liturgical Prayer in *Ma'aseh Merkavah*," *JQR* 77 (1986-87), 179-190.

[3] Altmann, Alexander, "*Shire Qedushah be-Sifrut ha-Hekhalot ha-Qedumah*," *Melilah* 2 (1946), 1-24.

[4] *Jewish Gnosticism*, 103-117.

[5] P. Schäfer, *Synopse Zur Hekhalot-Literatur* (Tübingen, 1981). This paper will follow the numbering in the *Synopse*.

[6] "Tradition and Redaction in Hekhalot Literature," *JSJ* 14 (1983), 172-81; *Synopse*, v-vii; "Aufbau und redaktionelle Identität der Hekhalot Zutarti," *JJS* 33, 569-82.

varied literature that spans many genres and stages of development. This is manifest in the literature's redactional properties. As Schäfer states:

> In the tension between tradition and redaction, the decisive weight must be placed on the tradition in each case.[7]

Diachronic form-critical and rhetorical analysis such as that undertaken in this study can thus recover those strata of the literature and the forms of religion it reflects.

Ma'aseh Merkavah actually consists of three texts, which I have designated as "sections." Each section is composed of sayings pseudepigraphically attributed to Rabbis of the second century C.E. These consist of prayers framed by narrative. The narrative purports to tell how these Rabbis acquired Divine visions and secrets. Section I tells how Rabbi Akiba learned the secrets of ascending through the *Hekhalot* to witness God in His heavenly court and His *Merkavah*. This narrative is continued in a later fourth Section (IV). Sections II and III tell how Rabbi Ishmael conjured the angels who imparted to him the secrets of acquiring wisdom. This paper will focus on the prayers in Sections I, III, and IV, which display close stylistic and thematic affinities.

The prayers which formed the basis for *Ma'aseh Merkavah* were probably composed in Palestine between the third and fifth centuries C.E. Sometime after their composition, these prayers came to include magical and theurgic formulae consisting of strings of Divine names, numinous phrases and biblical verses. The prayers were then placed into narrative accounts of the ascent of Rabbi Akiba and Rabbi Ishmael. They were depicted by the authors of these narratives as the powerful prayers through which these Rabbis ascended to the Hekhalot, protected themselves from the dangers of the ascent, and were able to achieve a vision of God. These narratives were probably composed and placed together in Geonic Babylonia, between the sixth and eighth centuries.

Prayer in *Ma'aseh Merkavah*

Prayer is generally regarded as an important testimony to the experiential, mystical character of Hekhalot literature. Merkavah prayer has been seen to be characterized by the use of repetition of synonyms, a hypnotic rhythm, and a numinous quality. According to Philip Bloch, Gershom Scholem, and others, Merkavah prayer

---

[7] "Tradition and Redaction," 181.

employed these qualities to induce a trance.[8] Inspired by Rudolf Otto's category of the numinous,[9] Scholem saw in the style of the prayers a "polylogy" directly intended to aid the mystic in his vision of God.[10]

These descriptions of the character and function of Merkavah prayer were based to a great extent on *Hekhalot Rabbati*, the text which has been used most often as evidence for Merkavah mysticism.[11] Prayers in *Hekhalot Rabbati* may indeed have been composed for the purposes of engendering a mystical trance. *Ma'aseh Merkavah*, however, exhibits a rather different set of stylistic and thematic dynamics, with different implications for the role of prayer in Merkavah mysticism. The prayers which formed the basis for *Ma'aseh Merkavah* were not meant primarily to lift the worshipper from earthly contemplation to heavenly ascent, but rather to express his participation in an earthly liturgy corresponding to the angelic liturgy. Thus their primary purpose was evocative rather than instrumental. Only later did the authors of the narrative of the text attribute to the prayers the function of producing a vision of the Divine world.

Thematic and interactive rhetoric in the prayers

The composers of prayer in *Ma'aseh Merkavah* did not employ the elaborate repetition and polylogy described by Bloch and Scholem as their principal stylistic models. While such features do appear in *Ma'aseh Merkavah*, they are not the most prevalent literary forms in the prayers. Rather, the composers primarily employed prosodic forms common to Hebrew poetry in this period. These forms include a basic

---

[8] P. Bloch, "Die *Yorde Merkavah*, die Mystiker der Gaonzeit und ihrer Einfluss auf die Liturgie," *MGWJ*, O.S. 37 (1893), 18- 25, 69-74, 257-66, 305-11; Scholem, *Major Trends*, 57-63.

[9] R. Otto, *The Idea of the Holy*, (second ed., Oxford, 1950).

[10] The formal and poetic characteristics of prayer in Hekhalot literature have been analyzed by Johann Maier in an important series of articles: "'Attah hu 'Adon (Hekhalot Rabbati XXVI 5)," *Judaica* 22 (1966), 209-33; "Hekhalot Rabbati XXVII, 2-5," *Judaica* 21 (1965), 129-33; "Poetisch-liturgische Stücken aus dem 'Buch der Geheimnisse'," *Judaica* 24 (1968), 172-81; "Serienbildung und 'Numinoser' Eindruckseffekt in den poetischen Stücken der Hekhalot-Literatur," *Semitics* 3 (1973), 36-66.

[11] On *Hekhalot Rabbati* (§81-306 in the *Synopse*), see Scholem, *Gnosticism*, 6; Gruenwald, *Apocalyptic and Merkavah Mysticism* (Leiden, 1980), 150-173; A. Goldberg, "Einige Bemerkungen zu den Quellen und den redaktionellen Einheiten der grossen Hekhalot,", *FJB* 1,(1973), 1-49; Maier, "Serienbildung;" "Hekhalot Rabbati XXVII, 2-5."

rhythm and an elementary parallelism of stichs.[12] This parallelism and rhythm can be found in petitionary prayer of the statutory liturgy, liturgical prayer from Qumran, secular funeral poetry of the Talmudic age, and personal confessions attributed in the Talmud to the Rabbis.[13] Certainly not all of these genres had as their object the direct apprehension of the Divine Presence. Rather, these formal elements were characteristic of rhetorical style in the Hebrew poetry of the age, and are shared by the various genres.

Moreover, the composers of prayer in *Ma'aseh Merkavah* also followed ordered procedures for arranging their themes. The survey of forms and themes in the prayers undertaken here yields striking patterns of progression. These patterns are evidence of a rhetorical model, a system of rubrics which were employed by the authors in the composition of prayers.

This pattern is summarized here. The individual forms are then described in detail:

(1)   The prayers open with a blessing *(berakhah)* or other form of address to God.

(2)   The prayers then describe, often in majestic poetry, God's establishment and creation of the heavens and earth.

(3)   The poetry then concentrates on one aspect of the creation: The heavenly beings, especially the angels, and their continual praise of the enthroned God.

(4)   At this point many of the prayers stress the correspondence of the angelic praise with that of the human worshipper.

(5)   This leads to the worshipper's declaration that he will recite God's glory or pronounce the name of God.

(6)   The prayers close with a liturgical blessing.

Opening

The prayers open with a direct address to God. This address takes three forms. One, which may be called a vocative form, consists simply

---

[12] These forms and their historical background have been identified and analyzed by A. Mirsky in *"Ha-Shirah bi-Tequfat ha-Talmud," Yerushalaim: Shenaton le-Divre Sifrut ve-Hagut* 3-4 (1970), 161-70; *Mahsevetan shel Surot ha-Piyyut* Jerusalem, 1968-69; *Re'shit ha-Piyyut,* Jerusalem, 1965; *"Toldot Ha-Shirshur," Tarbis* 28 (1959), 171-80; *"Gidere ha-Piyyut shel ha-Payetanim 'Alume ha-Shem," Peraqim* 1 (1969), 109-14.

[13] See Mirsky, *"Ha-Shirah."*

of a name for God: for example, §548, a so-called "Prayer for Mercy," simply begins, "'El RWZYY YHWH."

A second, more prevalent form, is the use of a second-person *hitpa'el* verb, or a series of such verbs. These are usually verbs of praise such as *titbarakh*, "may You be blessed," *titqadash*, "may You be sanctified," and *tishtabah*, "may You be praised." The opening address is sometimes followed by a series of epithets for God. An example can be found in three prayers in Section III. The first prayer §587, begins:

> May You Be blessed, (*titbarakh*) O God, great, mighty, and strong, exalted in beauty, magnificent in glory..

The following two prayers begin in a similar way, with all three yielding this pattern:

Prayer	Address	Praise
§587	May You be Blessed,	O God, great, mighty, and strong, exalted in beauty, magnificent in glory...
§588	May you be sanctified,	O God of heaven and earth, Lord of lords, magnificent of the magnificent, God of the Cherubim...
§589	Blessed be Your name,	O Strong king...Lord of miracles, Lord of the extraordinary...

A third form of opening for a prayer is the *berakhah*, the liturgical blessing, a form which is discussed below. *Berakhot* appear at the end of most of the prayers in *Ma'aseh Merkavah*. However, blessings are less prevalent in the openings of prayers.

God's establishment of heaven and earth

The prayers proceed from this opening address to the second theme, that of God's establishment or creation of the heavens and earth. This theme is often expressed in a series of parallel lines.

A set of verbs, usually in second-person perfect, is used to express this theme: *kwn* (establish); *ysd* (found); *br'* or *ysr* (create or form); and *sym* (place). The following passage from §590 (in Section III) illustrates how these terms are used:

> You have established (*konanta*) Your throne in heaven,
> You have placed (*samta*) Your dwelling in the lofty heights;
> You have placed (*samta*) Your Merkavah in Your celestial reaches,
> in the bright clouds.

In such passages this theme can be coupled with the theme of God's sovereignty, transcendence, or superiority over heavenly beings. §587 links these themes in a particularly striking way:

In glory You spoke and the world came into being;[14]

With the breath of Your lips You established (konanta) the firmament.

and Your great name is pure over those above and all those below.

The first line praises God's creation of earth; the second, His creation of heaven; the complementary third line stresses the transcendence of God's Name over both.

The angelic hosts and their praise

The next form is followed invariably by passages describing the praise of God by the angels or other celestial beings. The theme of angelic praise is one of the most constant in the prayers in *Ma'aseh Merkavah*.[15]

The language used to express this theme varies widely in style. In §548 in Section I, the passage describing God's establishment of creation is followed by an extended description of various classes of angels giving praise:

With force and might,

song and hymn, clouds of fire,

fearsome Soldiers, awesome Captains,

a thousand thousand thousand

and a myriad of myriads of myriads

give praise and approbation

---

[14] *'Atah 'amarta ve-hayah ha-'olam*. On this common rabbinic expression for God's creation, see Marmorstein, *The Old Rabbinic Doctrine of God* (Second ed., New York 1968), 89. The term is also used in the opening prayer of the *pesuqe de-zimra'*, the Chapters of Psalms which open the statutory daily morning service: *Barukh she-'amar ve-hayah ha'olam*, "Blessed be He Who spoke and the world came into being."

[15] The antiquity and importance of this theme in prayer literature can be seen in the angelic liturgy at Qumran. See C. Newsom, *The Songs of the Sabbath Sacrifice: Edition, Translation, and Commentary*, (Atlanta, 1986). See also J. Strugnell, "An Angelic Liturgy at Qumran—4Q Serekh Shirot 'Olat Hassabbat," *Supplement to VT*, VII (1959), 318-45; and L. Schiffman, "Merkavah Speculation at Qumran: The 4Q Serekh Shirot 'Olat ha-Shabbat," in J. Reinharz, et al., *Mystics, Philosophers, and Politicians*, (Durham, NC, 1982), 15-47.

to Your great, mighty, and awesome name.
Before You stand all the Mighty Ones.

This passage is marked by its accumulation of terms for angels and its extravagant numbers, forms which are seen as characteristic of numinous prayer in Hekhalot literature.[16] This style is chiefly characteristic of Hekhalot Rabbati, but of secondary importance in *Ma'aseh Merkavah*. For example, the corresponding passage in §587 is more measured:

and angels stand in heaven,
and the righteous are sure in their remembrance of You.

This couplet is notable for juxtaposing the angels with the righteous on earth, a theme which, as we shall see, figures prominently in *Ma'aseh Merkavah*.

Doxology and declaration of praise

Doxological or liturgical formulae often appear in the latter portion of the prayers. These doxologies include the *qedushah*, (Is. 6:3), liturgical responses such as "Blessed be the Name of His glorious Majesty for ever and ever," and doxologies not found in the statutory liturgy.[17] These formulae are often introduced by passages in which the angels or worshippers are depicted reciting the praise of God or the Divine name. These passages employ the verbs *magia'*, "present" or *mabia'*, "express," or the verb *mazkir*, "recite."

This pairing of the description of the angels presenting praise to God with a doxological formula is illustrated in the following passage from §555, a brief prayer in Section I.

From this one, "holy" and from that one "holy,"
and they present song perpetually
and pronounce the name of GHWRY'L YWY, God of Israel,
and say: "Blessed be the name of His Majesty's
    Glory forever and ever from the place of His *Shekhinah*."

Here the *qedushah* is described, though it is not quoted. The doxological formula follows as a response to the qedushah.

---

[16] Maier, "Serienbildungen."

[17] The doxological form has been analyzed by Eric Werner, "The Doxology in Synagogue and Church," *HUCA* 19 (1945/6). One passage in the text, §555, is a veritable lexicon of such doxologies, which are said to be recited by the *Merkavot* of fire.

At this point the worshipper declares that he will praise God. This declaration takes the form of a first-person imperfect verb, or by a word for "therefore" (*'al ken or lefikhakh*). In §596 the worshipper declares: "Therefore (*lefikhakh*) we shall bless You...." In §589 the angelic praise is introduced by, "Therefore, (*'al ken*) the Mighty Ones of Heaven give praise before You."[18]

Closing praise and blessing

Almost all of the prayers in *Ma'aseh Merkavah* conclude with *berakhot*, liturgical blessings. These benedictions are often identical in form to the blessings of the Rabbinic liturgy. However, only one of the formulae corresponds to a known *hatimah*, that is, a closing blessing of the statutory liturgy. This is the blessing, "*ha-'El ha-qadosh*: "blessed are You, O Lord, the Holy God," which concludes the *qedushah* in the statutory *'Amidah*. The other blessings are not associated with known liturgies. However, it is important to remember that, as Joseph Heinemann has shown, the *berakhah* was used both for statutory and nonstatutory prayer. There is ample evidence from this period for blessings recited privately, and outside of official Rabbinic control.[19]

Several *berakhot* echo concerns manifest in the prayers themselves. For example, two of the closing blessings praise God as "magnificent in the Chambers of Song" (*'Adir be Hadre Shirah*), thus reflecting the motif of praise of God in the chambers of heaven.[20] §585, a brief prayer in Section III, focuses on the *Hayot*, the Holy Creatures, and other heavenly beings. The prayer closes with the blessing: "Who forms all creatures in truth (*yoser kol ha-beri'ot be'emet*)." It was not, therefore, the liturgical associations of berakhot that led the composers of the prayers in *Ma'aseh Merkavah* to include them but their content.

---

[18] §551, *Alay le-Shabeah*, which is based on a prayer from the Babylonian Jewish statutory liturgy, also contains a passage beginning with *'al ken*. However, there the phrase introduces a passage of Messianic hope, not the protagonist's praise. Nonetheless, *'Alay le-shabeah* does include a first-person declaration: "And I shall sanctify Your name." On the history and structure of the prayer, see Swartz, "'*Alay le-Shabbeah*."

[19] See Heinemann, *Prayer*, 77-103, 156-192. On pp. 74-76 (pp. 288-90 in the Hebrew Appendix), Heinemann demonstrates the wide variety of blessings for ritual occasions. On the origins of the liturgical blessing see also W.S. Towner, "'Blessed art Thou, YHWH': The Modulation of a Biblical Formula," *CBQ* 30 (1968), 386-99.

[20] §551, *'Alay le-Shabeah*, and §548 in the version in MS. NY JTSA 8128.

The rhetoric of the prayers and its implications

When these themes are taken together, they form a coherent expression of interaction with and praise of God. The opening address or blessing serves a function of salutation.[21] The *berakhah* also offers the prayer a liturgical anchor; that is, both the opening and closing *berakhot* delineate the prayer as a unit, and serve to signal the main theme of the prayer. God is then reminded of His creation of a twofold cosmos, consisting of heaven, with its celestial hosts, and earth, with its human community of worship. The focus then narrows to those two communities—the angels and human worshippers.

The prayers thus shift from the theme of creation to the description of the angelic hosts, and follow with the theme of the earthly community of praise. This progression serves both to remind God of His role in creating the worshipper and to suggest that the prayer of humanity is on a continuum with the prayer of angels. Thus a two-way channel is established: From the creative power of God to the authority, or permission (*reshut*), of human beings to sing God's praises.

These passages stress the uniqueness and transcendence of God throughout. Forms and phrases expressing this are found frequently in the prayers; an example is the recurrent form which consists of phrases beginning '*En ke-*, "there is none like [You or Your name]." This motif serves to stress that it is God, not the angels or the Throne, who is to be praised.[22]

Having erected this framework, the worshipper is then in a position to declare and participate in the Divine liturgy. He does so in the doxologies and supplementary passages of praise which follow. Here too, the doxology form represents the worshipper's appeal to others to participate in praise more than the detailed praise itself. In this way the prayer completes its function and character as liturgical poetry; an eternal pattern of Divine worship is both evoked and invoked in these passages. The closing *berakhah* reinforces this statutory quality.

---

[21] Cf. the function of greeting in the biblical cult, performed by the *Shelamim* offering. See B. Levine, *In The Presence of The Lord* (Leiden, 1974).

[22] Other Hekhalot texts depict the traveller who errs by worshipping an angel instead of the enthroned God. In 3 Enoch, §20 (=§856) this is the error of the arch-heretic Elisha ben Abuya. See P. Alexander, "3 (Hebrew Apocalypse of) Enoch," in J. Charlesworth (ed.), *The Old Testament Pseudepigrapha* vol. 1 (Garden City, NY, 1983), 223-315; see p. 268 on this passage. Cf. A/2, lines 13-18 in the Hekhalot fragments from the Cairo Genizah in I. Gruenwald, "*Qeta'im Hadashim Mi-Sifrut ha-Hekhalot*," *Tarbis* 38 (1969), 300-19 (= P. Schäfer, *Genizah-Fragmente zur Hekhalot- Literatur* [Tübingen, 1984], Text 8, 2b).

Prayer in *Ma'aseh Merkavah:* conclusions

The prayers of *Ma'aseh Merkavah* cannot be characterized as spontaneous outpourings of the soul in mystic apprehension of Divinity, nor as meaningless polylogy geared toward engendering a trance. These prayers are saturated with literary convention. They were carefully crafted, employing poetic techniques which had developed long before their composition. Moreover, they reflect a distinct set of themes and have a specific rhetorical task: To persuade God and the worshippers that the prayer of the human community is as fitting as that of the angels.

This praise was probably seen by its composers as occurring on earth. A two-tiered structure informs the passages which speak of creation and of God's creatures and their praise. In prayers such as §587, the parallelism of these passages aids this concept:

Angels stand in heaven,

and the righteous are sure in their remembrance of You.

This idea of corresponding communities is also a feature of a statutory version of the *Qedushah* from the standard Babylonian Jewish liturgy:

We sanctify Your name on earth

as they sanctify it in the heavenly heights

as is written by Your Prophet:

[Is. 6:3]

In this statutory version, the praise of God is carried out not in the direct presence of God in heaven, but on earth in the liturgical community. So too, the righteous of our passage, the worshippers in *Ma'aseh Merkavah*, praised God from their community on earth.

The formal features and themes described here, though rooted in convention, do not lack an affective dimension; they are, in fact, essential to the expression of numinous themes. The prayers, while not geared to trance-induced ascent, are nonetheless oriented to the evocation of awe of God in His majesty—Otto's *mysterium tremendum.* The prayers require the worshipper to imagine the celestial array. But direct petition of God is seldom seen in these prayers, even when called for by the narrative context.[23] The poet thus evokes the Heavenly court; he does not approach it. God and His abode are still distant and

---

[23] Section I, for example, contains a prayer which the narrative refers to as the "Prayer for Mercy" (§548). However, a plea for mercy is absent in the prayer.

utterly separate from the world. The prayers of *Ma'aseh Merkavah*, with their stately progression of themes and phrases, emphasize this distance, while assuring the worshipper that his praise echoes that of the Divine temple.

Historical conclusions

The prayers described here display close stylistic and thematic affinities, and were probably derived from a corpus of liturgical mystical prayers. These were probably composed and transmitted orally and then collected in anthologies.[24] Such anthologies can be found in some of the earliest manuscripts of Hekhalot literature. An example is a collection of *qedushah* hymns found in an old manuscript in the Cairo Genizah.[25] The prayers in that collection also found their way into *Hekhalot Rabbati*.[26] So too, the prayers which formed the basis for *Ma'aseh Merkavah* were probably handed down to the composers of the narrative by tradents who claimed them to be the hymns which they or their legendary forbearers, Rabbi Akiba or Rabbi Ishmael, used to ascend to heaven.

This study has shown that the prayers in *Ma'aseh Merkavah* originally stressed the relationship between the prayers recited by the worshipper and those of the angels in the direct presence of God in the celestial court. Only later did the redactors attribute a theurgic function to those prayers. At issue in marking this evolution is locating a fundamental step in the history of Jewish mysticism: At what point did the visionaries of ancient Judaism attribute their visions not to Divine initiation, as in prophetic and apocalyptic texts, but to their own efforts to cultivate the ascent? The history of Merkavah mysticism indicates that this step occurred after the destruction of the Second Temple and during the formative period of classical Rabbinic Judaism; the history of *Ma'aseh Merkavah* suggests that this process occurred in stages.

As Baruch Levine has shown, the Temple functioned as a specific locus for the approach of the localized, potent Presence of God when

---

[24] On the role of oral composition in ancient Jewish prayer, see Heinemann, *Prayer.*

[25] Cambridge University Library, Taylor-Schechter Box K21.95 S. The manuscript has been published by Schäfer in *Genizah-Fragmente*, 9-32.

[26] On this manuscript and its implications for the text of *Hekhalot Rabbati*, see Schäfer, "Tradition and Redaction," 176.

invoked by the priests.[27]   The elaborate rituals of purity served as an equivalent of a sanitary environment for the Presence.   This procedure for bringing God near to humanity was at the heart of the Temple system.

The Qumran community, under priestly leadership and in self-imposed exile from the Temple institution, faced the problem of approaching the Presence of God apart from what they saw as a corrupt Temple.   Among their strategies for compensating for this absence was the liturgy of the Sabbath Songs. In these songs the earthly community visualized the angelic sacrifice and the liturgy that accompanied it.[28]

An analogous problem was faced by the composers of prayer in *Ma'aseh Merkavah*, who lived at a time when the Temple was destroyed and the potent Presence no longer appeared on earth. The response of the central shapers of Rabbinic Judaism was to insist that liturgical worship, study of Torah, and a life in accordance with *Halakhah* were effective compensation for the absence of the Temple. This response is epitomized in a famous formulation attributed to Yohanan ben Zakkai:

> ...we have another means of atonement, effective as Temple sacrifice. It is deeds of lovingkindness, as it is said: 'I desire mercy and not sacrifice.' [Hosea 6:6][29]

In this formulation, the function of the Temple in bringing the presence of God to earth is not addressed.   Obedience to and study of Torah were seen as appropriate substitutes for the statutory obligation of sacrifice and its power to atone, but not for its role as an earthly home for the Divine Glory.   In the same way, the Mishnah tractate *Berakhot* associates the services of the daily liturgy with the times for sacrifices.[30]   This association, however, does not grant the synagogue liturgy the function of inducing the presence of God to come to earth.[31]

---

[27] *In The Presence of The Lord;* "The Presence of God in Biblical Religion," in J. Neusner (ed.), *Religions in Antiquity: Essays in Memory of E. R. Goodenough* (Leiden, 1968), 71-87.

[28] See Newsom, *Songs of the Sabbath Sacrifice.*

[29] *'Avot de-Rabbi Natan* (ed. Schechter) 11a. On this passage see J. Neusner, *Development of a Legend: Studies on the Traditions Concerning Yohanan ben Zakkai* (Leiden, 1970), 113-14.

[30] On *Berakhot* in the Mishnah and Tosefta see T. Zahavy, *The Mishnaic Law of Blessings and Prayers: Tractate Berakhot* (Atlanta, 1987).

[31] It is true that statements appear in Talmudic literature that "Where ten are praying, the *Shekhinah* is with them," (b. *Berakhot* 6a), and that similar statements are made with regard to study and sitting at judgment (ibid.). But

Apparently, this response did not suffice for the composers of *Ma'aseh Merkavah*. Like the composers of the Qumran Sabbath Songs, they created prayer that assured them that their worship was being held in conjunction with the heavenly liturgy—that even in the absence of God's Potent Presence on earth, heaven and earth were in consonance when God is blessed both by angels and human beings.

Later, the formulators of the theurgic and narrative strata of *Ma'aseh Merkavah* would take an additional step in satisfying the longing for the Divine Presence. They asserted that the human being could actually ascend to heaven to participate in the heavenly liturgy. It was only necessary to be prepared with the proper moral qualifications and the proper theurgic apparatus. The purpose of *Ma'aseh Merkavah* was to provide the prospective traveler with such an apparatus: Prayers which were thought by the practitioners to have been employed for the vision of God, and which were imbued with numinous language and fortified with powerful names and phrases. *Ma'aseh Merkavah*, then, attests to the belief of successive generations in specific powers of affective prayer to bring them to an apprehension of God.

---

these statements function primarily as exhortations to prayer and study, not as recipes for conjuring the *Shekhinah*.

Index

DATE DUE

MAR 1 3 2008			